APPARENTLY

APPARENTLY

*This Is
What Parenting
Feels Like*

SUE DVORAK

apparentlythebook.com

Bible quotes on pages vii, 82, 204, 233, 329, and 334 from *New
Revised Standard Version Catholic Edition*; quotes on pages 79
and 339 from *Revised Standard Version Second Catholic Edition*.

Published by GFB™, Seattle
www.girlfridayproductions.com

Produced by Girl Friday Productions

Cover design: Kathleen Lynch
Production editorial: Reshma Kooner
Project management: Emilie Sandoz-Voyer

ISBN (paperback): 978-1-964721-82-8
ISBN (ebook): 978-1-964721-81-1

Library of Congress Control Number: 2024927344

First edition

To

Marie-Annette and Peter
my grounding

Marcel
my helpmate

Emily, Adam, Madeline, Eva, Levi, and Veronica
my teachers

"... and he set out, not knowing where he was going."
Hebrews 11:8

CONTENTS

INTRODUCTION

This is a book for parents of babies and young children. It's also a book for parents of older children, and for weary parents of teenagers, who were up way too late last night waiting for their kid to get home, then later still, giving him shit. This book is especially for older parents whose children are grown now, whose hearts are soft and battle-scarred and full of memories to be sifted through. This book is also for moms and dads whose own parents are getting seriously old now.

This book could be meant for anyone who wants to think about parenting, because we all can. We were all parented, one way or another. Maybe we want to think about that.

This might not be as good for people who fully intend to have children, but haven't quite gotten around to it yet. Hard to say, really. Truly, though, anyone who wants to join is welcome. There's plenty of room on the bench: we can all just scooch over.

Is it rather bold, writing a book intended seemingly for almost everyone? Hell yeah!

Is it considered a mistake, writing a book seemingly aimed

at everyone, about a ridiculously universal topic such as parenting? Also, unfortunately, hell yeah!

But it's there, within that vast, rugged, and beautiful landscape, that my stories are found.

What is this book about? Okay, that's more complicated. This book is about *being* a parent, or, at least, my experience of it. I have felt compelled, driven actually, to sit in the quiet and think about it—what it's been, what my kids were like, what happened, what I learned. I want two small, fat, sticky hands pressed on my cheeks to turn my head and my attention toward that earnest little face with clear eyes and messy hair and food across one cheek, to hear again the plaintive, "But, Mommy, I don't need a *m-o-p*," after my husband pointed out that "someone needs an *n-a-p*." I want to try to remember, really remember, the pain and the joy and the mess. I want to ponder what I think about it.

Those of you with babies and young children, who still believe you must do all things well, will be alternately encouraged and horrified by my recounting. Might parents of school children, chest deep in this game, see some of their own stories within mine? Maybe. I'd love that. Were any parents of teenagers to snort aloud, or shed a tear, that would be a W. But let's not set the bar too high—always a mistake when it comes to parenting. If older parents, whose kids are grown up, more or less gone now, were to remember a few things they'd forgotten, I would be pleased. That would be enough.

The thing is, I'm doing this regardless. I would love to have you join me, though, to think about your stories too.

It matters so much to us, this being a mom or being a dad, but we don't get to think about it much while we're busy doing it. We are just getting the hang of the stage our child is in when he or she moves to the next one, and we begin all over again. Parenting keeps moving, and there's not enough time to think about it while it's happening.

I know this might seem murky. But parents don't have time for me to blather on about what this book is about. We all have other things we need to be doing, all the time. Let's talk about the meaning of this later . . . somewhere near the end perhaps? That would be better.

Honestly, I think we should just get started, without really knowing what we are doing. Like parenting.

Let's go. Get your stuff.

BABIES

YOU

Light spills into the dark room
Harsh from industrial bathroom, soft
    from window to the city

Distant beeping, muffled voices, footsteps
    briskly by
On my side, sheet thin over plastic mat-
    tress holding me up to see
To see
Into glass box on a cart, close as side rail
    allows

A solitary form, cloth parcel in a glass box

I roll over, prop and kneel
Scent of briny bleeding, earthy, old as
    time
Hunch and reach, clutch the parcel
Poised, poorly planned, dumb
She-wolf in blue gown, without instinct

Lift

Small bundle,
Held with just my hands
Light but dense, weighted

Head a tiny halo of pale fuzz
Dainty face size of my palm, fine, pretty,
Serene, defies the violence of birth
Perfect buds of lips in miniature
(she'll enjoy putting lipstick on these, my
    aunty said)

Can't resist
Unwrap the flannel
A scrawny cherub not imagined,
Tiny fists curled, damp, resist opening
Fingernails as teardrops in size and shape,
    luminescent, paper thin,
Downy limbs that pushed me,
Pressed me from the inside, I stroke
Now on the outside

Startle

Stretch out against the shock of my touch
Tiny face crumpling
Neck reach, fleeting grimace at the world
Pursed lips suck, then slow, slowing. Stop.
Relax, curl in.

Rewrap.
She gazes, a mystic wise
Both gazing. Equals.

Love crashing
Desire without danger of myself or another
Danger around us, outside, shared
She-wolf in blue gown, without instinct
Babe in flannel, swaddled

Lay her close, lie beside
Arm atop, a shield. Warm.
Floating, sounds fade
Desire without threat
Love crashing

EARLY DAYS ON THE JOB

BIRTH

Childbirth is a happy crisis. If "Mom and Baby are doing fine," it is the happiest of times, but a crisis nonetheless. You prepare but don't feel ready. People seem unclear about their roles. Events are unforeseeable. Communication can be poor. Response to stress is unpredictable: my husband stopped to gas up the car on our way to the hospital while I was in labour with our third birth.

Though, in truth . . . I kid myself, pretending that was a stress reaction. Gas prices were good that night, and Marcel likes saving money on gas.

In the giddy moments after a birth, the sense of crisis finally wanes, and joy bursts forth unencumbered. Manic joy for sure, but joy, gushing and pure.

Minutes after our first child was born, I announced loudly, in an "outside voice," or more a "gymnasium voice," from my propped-up position in bed, "I've never even *been* to a birth before!!" The adorable (was he?—I possibly embellish), childlike-appearing medical intern, who'd been stationed at my crotch for ages and delivered the baby, stretched up from his post down there and responded in an equally euphoric way, "Me neither!!" We smiled at each other, similarly relieved it was finally over, both extremely pleased with the outcome.

Delivered the baby.

My baby.

And there it is. As my husband says, a new person joins us, and he or she does not come in through a door. Crazy Town. Entirely ordinary and utterly miraculous, mind-blowing if you really think about it. Certainly, there's a lot to deal with at the time, so reflections on the transcendence of birth are interrupted by practical problems, like caring for a newborn. You shift about in bed, or wander around the room, trying to adjust to a) there suddenly being a baby and b) coping with the reality that it belongs to you.

I shuffled about in my blue hospital gown, left hanging undone at the back because . . . after what I'd just been through, what did it matter? I was wearing crazy-huge, fishnet hospital-underwear things, with two mammoth pads, and even a liner sheet of sorts, placed inside them. Do not think fishnet as in lingerie; think fishnet like the fishing industry. This rowdy, multi-pad/fishnet rearview situation was on full display, and here's the weird thing: I did not care. At all.

The onslaught of hormones that flood a woman's body after birth includes one with the helpful effect of causing the new mother to not give a rip what she looks like, or what people think of her. It's fantastic (only lasts a few weeks). Following the birth of my babies, I could have stood in my gaping gown on the busy street corner just outside the big downtown hospital, with my giant caboose of fishnet and pads and such exposed for all the world to see, and cared not in the slightest.

"Mom, that's very private, that babies are born out of pa-jiimas . . . no, I mean out of ba-jiinas.

That's private."
—Adam, 3, out of the blue, days after
hearing how and from where babies are
birthed

THE DAYS AFTER BIRTH

Quite a few things happen right after a birth. First, again, there's a baby. So there's black-tar poos, the clamped umbilical cord, doll clothes and miniature diapers you press to your lips after each change, anxious that they be wet. There are forms to fill out, and big glasses of apple juice with ice, which is delicious and makes you wonder why you haven't drunk apple juice since you were a child.

Oh, and the baby is hungry or, worse, not hungry. Ah, yes.

You will have read that "following birth, the mother's breast milk will come in."

Terrific! Handy! you will think.

Not so fast, girlfriend.

They are not up-front with us, in full disclosure, that milk will come in, "causing your breasts, regardless of their normal status or size, to transform into boulders of rock-hard, painful granite affixed to your chest wall upon which a baby must suck."

I have small breasts. I would have liked larger. When I was young, I thought women somehow "decide" what kind of boobs they wanted. I decided to have glorious, beautiful, full breasts, not too big, and not long (apologies, long-boob gals). Shame, but yeah, that didn't happen. Why shame? Well, I'd look better in my clothes—there'd be a point to wearing a nice wrap dress. Maybe I'd have had more fun? Hard to say. I've spent a lot of time feeding babies with these measly ol' boobs of mine, so, though not abundant, they get the job done. Besides, it's okay, I have good arms.

All young women: *Who cares about arms?*

All older women: *We do.*

One time, many moons ago, a woman in a store said to me, "You have lovely arms." I said, "Oh, thank you!" Inwardly I thought, *That's a weird thing to say.* Years later, I regret thinking that, and also regret I didn't hug that lady and tell her that I love her.

So there I was, with my small, concrete breasts and a starving, newborn baby. And she couldn't latch.

Latch. Echhhk. That freakin' word I'd never used in my life until the moment my daughter was born, then heard, or said myself, about fifty times in the first twenty-four hours of her life. Just hearing the word still causes me stress: latch—ughh. The endless latch-talk made me want to tell everyone to piss off. But they were right. She couldn't latch and I couldn't get her to. We were both distressed, crying over a shared, common problem, as would be the case again in years to come.

We'd solve the problem together too, I discovered, this time and over those same future years.

A doctor from South Africa insisted we try cabbage, meaning the use of cabbage leaves held pressed to my petite, granite breasts, to soften them. Yes, cabbage leaves, and no, he didn't seem to be joking. We got a cabbage and I did just that. (Where the hell did a cabbage come from? I have no idea. Did Marcel go to a store from the delivery ward? Did the hospital, which doesn't even have an apple or banana lying around, somehow have a cabbage? Am I hallucinating that this happened?) I sat with cabbage leaves applied to my chest, accompanied by the distinct feeling a guy was about to burst out from behind a vinyl hospital chair and holler, "You're on *Candid Camera*!!" I've never seen that show, but my entire life I have heard people say those words, whenever someone was caught doing something strange. It was like a show made of lengthier, embarrassing TikToks, I gather. Apparently this stuff never gets old.

The cabbage became wilted after a while, and maybe my breasts were softer? Did that mean it was working? Though, if you pressed cabbage leaves on a man's pectoral region, and he relaxed a while, they'd probably be wilted too (the cabbage I mean, not the pectorals). Honestly, I am not recommending this; I can't remember any of it properly.

I do remember one thing for certain: a nurse wheeled in a cart with a contraption upon it, one that looked like part of an engine . . . a bilge pump from a ship, or maybe old farm machinery.

It was a Breast Pump. Yes, exactly—what the hell.

Once tubing and attachments were in place, the ultimate, classic, metal, comic-book-worthy toggle switch was flipped to the On position, and that puppy started up, a-hummin', a-drawin', and a-swooshin'. Holy Hannah, it felt like it might pull my entire breast right off, up through the funnel-shaped plastic, and—zip!—it would be gone. Now, *that* would be a story: *So I went in to have a baby the other day, and a funny thing happened . . .*

Using the breast pump, and kind assistance, and one hungry baby, we toiled at getting the block-o'-boob situation under control and feeding said baby. Obviously something worked because we left the hospital the next day.

All of this begs an obvious question: How could I be so useless at breastfeeding my own offspring??

The entire planet of womenfolk, since the beginning of time, have figured out how to do this. Should there not be some vestige of instilled knowledge woven into my genetic coding, passed down through the centuries? One would think. Really, though, there was nothing. No helpful instinct kicked in, no knack that came to me unbidden, like a song in my head

I could already hum. Nothing. Just sweating it out, trying to get the damn breastfeeding latch going.

Weird.

One wishes that more of parenting was pure instinct, as in the animal world. Animals are compelled by their very biology to do the exact right thing, while we humans stumble about in the dark, coming at necessary tasks sideways and at all manner of odd angles, some just plain wrong. It's sad to think of what human children endure because we parents have no idea what we're doing in *really* important matters, while polar bears and whales are just taking care of business.

I suppose we should be careful what we wish for. Compelled instinct would be fabulous for things like innate breastfeeding abilities and embedded baby sleep solutions, but then a bummer at, let's say, cocktail parties, where instinct would force us to "point," like a hunter-retriever dog, at the prize game of the most handsome, virile-appearing man in the room, frozen, one arm outstretched, finger pointing, one leg extended out behind, fixed in place next to the appetizer table. Yeah, instinct could be awkward too.

Despite all this, on Day 3 with Baby 1, we went home from the hospital, lacking any helpful instincts whatsoever. Except love. Big, huge, crazy, unstructured, out-of-control love, crashing, wild, and lacking direction.

GOING HOME

The occasion of going home from the hospital with your newborn is one of the strangest moments of your life. You keep waiting for someone to come sprinting up, waving and yelling, *Whoa, whoa!! Hold up, wait—hang on!* and stop the foolishness. Seriously, everybody thinks this is a good idea? Two people who don't know what they're doing, taking a *newborn* with them, to become its primary caregivers?!?

I remember being in the passenger seat on the drive home from the hospital, after Marcel finally affixed the foreign device, the car seat, in the back of the car for the first time, with the little foreigner, Emily, secured within. We were in a slow-motion movie. Yes, a foreign film . . . without subtitles. Buildings floated by us, and we over a bridge, with people everywhere, all around, crossing streets, on the sidewalks, and in parks, acting as though everything was normal.

It was not. There was a baby in the back seat. And it was mine.

I wanted to roll down the window and yell:

ARE YOU GUYS NOT PAYING ATTENTION?? *How can you act like everything's normal? Do you not realize there is a* BABY *in the back seat of this car? Right here?!* I have experienced this surreal moment a number of times, six to be exact, and each felt equally crazy. *How is there a new person in the car with us?*

Back home following that first new-baby trip from the hospital, Marcel and I sat on kitchen chairs pushed away from our small table, under the glaring fluorescent kitchen light of the place we were renting. We shoveled hot Chinese takeout straight from containers into our mouths, not taking our eyes from the strawberry-blond, fuzzy-headed teeny tiny person on display in a car seat set directly in front of us on the gold-and-brown-patterned linoleum floor. Staring at her.

With later children, this introspection was interrupted by things like a preschooler asking for the tenth time, *What's the baby's name again?* or a toddler calling for help from the bathroom, which was weird because she wasn't toilet training yet.

During one of the first nights home with our first child, I remember stirring in the night to the distant sound of tires screeching, our neighbour's tires, or their friends' probably. Our neighbours had loud, raucous parties. I thought, half-asleep, *Wow, they are really screeching their tires.*

Gradually, through a fog, I realized, *Those are not tires. That is a baby. My baby. My baby is making tiny, tire-screeching sounds.* I got up.

YOUR NEW LIFE

NEW LIFE ROUTINE

Somewhere in there, in those first blurry, surreal weeks, which feel like ages while you are living them, something close to a rhythm, a new way of life, starts to form. It's subtle but it begins.

You wake up to a plaintive but demanding cry at 2:17 a.m.

Let me expound: *wake up* sounds simple, direct, and straightforward, but no. This waking up feels like drowning, in slow motion, but in reverse, toward the surface, from a pit of quicksand you are immersed in, pulling you back down, resisting your every movement. Your brain is disoriented, foggy, and it struggles to interpret the digital clock.

2:19.

What is that? A price? A speed? A ratio? Ah, no. Time. It's the time. You went to sleep about 11:58 so this feels difficult to understand. Plus, there's a baby screaming somewhere. Close by.

Here.

You get out of bed and lift that wailing, warm mass from the bassinet/stroller/cardboard box/crib/bed beside you and begin. To unswaddle, to soothe, to latch to a boob or provide a warm bottle, then you and babe settle. You slump, near coma-tose, and gaze at the little face you already love so completely, as if you've known and loved her all your life. In a stupor you stroke her tiny head of hair while she steadily feeds. You close your eyes, sitting there, propped heavily, gradually becoming part of the chair or bed itself. Months later, this routine be-comes more engaged in by the baby herself: she gazes right back at you, pats your chest, plays with your hair. One of my babies repeatedly pinched the skin along my side, with the little hand of her arm wrapped down underneath mine. Her pinchy ritual.

All this leads to the lifting and laying of that warm little body up against yours, the burping, the patting, baby's head bobbling on your shoulder. On to the other boob or more bottle, off to the diaper change, the clothing change. The re-wrapping, the pooing again and repeating of the change, the rocking or bouncing or settling, using wee tricks you yourself have discovered. A particular position of your arm, a comfort-able swaying motion, a jiggly bounce of vertical baby. You sort of start to know what to do. And you keep doing it.

In a stupor of fatigue, with eyelids lined with sandpaper, and, for breastfeeding moms, a deep ache between your shoul-der blades, you lay your baby down and experience a startling surge of exquisite tenderness for this little person, along with the sudden realization that you really need to go pee.

Getting to know your new baby-person in this way feels good—well, not the exhaustion part, but the developing of competence and knack part. This is what leads to a dad of a three-month-old casually saying to his aunty, "Sorry, no, here—like this: he prefers being held on his tummy against your arm when he's fussy."

Knowledge gained in the dark of early hours is sweet indeed.

That's the thing too: there's almost no wrong answer. I love seeing the different ways people do things with their babies, the "how to put her to sleep," "how to wrap her," "what to do" in a myriad of situations. All totally different, and "all good," as they say. A symbiosis of baby need, parent response, culture, necessity. One mom swears by something another mom would never do. Both approaches work wonders for their babies. Win-win.

Marcel is a wrapper, a baby wrapper. (No, not a rapper, and yes, he has made that dad joke.) Babies get the full burrito sausage-wrap when he is on baby duty. Our family jokes that babies don't cry when wrapped by him because they can't get a big enough breath.

Some people wrap babies into neat little packages to be tucked into one arm on, say, the back of a motorcycle in Mongolia in that *Babies* documentary a while back. Others have their babies loose and spread out. Modern babies are put in sleep sacks, bunting-bag affairs, like having your sleeping bag fashioned into a sleep outfit, so your blankets are built in. Some babies are put in front-facing baby carriers, baby coming at you on the street, arms and legs a-swingin' in the breeze. Other babies go everywhere in their stroller, which gets rolled into the apartment and babe sleeps there too. Lots of ways to sleep and wrap and carry babies. Each of us argue for our way, but really, you could find a continent where the entire population does the opposite of your argued position, and baby world is working out fine for them.

I hear my mom's voice saying, *Oh, babies have to be wrapped! They've just come from the womb, all snug and secure. They don't like being loose, their reflexes making them jump. Wrap that baby! . . . And, for Heaven's sake, why aren't parents putting knitted hats on their babies anymore? Their bare little heads are getting cold!* So I leave all that with you to consider.

This fledgling competency extends reassuringly to other areas as well. The stroller that once took a manual, an hour,

and a lot of swearing to open and set up, ready for baby instal-
lation, is now whipped out of a trunk with one arm, while you
hold said baby, and in later years, while arguing with a toddler
at the same time. Same with her little eating routine: *Oh, get
her to do the spoon herself while I pack the daycare bag, then
try to just shovel it in.* And his sleep schedule: *I'll put him down
now. He's tired . . . about to start screaming. I can tell.*

"I can tell." Legit baby skills, comin' out of nowhere.
Actually, coming out of the Doing. Like much of parenting,
the skills, the relationship, the knack, the synchronicity, comes
from the Doing. It's refreshing to realize that, for some things,
there aren't many shortcuts available. As long as humans roam
the earth, I think the Doing is how we get to know our children. The Doing is both the burden and the joy.

The next time you stagger about in the dark in the night,
carrying your baby and stepping on toys, think, *I am really
getting good at this. I am really getting to know my child.* You
are really getting good at this! Then go treat yo'self and crawl
back into bed.

How about Eggo waffles with lots of syrup at 3:00 a.m., to
reward yourself when you are equally dead-weary and starving? We had an entire, unopened box of frozen Eggo waffles
in the freezer when we brought our fifth baby home from the
hospital, and I ate the whole thing. Not all at one sitting, mind
you, but yes, "all by myself" (favourite toddler expression of all
time) over a number of weeks. This is not a suggestion really,
just an observation. Somewhere in the middle of each night,
after the nursing, patting, changing, and rocking, Levi would
be tucked back into the bassinet, a pretty, white wicker thing
with homemade liner pads, bought for my parents, living in
Australia back in 1962, passed along through various families
to us. I'd beetle to the kitchen, in the quiet of the house, to
pop a couple of those bad boys in the toaster. Warm, slath-
ered with butter and peanut butter and syrup, those dieticians'

nightmares were honestly the best thing ever. Delicious. I must have needed the calories, or at least the comfort, which probably made "getting back in shape after baby" a bit more challenging, but whatever. You do what you gotta do. (Try not to do drugs.)

Afterward, I'd climb back into bed, bone tired, cold, and clammy somehow, with freezing cold hands and feet. Snuggling up against Marcel's toasty slumbering form, I essentially used him to warm myself up. Generous soul, he never pulled away or even flinched, but simply made the brief sound of someone in pained distress. His warmth helped me fall back to sleep.

This odd little detail brings to mind something I heard thoughtfully expressed by a young father: that, despite wanting to help, he sometimes felt he was hovering outside of this new life routine because his newborn relied so heavily on his wife, who was breastfeeding.

My warming-up routine offers an obscure example, both concrete and symbolic, of how dads are difference-makers on their teams with a fresh, new recruit—teams that seem to have two players caught out playing extended overtime. By his presence, by not flinching at what is needed, in all the ways that need may show up, by providing warmth, physical and otherwise, to the mama and baby of his team, the father of a newborn provides key support, the support that helps keep their team in the game.

Which brings me to an important point, pertinent to this entire book. Marcel is the love of my life and my partner in all things. But he is not me, and I am not him. These are my stories, told from my point of view because that's the only valid perspective I can truly share. Marcel's stories about parenting would definitely be interesting, involve all the same main players, and potentially be unrecognizable compared to the stories found here. And that's okay.

Life is interesting largely because we all have different points of view; as we share our perspectives, we all learn more about the world. That said, I'm not terribly keen to have you learn everything "interesting" about me. So—don't hurry on your book, honey.

BREASTFEEDING (AND BOTTLE-FEEDING)

A couple months in, I'd finally gotten the swing of the whole breastfeeding thing, something I eventually came to love. It's . . . Pardon?

Wait, what? No, I . . . You think I'm saying babies should always be . . . ?

Whoa, that's not, no . . . hang on, please! I agree! Yes, yes, *either can be good*, breast *or* bottle! Yes, yes, there are plenty of reasons to choose bottle . . . for sure!

The important issue is the baby's nourishment—and the mother's sanity, of course. Bottle-feeding is better for a baby in *any* situation where . . . well, where bottle-feeding is better. How about when breastfeeding is not working? That's a good reason. Or what about, say, when breastfeeding is driving the mother insane? Mother's insanity is a bigger problem for a baby than being fed formula. Another good reason to bottle-feed is when breastfeeding is not possible, because life. There are many good reasons. I agree with you too, yes, the love festival part of breastfeeding can happen with a bottle: curled up in a chair together, eye contact, bonding, relaxation maybe. And Dad can do it too, and the babysitter, and Grandma, so that's good. Agreed, all good.

But . . . please, do you mind if I talk about breastfeeding for a bit, as a thing? Because it's quite a thing if you've never done it before, which includes everyone who has never done it before, which includes *a lot* of women. I come at this as someone so naturally terrible at it I had to go for *lessons*! I am not bragging here.

All my babies were "slow to regain their birth weight," which becomes a mother-centric crisis in Newborn Breastfeeding World. This phenomenon takes all of a new mother's natural insecurities, which are legion, and puts them on crack cocaine (This is only an expression, to be clear. Do not use crack cocaine while you are breastfeeding. Or any time if possible.) First time around, I did not know that yet, that our newborns were underachieving, sluggish weight-gainers. How is one to know these things?

Any whiff of a newborn being "slow to gain weight" (i.e., not transforming rapidly into a Rubenesque butterball) soon hints at an even more mother-terrifying "failure to thrive" scenario, a five-alarm fire in baby world. Where I live, this possibility alerts public health services, who deploy officious nurses who descend upon your home with baby scales and breast-pumping schedules and an air of criticism. Criticism produces worry, and nothing kills milk production like a hefty dose of worry, which, all together, swirls into a remarkably negative circle of events.

The public health nurse would set up her scale on our kitchen table and weigh the baby to see how many grams he'd gained in the past three days. All the while, I knew my narrow baby had produced a massive honey-mustard poo in the night, temporarily negating half his gains of the past three days. Disheartening, and totally stressful.

It took me a few babies to figure out that my DNA combined with my husband's produces a small human of particular shape for the first two months, specifically the shape of a tube, or "totally tubular," as my dear girlfriend called them. My babies all got chubbers a few months later, but for a while, they looked like long-distance-runner babies. Try convincing a skeptical public health nurse that your totally tubular marathoner baby is doing just fine. I was never able to do that, but eventually came to know it myself, a blessed reassurance.

THE CLINIC

In the early days with my first baby, back when I was a young and earnest mother, breastfeeding was a disaster. Luckily, I was sent to a breastfeeding clinic. The clinic seemed a barren place, sterile, old looking even back then, all hospital colours and lacking décor. This strikes me as funny, knowing now how utterly nonclinical, how earthy, physical, and human an experience breastfeeding is. I mean, clearly, cultures that nestle new mothers in blankets in cozy spaces, warm milky tea by their sides, near a fire, tended to by women of their tribe who show and help the new moms, are far ahead of this bare, heartless situation. Clearly.

I sat waiting in an exam room that was outfitted with a few ancient vinyl armchairs and not much else. I'd been instructed to remove my shirt and bra. I sat, half-naked, in the bare, office-like space, holding my baby and waiting, which felt strange. But then, a lot about all of this felt strange.

The "lactation specialist," a medical doctor who ran the clinic, strode into the room. She had an entirely practical air, a woman without pretense, accustomed to entering rooms with half-naked strangers sitting waiting for her.

She said hello, inspected my sorry little breasts a moment, then stood behind me. Without ceremony, she began to manhandle (womanhandle?) my breasts efficiently for a while with cold hands, chapped from frequent hand-washing, as I'd heard her do right outside the room. She turned her intent gaze upon my baby, putting on gloves and taking babe from me in a deft, expert manner, holding babe from underneath against one forearm, baby's head cradled in her hand. The doctor squeezed baby's cheeks, opened her lips, and peered into her tiny mouth, pulled baby's tongue to and fro.

Once this brief assessment was complete, with almost no conversation, Dr. Gal placed baby across my body. She stood close behind me, leaned over, reached around under my armpit near baby's head, and took my breast from underneath. She lifted and compressed my boob into a small, pointy torpedo. More or less hugging me, she reached her other arm around to help tip baby's head to the desired orientation. Stroking my torpedo-boob's cracked nipple against baby's lips a few times, the doc showed me to wait until baby opened her mouth—wide. Without warning, Lactation Doctor swiftly clamped that open-mouthed baby firmly onto my breast, sort of like being hit in the chest with a baby, becoming yet another thing that felt strange.

Lacto Doc could tell immediately the latch wasn't right. She inserted a finger into the corner of baby's mouth to break the suction. She repeated all this a few times, making it clear that the toe-curling nipple pain of a latch too far out was not correct, while warning me that even a good latch would hurt a few moments, but only in the beginning weeks. This repeated lifting of torpedo-boob and surprise whamming on of baby eventually resulted in a good latch. Pressed there, baby began steady, firm, slow sucking, a deep pull that felt secure and full. My lactation guru stood a moment, watching, squatting down low to inspect baby's mouth, throat, and swallow. She told me to listen, pointing to baby's swallows. We listened together silently a few moments to the steady, deep clicking sound. She instructed me to stay there, until baby decided to be done, then burp her, and we'd do the other side. She gave the briefest inkling of a smile, and then Lactation Doctor was gone.

I sat in that heartless room, with my baby's sucking pull on my breast and the letting go of milk rushing in to fill the void, to feed my baby. I felt overcome by a wave of affection for my lactation specialist doctor. Her no-nonsense, zero-nurturing style was perfectly comforting to me somehow. It was easy to take, completely nonjudgmental, and just what I needed. I felt like crying, but then, I felt like crying a lot in those days.

There was a job that needed to be done, and this gal knew how to do it.

She—this frightfully efficient lactation physician—she was my nurturing kinfolk by the fire, using her practiced hands, sharing her knowledge, albeit all Western-style, with me, wearing a white lab coat no less. Her children, if she had any, were long past breastfeeding days. Who knew what burdens she carried? She looked tired but was really good at what she was doing.

I love women like this one. Don't get me wrong: I love effusive, overtly nurturing women too, but I have a huge soft spot for efficient, deadpan doers. You know, the serious, seemingly less emotional women who run the ranch, or head up the corporation, or teach hundreds of anxious new mothers how to breastfeed successfully. That sort. Bless up.

With that session and a follow-up with my lab-coated tribal sister, eventually it all began to work.

The latch finally works easily, without startling baby maneuvers or any pain. With nursing comes a pulling sensation deep in the chest wall, followed by a soon-familiar tingling rush of milk's magical "letdown," excellent to feel while nursing a baby, terrifying while seated in a meeting with adults, wearing a nice blouse. The baby swallows valiantly, a deep, strong, distinctive sound in the back of her throat, her entire being intent on taking in the crazy rush of milk that happens until everything settles into steady homeostasis. Swallow click, swallow click.

Getting it right is satisfying, a relief, like what viewers observe happen when breastfeeding finally starts to work for Pam and newborn CeCe in the TV show *The Office*. The mom relaxes and lets go awhile. She has to; she's "just sitting there" with a baby attached to her body. As she studies the folds of her baby's ear, her mind wanders through thought, a strangely refreshing thing to do, like a spontaneous mindfulness exercise, or the effect of a mild calming drug, one that nature cleverly supplies. Breastfeeding becomes an experience of being sufficient for another, of providing, on a most primal level.

Any nursing mother *Oh, hey, pass me that hungry baby and I will feed it . . .* with my body.

There comes a sense of kinship with women up and down the centuries, babe at breast, nurturing the world sort of. Yet, again comes the paradox of parenting, always: mystery entwines with reality. You nourish your offspring with your own body, a transcendent experience, like an animal in the wilderness, while simultaneously, say, writing a cheque in line in a grocery store checkout, as my sister did once (. . . said nobody ever in the past three decades).

Another example of reality? A nursing woman might sometimes find herself leaning awkwardly over a well-secured baby car seat, in a moving vehicle, feeding an apparently starving, strapped-in baby. The mom isn't driving, someone else is . . . but Mom's not wearing her own seatbelt, come to think of it. Is this a good idea, allowing the mother to be dispensable in this situation?

A woman living this kookiness might reasonably once again yearn for larger breasts, even covet the previously dismissed pendular sort, or simply wish she were bottle-feeding. Any of those would be better than this bizarre, hunched-over-baby situation, which occasionally occurs when the spouse-partner-person values "getting places quickly" differently from the nursing person. Nobody asks the baby's opinion; however, the baby is excellent at making his or her viewpoint understood.

I digress.

The unique experience of breastfeeding links mamas all over the globe, all the time: women nursing babies on subways, in grass huts, in entry spaces of daycares, in bungalows, on park benches, in apartments on the fortieth floor, wherever. So . . . not unique at all. We are women, hear us roar. Then hear the baby burp! That's important too; a good burp saves a lot of grief all around.

Enough already. Sorry, I'll wrap up.

Breastfeeding is interesting, a cool experience eventually, inexpensive (free, except for the outrageous amounts of food a nursing mother eats night and day), nutritious for baby, sometimes awkward, a way of life, environmentally sustainable, and battery free. It pisses some people off for unknown reasons, and it's kind of weird in a good way. It's also been done by human mothers on planet Earth since the beginning of our species, so there is that, but let's not go there—too complicated to address that discussion. Too tired. Bottle-feeding is also good, in the same way that driving a car is often better than riding a horse. People like horses, but cars are really handy.

All nurturers of babies, unite!

ADVENTURES WITH BABY

THE SMILE

An early adventure occurs when your baby smiles at you, really smiles, for the first time.

You: *Hey—was that . . . ??*

You feel your heart melt and somehow expand in your chest at the same time, bursting out of what must have been some restricted state, based on how this feels, as if, like the Grinch Who Stole Christmas's, your heart somehow "grew three sizes that day." Your baby lights up, all animated eyes and toothless gums, and smiles at you, transfixed, as though you are the best thing he'd ever hoped for.

And you fall more in love, again—which you had not thought possible before that moment.

And that just keeps on happening.

PARENT AND CHILD ON AN OUTING

On you go, feeding and changing and jiggling and carrying this small, new person in your life. Your competency builds, eventually leading you to become Parent and Child on an Outing. You decide to head out together into civilization by choice rather than necessity. Not to pick up a prescription at the drugstore before it closes, not to get basic rations at the grocery store or mail some godforsaken thing; nothing like that. This is for fulfillment!

You're fairly sure of how to do all this by now, this dressing baby in her impossibly cute mini-clothes, packing up stuff as though she's travelling abroad, settling her into her stroller, or her car seat in the car, or her baby carrier on the subway, or her sling-thing on the bus.

Off you go with your little person.

And it's fantastic. There you are, hip Mom wearing sunglasses to hide the bags, or Dad in baseball cap to hide the hair. You are total cool chic . . . as opposed to, of late, uncool derelict. You're all over this baby thing, like a freakin' Instagram celebrity person.

You hand babe her little sucky, melty cookie *just* before she begins fussing because, well, you know. You can see it coming. You're actually sitting! . . . sipping a coffee . . . outside! . . . with people! Or walking, outdoors, in the sun! Or in a store! . . . out in the world! . . . to buy something! . . . you've wanted! . . . for months! Things are going great.

Sometime later amid these pleasantries, your baby girl, gurgling and making bubbles, hits herself on the head, hard, with her firm, round, teething ring. She hesitates momentarily, then decides. Her face crumples, because that hurt, a lot, suddenly making her realize she's much more tired than she originally thought, as you both wait in a lineup to purchase new leggings you've wanted, without even trying them on. That crumpled face? You know that too.

She starts to cry, a grating sound that builds to intense, piercing shrieks, designed by evolution, we assume, to get everyone's attention, which it does. You reach for the soother and fumble, dropping it . . . onto a dark, sticky patch of something on the floor. You consider wiping the soother/dummy/pacifier/

nu-nu/binky/soo-soo on your clothes, but you don't want that thing touching your clothes. You hesitate a sec, considering whether you might suck on it yourself, "to clean it" (which is not a thing). The thought grosses you out, seems like it would be disgusting for *you*, and so probably, no, you guess you can't give it to your baby. You guess.

She's really revved up now, red faced and frantic, arms held aloft from her body, shaking spastically with her screams. People glance at you, like maybe you could stop it somehow . . . but for some reason *aren't*?

You (inside your head): *What?! People! I want this crying to stop more than anyone in this department store/coffee shop/library/guitar store! Seriously, lay off!!*

There will be no stopping her. You can tell.

You pack up hastily, wobbling the stroller or bouncing her in the baby carrier, a screaming babe strapped to the front of your body. You are sweating, also suddenly feeling way too tired to be doing this. You wish you were at home, curled up on the couch in your crap sweats, no new leggings, patting her to sleep. You make it home after forty minutes of baby-shrieking hell, feeling bad that your Parent and Child on an Outing did not go well.

Stop.

Don't do that. Don't feel bad—it doesn't matter. Get her settled, put on your comfy clothes if you're not wearing them already, make a cup of tea, sit down, and chill for a bit. You did great! Go, you.

It doesn't matter that she cried. Shrieked. Babies cry, all over the world, all the time, and this time it was yours. No big deal. Nobody's "fault." You are awesome; you did a good job. Hell, two months ago you knew nothing about babies, and now you're swingin' one around like a pro, nestled in the crook of your arm while you do other things. Knowing how to wrap her. Changing diapers with your eyes closed, when moments ago you didn't even know which was the front of a diaper and which was the back. Taking her on outings, for fulfillment.

I'm old enough to feel all mother-mode about *you*. You are doing great, and you need to trust yourself, Dad or Mom. Trust your instincts. You know your baby better than anybody else, and that will continue. That, *that*, is the beginning of feeling good about parenting. Really, I mean it. Trusting what you know will become your number-one, absolute best resource for the rest of your parenting life, hands down. Your instincts, if you pay attention carefully, will help you to know what's bothering her when she is eight, or notice something unusual about his illness when he is eleven, or decide she should not stay over at a certain friend's when she is fifteen.

But let's not talk about that yet.

Here is what's important: trusting your own instincts is worth more than a tower of parenting books. Hone those instincts, darling parents of young children, and start trusting them. This is your baby, and you are doing great. You know what to do, or at least, you're learning fast.

OUTINGS GONE WRONG

This will make you feel better.

Marcel and I had an "outing gone wrong," a fantastic one, with our fifth child: a work-related trip for Marcel to a bougie resort in Hawaii! What a treat! Neither one of us, nor the baby, had ever visited Hawaii before. We were old hands at the parenting-baby thing by then, not phased at all by a flight, or what to take along, or how it would go. Easy-peasy. This was one simple flight, with one baby, for a holiday no less! My beautiful parents, to whom I am eternally grateful for this and much more, had come to look after the remaining team at home.

Just sitting on an airplane for five hours was thrilling

enough. We settled into the flight, with our smiley, chubby five-month-old guy nestled upon us. He was adorbs, the kind of baby you'd love to see, though in this case, from far away, because, let's face it, nobody wants to sit anywhere near a baby on an airplane. Obviously.

Things were fantastic, us being carefree, maybe even fun, parents for a few hours. Our little man proceeded then to have the most incredibly massive poo ever to occur in the history of babies. This poo had to have been litres, or gallons really, or many pints, or honestly a bunch of whatever measurement you use, because there was just so much. Everywhere. Bright orangey, mustard-coloured too, which, actually yes, *is* important to the story. Because the poo shot up the back of his entire outfit, and into his hair, and all over the front of my shirt, my white shirt, as he sat against me. There was even some poo sinking down into the crotch of my pants, a charming touch, all rendering me not quite so appealing-hip-parent-mode as moments prior.

Dripping with poo, I carried him forward in the cabin to the airplane bathroom and waited in line, holding a package of wipes and our little guy's handy change of clothes, my appearance likely horrifying any passengers who glanced up. Actually, they might not have been horrified at all, only curious as to how I spilled an industrial-sized tub of mustard on myself on an airplane. Had I demanded of the flight attendants that I wanted *more mustard, dammit!*? Who knew?

Okay, so, airplane bathrooms. Yes. Try holding gurgling, chubber babe over a sink the size of a dinner plate at a cheap buffet, to rinse him with a press faucet that's timed to run for three seconds per press. Not efficient. About fifty baby wipes later, he'd been swabbed down, a sticky sheen of mustard still plastering his abundant hair to the back of his head. A trendy new baby hair product? Let's pretend.

Naturally, I'd brought along a change of clothes for baby,

but not for myself, silly me. In a state of illogical desperation, I tried rinsing my own shirt in the same miniature sink, while still wearing it, while holding a baby.

Passenger (outside the door): *Uh, hello? Is someone still in there?*

Me (falsetto voice, not sure why): *Oh, yes! Just a mo-o-ment!*

Passenger, quite a few moments later: *Uh . . . are you okay?*

Me (much too cheerfully): *YES! Everything is FINE!!!*

I emerged a disaster, sweating, wet shirt, huge stain, a lot of laundry, holding a baby with weird hair who began crying, as though he wanted to stay in the closet-bathroom. I squeezed past a lengthy lineup of passengers waiting for the bathroom, undoubtedly annoyed at my campout in there.

I passed the fresh-clothes boy to my husband, who had a look of aghast/feigned sympathy on his face. I settled into my seat, attempting to pull myself together, thinking, *Well, that was terrible.* Little did I know we were just getting started.

We landed, did the luggage pickup, and the "special cargo" lineup for the ratty stroller, then the get-a-taxi, in our scorching-hot new environs. As we whipped along a freeway through desertlike relative nothingness, the taxi began making worrisome sounds. I have no idea what actually happened, mechanically speaking, but the taxi broke down. We stopped on the side of a barren freeway, in the blazing heat. Thank goodness I had my paltry breasts with me to feed the chubby baby; this garden-variety type of problem becomes a top-level crisis when your baby needs a bottle—now—and you don't have one.

We waited there. After a surprising amount of time, a new taxi arrived. An argument of taxi drivers ensued. For reasons I cannot remember or never understood, Marcel had to transfer all the luggage from the original, broke-down, dirty taxi into the new dirty one. We were dripping sweat, our perpetually cheerful baby crying as much as we were sweating. I was extremely thirsty and getting very hangry.

The moment of arrival at the exclusive resort: picture it in your mind's eye.

A luxurious, open-space lobby in a tropical setting. You are lounging on elegant furniture, surrounded by rich fabrics, palms, and real artwork, an elegant, tranquil space. Slow-turning fans overhead stir warm air that caresses you softly with its movement and a delicate floral scent.

A couple stagger in. They are ne'er-do-wells, red faced and disheveled, carrying a baby and crappy luggage, pushing an ancient stroller, which, suddenly even to them, does not appear clean. Their damp hair is plastered to their heads, and their wet clothes to their bodies. The woman, one cannot help but notice through her wet shirt emblazoned with a large, strange, Eye of Sauron gold-coloured logo, is wearing a lumpy, multi-seamed, nonattractive bra with wide straps and numerous clips, like retro but not sexy, one flap clearly undone, giving her a lopsided shape. (There's an alarming stain located on the front of her trousers, but classy people like you won't mention that.)

The man is wearing formal business clothes that look as though he's been camping in them, then went swimming. Then rolled in dirt. The baby is naked, wearing only a disposable diaper, as though they gave up on dressing him at all, let alone in the designer-baby ensemble you expect in such an establishment. The baby is cute, but his hair is gross, like he's had sauce spilled on his head.

The Clampetts come to town (look it up, Millennials, Gen Z, whatever gen's next). That was us, seasoned, experienced parents: full disaster zones.

Don't be hard on yourself. Things go badly sometimes. Who cares? Your baby certainly doesn't. You probably don't have a bull's-eye of poo in the center of your shirt either, so take that as a W. (If you do, I'm sorry about that. Just throw it away; you probably have enough shirts.) Do not spend any time feeling bad when "things don't go well" when you're out with your baby. Babies are more resilient than we think and, many days, more resilient than we are.

SLEEP, AGAIN

Sleep. We have to talk about sleep again. Your sleep, not the baby's.

Sleep is the drug, and you are the addict, and you cannot get a good fix.

You manage tiny hits here and there, to keep you going, almost making you feel more desperate rather than ever so slightly satisfied. Out of the blue you randomly get a huge dose of sleep the drug, sumptuously reminding you why you love it so much, making you feel like Superman for the next forty-eight hours, bringing your world back to HD Technicolor once again.

You will meet other parents, hear of theories, be given books, etc., all of which assert that it's possible "to have babies and young children sleep completely through the night, reliably, all of the time!"

Not really.

I mean maybe, or sometimes, but not usually. Especially if you have more than one child, counting on the idea that fabulous sleep will regularly be a go is like planning your retirement around a lottery win: probably not a good idea. Love the win if you get one; plan for life without it. Sure, it's possible you hit a homer right out of the park and win a baby and/or toddler who sleeps solidly through the night, like all the time. Get down on your knees and praise the Creator of the Universe if that blessing has been bestowed upon you. You win. The rest of us just cobble together routines and patterns of coping, with varying success.

"Normal," in contrast, is a procession of activity that occurs during the night, beginning the day this small person emerges from a woman's body and continuing until that small person is about three years old, occasionally longer. (Multiply this by the number of children you have, using special math to account for some overlap of ages. Maybe someone can help you with this assignment; it's more complex than it initially seems, almost impossible if you haven't had enough sleep.) "Nighttime" begins to exist as a completely different entity than it's ever been before, unless you worked graveyard shift in a pediatric Emerg Department, or had a job supervising overnight pajama parties for the very young.

There is a "settling the baby" period that lasts for months, or years. Again, there's no shortage of books, or approaches, or blogs, or coworkers to advise you on this issue, but ultimately the goal is that both baby and you survive as unscathed as possible. Bearing in mind that older babies cannot possibly *need* nutrition multiple times per night, there still might be stretches of time when baby seems to need you, to change a diaper, hover nearby, provide a few pats, lurk about in the shadows a while, and tiptoe out again. (I know!! Fifty books say not to do that, I know! . . . I used the word *survive*, didn't I?)

Marcel and I would each fake that we were "about to get up," a standoff of fraud waged in hopes that the other would cave first and respond to the baby's wails. My clever husband came up with a fantastic idea for a product that we'd invent if we weren't so damn tired. This ultimate parenting gadget, the Neglect-o-Matic Parent, would be a life-sized, cardboard photo-replica of the parent, set up with wires and pulleys and such, with a large padded mitt attached to an articulated elbow joint.

Crying baby? Parent would just roll over in bed, pull a

string (or press a button if prototypes went better than expected), and presto! The Neglect-o-Matic Parent would glide out of the corner of the child's bedroom, the big ol' mitt giving a few good pats, the recorded parent voice offering a few coos while the real parent snoozes on.

Venture capital people: call me.

BABIES, IN GENERAL

DIFFERENT TYPES OF BABIES

Babyhood whips by. Baby's rolling turns to double leg throws (try it yourself), moves to sitting, turns to crawling, then things really get going. All kinds of fun, your babbling, smiley little person on the go.

If someone were to ask, *So what are babies like?* the answer, of course, is "it depends." It depends on the baby! They're all entirely different, just like people. The key is figuring out what *your* baby is like.

Here are examples of some of the options apparently available.

CRY(ING) ME A RIVER BABY

Some babies find the world largely irritating, inside their own little body and outside it too. They're gorgeously content at times, but it seems their sensitivity set point got bumped up on their way into this world. A gas bubble through new bowels is perceived as violent, internal damage. Loud noises are like bombs exploding nearby. Seams or tags on wee sleepers jangle nerve endings. This baby battles against the letting go of sleep, resists that giving in. So he cries. And cries. You are present as a basic support system and accompaniment, but you cannot take his angst away. You cannot make the crying stop. Your job is to model calm acceptance and total chill vibes, to help your baby do the same.

Yeah, I know. Good luck.

During one particular visit at my parents-in-law's house, in the wee hours of a few consecutive nights spent in a crammed, but thankfully removed, basement toolroom, Marcel and I had a number of "dynamic" conversations about our crier sort of baby. Our baby really needed to cry out this baby stress at night, which became incompatible with, say, quiet or sleep. My husband was making the well-supported argument that whatever we did made no difference, which he demonstrated through employing various baby treatments. Cuddling with a small jiggle, swinging said baby in a deep rhythmic arc, holding our small bundle high overhead with two hands, wrapping him and placing him on the floor under a work bench; all brought about the exact same result.

Crying.

I tried to make the less obvious argument, not possible to demonstrate, that it was our job to just stay there and do the thing. In the end that's what we took turns doing, each persevering with some thing until the jiggler/rocker/walker/sitting-slumped-er of screaming baby was perched teetering upon the precipice of total insanity, needing to tap out. We'd switch, a crash course in compelled patience.

I'd like to share something with anyone who has an inconsolable crier baby. I know it feels like all the crying you and your baby endure together points toward a horrific future looming ominously upon your shared horizon. It doesn't. Banish that fear.

Rather, it's more like those difficult times bond you together somehow, in a manner both distressing and exhausting at the time, but still. You get through it together, gradually forming a mysterious connection between you, impossible to define but real, almost a way of understanding someone without knowing why. I've considered as well an observation that there seems to be a correlation between an acutely sensitive baby and an adult who uses that sensitivity to be attuned to others: the crier baby who becomes the intense preschooler, who becomes the curious, analytical child, then the introspective teenager, who becomes a thoughtful, emotionally attentive adult.

This has been my experience with a crier baby. Hang on to this idea.

There is also an excellent possibility that all the crying (the baby's) has nothing to do with anything, ever. There could be that.

Either way, hang on.

SOCIAL CITY BABY

Some babies are social creatures, the life of the party. They start making eye contact early and soon follow your gaze to check out what you're looking at, because they want to see it too. These babies work the room, collecting business cards and networking like nobody's business. Toys are only as good as the ways in which they can be employed to interact with people. Peekaboo becomes a full-time job for these guys. They are sweet and charming, but beware, they're good at getting what they want and will soon be in charge of everything if you're not careful.

We had a social baby who, after the briefest of shoulder checks to scan for general proximity of humans, would, from a sitting or, later, barely standing position, tip her head back and fling herself backward into the abyss, counting on someone to catch her. This maneuver, similar to the backward fall from a ten-metre platform at the beginning of an Olympic back high-dive, caused many a nearby adult to yell, "Oh God!" and dive too, to catch her.

FYI, this behaviour served as no indication of our baby's future adult personality. She's an extremely considerate person, never forcing people to catch her anymore, that I'm aware of.

CONTEMPLATIVE BABY

Some babies are serene, wise old sages, contemplating you and the world around them as Zen masters from another paradigm. With their eyes wide open way too often it seems, these babies observe things quietly for hours, taking it all in. You rather expect these babies to begin speaking full sentences, in a language different from the one you speak. Their eyes track your movements knowingly, like a spy who's not allowed to write anything down and must store mental notes about everything.

I felt the peace of my old-sage baby only a few days into her young life, as she accompanied me on a couple of medical visits, strapped into her car seat on the way to the Emergency Department and then to a specialist's clinic. I had some complications, and she needed to come along of course, me being her food source and all. There she was with us, this new person, carried along by my steadfast husband, attending various waiting rooms, propped and present in the corner of examining rooms. Unexpectedly I felt her as a comfort to me, my baby quietly gazing upon the scene, or sleeping there in the hubbub. I remember looking at her, there in the back seat as Marcel drove us all home, feeling grateful for, and strangely comforted by, the presence of her teeny self.

How odd that a four-day-old baby could be a source of reassurance at a tense time and the days that followed, but she was, my baby sage.

She's still like that.

"LET'S GET PHYSICAL" BABY

Some babies are snugglers, as though they just cannot get close enough to you. They are baby koalas clinging on to you in the highest branches, curling their little bodies to meld to yours as thoroughly as they can. They are all about touch, these miniature people, and contact, pinching with teeny fingers and rubbing their fuzzy head on you. A physical baby is not clingy so much as forthright. She wants that input and she knows it; she shows you what she needs and seeks it, which is a super-helpful way to be in the world.

A kiss from our physical type of baby was like being eaten, as it often became a good suck on the hard angle of our chins. She'd use us as a surface to wipe her runny nose. I remember her giving me a kind of a headlock, her little arms and whole body pressing in around my head and neck with surprising tenacity—she could actually squeeze.

She still gives great hugs.

You don't have to guess at physical baby's "love language." For now, their love language is you.

CHAMPING-AT-THE-BIT BABY

Some babies are annoyed as hell at having to be a baby, at being small and less able to direct things in their world. These babies do not love being cuddled. They will push and arch away from you if you're getting all up in their grill, like they have appointments to get to, ones definitely not scheduled to take place in your arms. This being-held baby business is putting a real damper on things for her, so if you'd just get her a briefcase, or maybe a travel backpack, for her stuff, she'd be on her way, thank you very much.

I remember our family sitting together in a big booth of a family restaurant, on the rare occasion of a late lunch out on a Sunday afternoon, with me holding this type of baby, at five months of age, in my arms. I kissed her squishily on the cheek, as one does when holding a nice baby. I remember being shocked, even hurt, as she frowned at my kiss and rubbed at her cheek with her quick little hand, wiping away all of that gushiness-for-baby stuff she did not relish being the recipient of. We all laughed. I tested the kiss again, to the same result.

We still just kiss her anyway. Now I think she likes it.

HAPPY-GO-LUCKY BABY

Some babies are inexplicably happy, just as inexplicably as "the world is irritating me" babies. You are not responsible for your baby being either of these, by the way, criers or happy models. This is the baby's deal, not yours. It's not about you (get used to that concept).

Our baby of this sort wakes up happy . . . in a hot, stuffy room in summer . . . with a full diaper he didn't mind . . . with another small person crying in the same room. Happy, everything's good. Pasta with sauce that has too many capers by mistake? Yup, that'll be fine. Drink water out of a cup? No prob. Oh, sleep now? At this different time and place? Really? Uh, well . . . okay. It's downright weird.

Our baby of this sort would be lying on a blanket on the floor, playing happily with a toy, when a rogue sibling cruising by would grab the toy. This baby would then simply roll over and play with the frayed edge of the blanket he was lying upon.

There is nothing you have done to deserve this sort, please realize. He just shows up.

To a great extent, ours of this type has continued on in this way, though it would definitely not go as well for you now if you were to grab a favourite toy out of his hands.

These are just a few examples, in my experience anyway, of the countless different types of babies that exist. The key, and the fun, is figuring out what type of baby *you* have. The details become ridiculously difficult to remember in the future so maybe you should write some of it down. The feelings become written on your heart though—maybe that will cover it.

YOUR BABY

There is one thing *every single baby* on planet Earth has in common though: his or her babyhood is brief. A year and a bit. That's it, my friends, then: babyhood: check! Done—it's a wrap. It is exhausting, and intense, and feels like a long time when viewed from the vantage of 3:00 a.m., but babyhood indeed goes by in a flash.

Try, try, try to roll with it. Try to take it all in. Pay attention. I know, a lot of us suck at letting go, at just "being." But now is the time, if there ever is one. Think about it: you have a freakin' baby in the house! Yours! . . . *How often will that be true?*

Do me a favour.

If you have a baby, go get that little bubaloo and stick your face into her neck. Settle into the small, sweet curve of softness found in the space between her round cheek and the fresh fold of her little ear, and the tiny shelf of her shoulder. Stay there and breathe a while. Wonder at her hands, grabby and moist, with their dimpled knuckles and miniature fingernails. Look into her eyes, pure and perfectly clear. Feel her weight, not heavy yet, but significant, a presence somehow. Feel her warm head with its soft hair against your cheek, and her body breathing against your chest, and close your eyes. This little person you will know and love and intertwine your life with for the rest of your days, drink her in.

A baby—but not for long, baby.

YOUNG
CHILDREN

ONE, TWO

one, two
potty for poo

three, four
wipe kitchen floor

five, six
kisses and licks

seven, eight
close the gate

nine, ten
do it again

COPING

OBSERVE IT

Toddlers. What an apt description: to toddle. When was the last time you saw an adult toddle, except at an event with an open bar? These small people hurtle, and teeter, pee, slump, and fall, climbing about in your life, willful, nonsensical, and erratic, as if they too overvisited the open bar. You feel your own existence become ludicrous as well, in a distracted, oddly lovely kind of way. Or maybe it's just helpful to look at it as such.

"Young childhood," let's say, eighteen months to five years old, covers three and a half years. Let's imagine you live to be eighty-seven years old (a vibrant, healthy eighty-seven-year-old—you're welcome). Toddler Crazy Town will occupy 4 percent of your lifetime. That's it, folks: 4 percent. Might knowing this help you be okay with sitting on the bathroom floor for twenty-five minutes, reading the same book over and over, next to your cute little person seated upon a plastic potty, "waiting for poo"? Maybe?

A helpful technique for coping with all this, with tantrums, theirs and yours, with risks, hilarity, exhaustion, and sweetness so pure it makes your heart ache with an unnamed homesickness, is to *observe your life*, not just live it.

Observe.

Watch your life unfold around you, as if you are immersed in a theatre play happening in real time. You are one of the actors, and it's an extremely weird play. Observing your life this way makes everything easier to bear, and more likely you'll remember any of it years later, which honestly, and surprisingly I know, you will really want to do. Trust me.

March 10, 1998: it's early morning in late winter in our kitchen. Three-and-a-half-year-old Adam is kneeling on a chair eating his third Weetabix. Almost two-year-old Madeline is in her high chair, putting huge spoonfuls of cereal into her mouth and all over the tray. Five-year-old Emily is sweeping the floor. I have my foot up on a chair, and I'm clipping my toenails, a gross thing to do in the kitchen but something I'd been meaning to do for a week.

This scene, of being surrounded by these people who, only a few years ago, did not exist, all talking, making noises, doing their own thing while I cut my toenails in the kitchen all before 8:00 a.m. on a weekday, suddenly strikes me funny. I start to laugh. Emily demands, "What's so funny?" I try to explain it to her. She stares at me and says flatly, "I don't get why that's funny," which makes me laugh even more.

Once her sweeping is done (i.e., debris moved to new locations), Emily prepares the dustpan. Adam bolts over immediately and tries to grab the dustpan from her, because he usually "does the dustpan" for me, to help me (not really helping me). A battle ensues (see? observe), two small bodies and wills in hard combat over possession of a plastic dustpan at 7:35 a.m.

Using parental wisdom . . . or maybe brute force? . . . I separate the two, and let the Sweeper continue with her pseudo-sweeping experience, while the three-and-a-half-year-old sits on the floor becoming the Crier, bellowing a loud, monotonous foghorn of a defeated, angry cry. The youngest, still working on her breakfast, somehow ejects her bowl. It becomes an airborne projectile, lands in the middle of the kitchen floor, and sprays cereal everywhere.

The five-year-old freezes, stands up slowly, drops her cleaning equipment, puts both hands on her hips, and exclaims loudly, "Aaaah! . . . I JUST swept the kitchen floor!!"

I don't know whether to laugh because the situation is funny, or cry because my life is ridiculous, so I sort of do both. This causes the children to stop everything, become still and quiet, as children almost never are while awake. They stare at me, shifty eyed, uncertain whether they should laugh too but obviously trying to suppress a sense of being terrified. All of this leaves me . . . well, it just leaves me—right there.

This is the "observing" I am talking about. Observe the oddness, the wonder, the banality, the mess of the moment. It will all pass, dear parents, I promise you, becoming only a vague memory to ponder in the future. If observed well, the memory will still make you laugh and cry, years later. Having young children is sort of terrible, and sweet, and boring, and bizarre. It tests you, and makes you care more than anything else ever has. You might as well feel it: the best part of life is feeling it.

"Mom, my heart is telling me I'm full."
—Adam, 3, toward the end of a meal
Me: "You mean your stomach?"
"Yeah, my stomach."

This later became:

"Mom, my knee's telling my stomach that is telling my brain I'm tired."
—Madeline, 4

PAY NOW OR PAY LATER

In the midst of observing and feeling, there's a lot of "participating" that occurs during the early years: the heavy developmental stage of a lengthy project called life.

It is helpful to keep in mind an appreciation of the sheer volume of work that goes into any great endeavour. Consider what it takes to get a clever idea for an invention from imagination to patent secured, what it takes to get a theatre play from nagging story idea to script written to stage production, or a symphony from hummed tune to orchestral performance.

A freakin' ton of work, that's what.

Same-same with parenting a young child: also a ton o' work. Much of this work is seriously not fun. Of course not. Nothing worthwhile is always fun—if it was, then it wouldn't be worthwhile. We humans resist this fact for obvious reasons, but anything worthwhile involves the arduous.

Your kid is flat-out adorable. Of course. Also, somewhat unruly. That's the thing with two- and three-year-olds: they're super-cute, tough customers. The work of parenting is aimed at getting one's young child from a nonverbal, feral state of total narcissism to one in which he or she can communicate and cooperate with other people, such that, at four years old, another four-year-old will voluntarily play with her.

Note the word *voluntarily*. Other children will cut your child zero slack with the "choose to play with her" bit. Zero. It has to be easy for them. I'm not saying you need to teach your children to appease everyone, no. I am saying it's good to really focus on helping her or him learn to consider others, to temper impulses just a tad or more. To "take turns," as it were. This "learning to get along with others" is a parent-slog, of getting up, of saying no, of resisting the tsunami force of a toddler's or preschooler's will. This is not for the faint of heart.

I predict your next question, and the answer is yes. Absolutely, yes, children *are so* learning this at three years old. When else??

When your young child *really* wants to use the good kitchen scissors to chop all the heads off his sister's Barbies behind the couch, it's exactly then that the learning occurs. The parent's long-suffering "No, you can't do that" is definitely not welcomed by that three-year-old. But, in a few years' time, he'll find it equally difficult to accept his classmate's "No, you can't eat the Krispy Kreme doughnut you noticed in my *Frozen* lunch bag, just because you want to." (Update cultural references as required; mine are never current.)

If you work hard at stopping the scissor-decapitation incident, things will go much better with the Krispy Kreme incident. See? These two events become mysteriously linked over time. And *much* later, along the same time continuum, they become related to "No, you can't throw a pen—hard—across a boardroom because you don't agree with what someone just said." Also linked, same-same.

To recap: a freakin' ton of work. But *you* need to do it; no one else loves your kid enough to take on that struggle. Nobody else will go to the mat over this stuff—too exhausting, no skin in the game.

Marcel and I had a running joke to amuse ourselves. All hell would be breaking loose, and if we were both busy or, more notably, relaxing, the exhausted shreds of our consciences would have one of us call out to the other, "Do you think we have to get up?"

Uh, yes.

There seems an Energy Distribution Principle at work in parenting little kids: when choosing between two possible courses of action, the one requiring the Greatest Energy Expenditure is pretty much always your best bet. Unfortunately. I'm not sure why that's true, but it is.

We should assume some cosmic balance of energies within the universe has set out that screaming, "Cut it out, Crystal!!" at the top of your lungs from the couch, while Crystal proceeds to do whatever the hell she wants, will never be as effective as getting up and making Crystal stop the thing. Bummer, but true. As a guideline, that's how you know which parent thing to do: the one that's more work. You can pay now or pay later.

Suggestion: pay now.

GETTING UP

Never was this "getting up" dilemma more evident to me than when I was sitting breastfeeding a baby. Even frightfully young children quickly realize that a mother sitting nursing a baby is essentially trapped. They see you immobilized there and think: *Party time!* I literally watched that thought appear on each of my toddlers' faces, right in front of me, to varying degrees depending on their personalities. My calling to them was white noise, an artifact, meaningless. I was the parent on the bus who tells her child one hundred times to stop something, but does nothing to make it happen, and my less-than-two-year-olds knew it. This got so bad at times that I considered strapping my nursing babe to my chest . . . women all over the world manage this way, while labouring at all manner of tasks. Surely I could fight with a toddler while doing the same?

Instead I sat, busily categorizing the toddlers' activities, on the fly, into designations of "Ignore" or "Get Up," while new episodes of *Toddlers Gone Wild* premiered around me.

The "Ignore" category, narrow at first, broadened

generously with time, to encompass activities such as a toddler dumping crayons or getting a block of cheese out of the fridge, walking around gnawing on it while responding "NO" to all requests to put the cheese back, or dragging a chair to the kitchen gadget drawer, climbing up and removing all cooking utensils, distributing them over the kitchen and family room floors. You know, ordinary things.

I'd best discern what belonged in the "Get Up" category by imagining what *other people's* reactions would be if they saw what my toddler was up to. One should get up, even with babe on boob, if a toddler speeds by holding a sharp skewer, the one she'd seen adults use to unlock the faulty bathroom doorhandle that becomes locked by accident, the toddler heading over to work on the doorhandle themselves, standing on tippy-toe. Sometimes a toddler manages to open an older brother's toolbox left by the front door and starts investigating the drill. (Yes, my seven-year-old son had a drill. I cannot explain this.) This too belongs in the "Get Up" category.

Toddlers tend to like taking their clothes off to nurse a doll alongside you, curiously needing to remove their diaper at the same time. I typically put that in the "Ignore" category, which was sometimes a mistake.

The appropriate level of alarm was difficult to gauge. If a toddler got into the bathroom (despite the plastic doorknob safety cover) and stood on the stool applying toothpaste to multiple toothbrushes to suck on, I felt torn about stopping nursing, again, to get up. I mean, I didn't care about the toothbrushes, but a twenty-month-old teetering on a stool with a toothbrush in her mouth? And isn't it bad for kids to eat a lot of toothpaste?

Eventually the baby was fed. Somehow, those babies all survived. All but one are taller than me now.

"Daddy, whatever you do, don't poo in your
unter-wear!"
> —Levi, 3, crouched in upper hallway, very
> early in the morning, whispering down to
> Marcel, on his way to work

Later that day, in a meeting, Marcel shared
with his colleagues that he'd had a banner
day because he had in fact not pooed in his
underwear.

MORE ABOUT SLEEP

We need to talk about sleep again, meaning yours.

There will not be enough.

Even after the babyville years, it can be a parade of visitors
in the night, especially if you have more than one child, or a
few children.

Eventually your seven-month-old will sleep five hours in a
row many nights. Unreal, amazing, life changing for everyone.
However, if you happen to have a young child in the same family as gold-star-sleeper baby, devastatingly, on the same night as
the five-hour baby sleep, your toddler might be restless, or have
a fever, or simply wake twice during that five-hour stretch. She
will come a-tap-tapping on your forehead . . . because she can
climb out of her crib now and batters at the doorknob security
cover meant to keep her in, for twenty minutes, as you listen
from your bed, despairing. Your toddler manages to open her
door and bursts into your room while the baby sleeps.

Let me say that again: "While the baby sleeps."

Two-year-old Emily would call us from her crib, louder and
louder, until I was fearful she'd wake nearby five-month-old

Adam, so I'd get up and go to her. She'd smile at me there in the darkness, greeting me sociably, as two guests at a cocktail party.

"Hi, Mommy! 'Ow ar lou?!" she enquired, with Einstein hair and a salesman's smile.

Or maybe that toddler action happens on a night when the baby sleeps for three hours, twice. (You do the math.)

Parents with young children often talk about sleep as farmers talk about weather, with an edge of shared anxiety, as though discussing impending drought conditions. Couples engage in odd "reporting to each other about sleep" in the mornings, a sad form of reciprocal support.

That was a terrible night.

Yeah, or some equally scintillating response.

Why am I telling you this?! Why am I not saying how good it can be? Why torture you with negativity, dispelling all hope in this cold and lonely world?

Because false hope is a terrible thing, and the truth will set you free. Sort of.

The barren truth is that sleep tends to be extremely fragmented over the span of years during which you have a baby and a young child/children. I say this to reassure you that pathetic, ridiculous patterns of sleep, and nonsleep, are perfectly normal. I don't want you to feel bad: I'm trying to make you feel better! You are not doing anything wrong. (If you are up more than ten times a night with your baby and/or toddler, you are doing something wrong. If something doesn't change, you will go insane, utterly, entirely, stark-raving mad. Find someone you trust who knows something useful about babies and young children, or seek professional help to figure out what you're doing wrong.)

Moms and dads: tag team, develop coping plans, outsource help, buy quality undereye-bag concealer, do what you can to survive the pitiful sleep that may happen for a few years.

For a few years?? Chills the soul, I know, but yes, sometimes it does take years.

My personal coping mechanism? If you, my darling child, were installed in a bassinet, crib, or small bed, then I wanted you to stay there, between baby feeds, the comings and goings, diapers and burping, crying and such. But if you, my child, could break free and arrive in the night to our bed holding two inert lumps of parentness, and maybe even another kid, you were allowed to get in and stay if—that is *if*—it was possible to sleep with you. That simple: it had to be possible to sleep with you.

I would hear the monster-breathing beside the bed, or suddenly have an eerie sense of a face being approximately two and a half inches from mine, or, less subtly, have "HI MOMMY!!" shouted into my ear at 3:17 a.m.

I'd open one eye to see who it was, do a cursory sweep and clutch of the diaper area with my hand to check for leaking, and whip back the covers. That was all the child needed. My small person would scramble up, turn around a few times, kind of like dogs do, and settle in against me, as the little spoon of course. We'd fall back asleep immediately, if all went well. No philosophy whatsoever, just coping.

Freeze frame—stop right there. This is important.

Those exact moments within the gong show years of non-sleep, those 3.7 seconds it took to slip back into unconsciousness while wrapped around my child, are among the most precious of my parenthood, a soul-filling indulgence of contentment, momentarily the pinnacle. The memory of being nestled with my young child, each in turns over the years, wearing kiddie pajamas, their warm feet pressed against my legs, toes wiggling a bit, little hands holding mine, smelling of soap and spit and a warm sweetness as we drifted back to sleep, is a hazy gift. Joy amid the torture. Bliss even.

Start film again—reality check. If you, my child, sat on

your dad's head a few times, or put your dainty little finger up my nose more than twice, or turned over and over as if attempting to break some world record for turning in bed, Dad or I would abruptly throw back the covers, explode out of bed, and return you to yours. Or, on a particularly desperate night, go get in yours ourselves.

That reminds me of a side story about getting in the child's bed: in our family, the whole "having beds" thing got away from us. Let me explain.

When the day came that our oldest children transitioned from a crib (i.e., could climb out), and we deemed that attaching a cargo net from a Jeep over the top was unacceptable, even by our low standards (seriously, we talked about it), we bought a twin-sized mattress and put it on the floor. Done. No problem for toddlers getting in, no worries about them falling out, jumping on the bed not an issue.

We were a good four mattresses into this approach when it dawned on us, while climbing down onto one of these pseudo-beds ourselves in the night, that maybe we should get the actual frames . . . you know, also referred to as *beds*. Marcel felt inspired to put his carpentry skills to work and make a bed for each child. The first of these Dad-crafted beds was gifted to our eldest upon its completion some months later. "Ta-da!" A bed.

Emily (at school, about 8): "I have a bed!"

Everyone (staring blankly): "What did you use to sleep in?"

Every family does this differently. We continued like this for years, sleeping together in whatever haphazard arrangement was brought on by the night parade, an island of slumbering kinfolk, until the kids themselves began just staying asleep in their own beds at night, having gradually found themselves done with seeking nocturnal company.

I'm not saying you should do this; I'm just saying we did. Do your best. You will sleep again, I promise.

"Mom, did you have a good sleep last night?"
—Adam, 4, to me when Eva was a
newborn

"Well, yes actually, sweetheart, I did."

"I thought so. You're more like you used to be."

DISCIPLINE

This might be a good time to talk about discipline. It's heavy, but we have to talk about it sometime—might as well get it over with. Discipline, authority, guiding without damage, whatever you want to call it. I have a strong opinion on the topic because I've worked out the answer to the entire question! No kidding! Maybe it's been a secret that I've stumbled upon—I'm not even sure.

Full disclosure: the approach I'm about to describe has not been reviewed, reported on, or endorsed in any way that I'm aware of, by child psychologists, or pediatricians, or anyone legit. No experts were involved in the making of this approach. I encourage you: check with someone knowledgeable before believing my secret to raising children. (Be certain the person you select to advise you isn't crazy though, whether professional/academic or not. Remember, there are educated, crazy professionals out there too.)

Here it is:

THE SECRET OF PARENTING

Your child needs to know beyond a shadow of a doubt and with absolute certainty that you love him or her completely, always, and beyond all telling, such that you would take a bullet for him or her without hesitation if you had to

AND, at the same time,

Your child needs to know beyond a shadow of a doubt and with absolute certainty that you will never tolerate shit from, or allow yourself to be treated badly by, him or her. Ever. Period.

Both equally and fully:
Love abundantly and Take no shit.

TA-DA!! That's it. I'm sure there are no questions, so let's carry on.

It's your love that allows you to be the hard-ass they need you to be. And it's love that keeps the hard-ass-edness from being mean. Your child comes to realize you simply love him or her way too much to allow him or her to be despicable with you or anyone and get away with it. Not on your watch.

Now, "trigger alert," or whatever the correct warning procedure is (too late): here you are, parent of an enchanting toddler or preschooler, being assailed by a rude proposal describing parents being hard-asses and kids being despicable. Sorry about that. I know it seems too early for this discussion, but it's crucial to know this sooner rather than later.

Sooner is now. This whole discipline section is mostly a view to future concerns, but then again, we all know that a four-year-old can be quite the asshole if you let him.

There's a fabulous paradox of tension held in The Secret. In the midst of your loving smooches, your fulfilling of needs, your affirmations and favours, kindnesses and back rubs, and all the fun snacks you will make, your child comes to understand, and know, that you will not tolerate crap from him. He becomes certain that rudeness or meanness on his part will trigger your wrath. Enveloped within the great dynamic of love and care between you, he has to be a teeny, tiny bit afraid of you and not even know why. Not because you hit him, or are cruel to him, or because of some weird Oedipal guilt complex for "failing you." None of that.

More like, he knows for certain you will not let atrocious behaviour go, while not being at all certain what you'll do about it. Like that. Your children have to be a bit afraid of you (just a teensy bit) and not know why—and not ever want to find out. Weird, but there it is. How you achieve this is up to you. I am naturally mean and have the advantage of "mean eyes." You know, the ol' hairy-eyeball stare of death. I could stop my kids in their tracks with The Look, making eye contact with them across a room, hell, across a gym, telegraphing what I meant by it. They knew immediately, 100%, exactly what they'd better stop doing, or start doing. Pure magic, available to any parent, though admittedly more difficult for lovely, kind people.

When my children were young, I developed an odd, uncontemplated yet effective technique of chasing them through the house when I'd finally had it. This is not for everyone; in fact, I don't recommend it. I just did it. Do not imagine a loving mother skipping playfully after her children, all tinkling laughter and amused affection. NO, oh-h-h no. This was a red-eyeballed lunge, a sprint of rage, a she-wolf hunt across the kitchen, flinging around the corner and tearing up the stairs. The child would bolt full-tilt away from me, speed-climbing the stairs on hands and feet, with me going as fast as I could behind them. They'd fly into their bedroom, slamming the door shut, when they'd reached a critical threshold of "not being the best version of themselves."

Damn right they weren't.

I had no idea what I was going to do when I caught them. Neither did they.

I did not catch them. I cannot remember why.

I was reminded of this effective weirdness years later, when my kids organized a most cherished birthday gift: a booklet they called *Mom Memories*, a collection of six stories, one from each, of a particular memory of their mom, in celebration of my fifty-second birthday.

Sixteen-year-old Levi wrote this:

MOM MEMORIES

A clear and vivid memory I have of us, Mom (of many memories, don't worry), takes me back to my younger elementary years. After having definitely done something terribly wrong, and pissing you off past a very dangerous point, it seems as though I had only given you one option for a punishment. Having you right on my ass, as I sprinted the hardest I ever have up our sketchy stairs was honestly and truthfully one of the scariest moments of my life. The feeling of your hand slipping against my clothes as I get away by centimeters is forever engraved in my memory.

But now that I am done making my childhood seem so traumatic, I can truly express how much you, Mom, have done for me. A tiny speck, a taste of what I'm talking about can be shown relating back to the stair incidents. During a surprising number of situations in my life, I seem to vaguely ask myself, If Mom knew about this, would I be chased up the stairs right now? And it seems to yield the correct outcome most of the time.

Heartwarming. Somewhat embarrassing as well, but heartwarming.

Now, let us proceed with a tip to accompany The Secret.

THE ULTIMATE PARENTING TIP

If you say to your child:
If you A, then I will B! . . . B must happen if A does.
Must. Always. 100% of the time.
(Warning: The Ultimate Tip is exhausting. Just sayin'.)

One valid school of parenting recommends that parents never use the "If A then B" formula at all, and they've got a point. The structure of the formula essentially serves as an invitation, or a challenge, depending on the kid, to behave badly. The thing is, parents universally resort to this format when we are angry, so we might as well talk about it.

Examples might be helpful.

If you take your brother's Playmobile car again, I will throw all your toys in the garbage!

You will? Seriously? Your B will be throwing away all the toys? For keeps? And she'll have nothing to play with . . . forever?? I don't see this plan making things better for you at all. More importantly, your kid knows you won't actually do B— throw all those expensive toys in the garbage—any time soon. Thus: her interpretation? Carry on with A.

If you don't get in the car this minute, I'm going to daycare without you!

Umm, okay, so this makes no sense, for all kinds of reasons. In humility, we must pause, all of us, and admit we've definitely said things equally asinine, a multitude of times. You get a pass on a few of these, but if you keep it up, your child will move in for the kill. Begin immediately attempting to stop yourself from saying zero-sense things.

If you keep kicking the seat in front of you because you're mad, I'll take you out of the movie theatre.

Bingo. There it is—rubber meets the road. Fair conse-
quence, total pain in the ass for you. If the little kicker goes for
it again, *you must do it*: haul her butt out of that movie. Perfect
example.

Before doing any of this though, try something. Try saying, "Stop kicking the seat," just like that, and *really* mean it.
See what happens. Use your mean eyes.

The Ultimate Tip is challenging, no question, but it's im-
perative. If you consistently never do whatever the hell you
said you'd do—the B thing—your child will come to learn that
you are not good for your word . . . and that, my friends, is
an irredeemable problem. She learns that you are a pushover,
dead in the water in parenting world. A boundless childhood,
brimming with potential "A behaviours" of her choosing, A's of
anarchy and total freedom, manipulation and asshole-edness,
stretches out in front of her. And she knows it. Not good.

Here are two pointers to help with The Tip:

- Pointer #1: Be certain the "A behaviour" (the
  thing you've identified as a significant infraction)
  actually *is* a significant infraction, i.e., matters. I
  got this wrong for a lot of early years, I am sorry
  to say. Leave the small stuff, be reasonable, don't
  set the bar at a ridiculous height.
- Pointer #2: Make sure your B statement (the thing
  you will do) isn't nutso. Easy mistake. Screen the
  words you are about to blurt for lunacy.

That's it.

The Secret? Love abundantly and Take no shit.

The Tip? If you say, "If A, then B," you gotta do B if A
happens.

Good luck. This mostly applies when your kids are older,
but you have to start now, while your children are young. It's

all hard. Just do your best. Given all the secrets and tips, endless recommendations, and advice out there, there is no one way to do things.

Despite your best efforts, many days will go horribly, which is my thinly veiled way of saying that, many days, I was horrible. Terrible, ranting, horrible.

But we regroup, get some sleep, try to figure out where things went wrong. We snuggle and kiss our young child, apologize for our atrocious behaviour, and get back in the ring, again . . . like a boxer! Sort of. Or actually, maybe no, not like a boxer at all. How about something with that same "sporting spirit," let's say, but without all the hitting . . .

Tomorrow is another day! If you do the loving part well, your child will forgive you for all the rest. Children are generous like that.

> "Oh, I don't matter about that."
> "No, it doesn't matter me."
> "It's okay. It can be yes. It can be no. I
> don't matter."
> —both Emily, almost 5, and Adam, 3, in
> moments of selfless generosity

DISTRACTION

The issue with young children is not discipline so much as distraction. Avoid the fight: distract! We've all been there: "Here—have this!!" and handing your child some random object grabbed within reach. Doing the simplest of things with young children present becomes a challenge. Cleaning up a mess without "help." Getting anything done on a computer.

Going to the toilet. Making a phone call. You know, crazy stuff.

Have you also literally run away from your own shrieking child (what's with all the running?), through your home, while trying to discuss your credit card limit with an adult professional? I ran into the bathroom once and locked myself in, only to discover, as the door was battered by a wild, wailing toddler, that I was trapped in a space more echoey than anything I'd ever experienced. I cringed, as screaming echoed and reverberated off the walls while I explained loudly that I had not thought the latest charge was going through on *this* billing cycle.

Desperate times.

I am pleased to share a life-changing strategy, yards more fun than the discipline stuff.

GETTING SOMETHING DONE IN THE PRESENCE OF A TODDLER: THE COPING STRATEGY

Let's start here: Would you set off on a climbing expedition without preparation? No, you would not. Well, no more should you blithely think you can just "make a phone call" with a toddler or two around. Ha!

You must prepare Diversion Tools.

Collect three or four odd things, not overtly dangerous, that children do not normally play with.

One must be an old remote control, preferably one that doesn't operate anything. If the remote still has batteries, causing lights to illuminate, or beeping to happen, consider yourself blessed. Young children love things that are clearly made for adults. Toddlers and preschoolers somehow know that the good stuff, the *real stuff*, is usually black or metallic, shiny, and often sharp, like remotes, real tools, keys, and external hard drives. We insult their nineteen-month-post-utero sensibilities with the condescending, primary-coloured plastic crap made for babies. The baby toys piss them off. They want the good stuff.

Other potential Diversion Tools (all intended for children who no longer put everything directly into their mouths as their preferred method of figuring out what something might be):

- a manual eggbeater (Theoretically, yes, small fingers can become caught in the turning beaters, but most two-year-olds have trouble turning the handle while sticking their fingers in at the same time. Most.)
- an old-fashioned, real, rubber hot-water bottle with water inside, cap on tight (If you're an educational parent, into "multisensory stimulation" and such, fill it with warm water—much more fun.)
- snacks that rule out the possibility of choking (prunes cut into small pieces, tiny crackers that turn to goo when wet, those miniature boxes of raisins*)
- a real builder's tape measure

*The Raisin Box Aside: I must explain, to anyone who has ever wondered, why on earth companies would package and sell raisins in ridiculously tiny boxes.

The small boxes of raisins are not food. They are an activity. A desperate parent is not whipping out the most minute box of raisins as a helpful source of nutrition. Hell no! It is an activity, the Raisin Box Activity, guaranteed to provide the beleaguered parent with a minimum ten full minutes of uninterrupted survival time, like a spare oxygen tank for a scuba diver.

Handed a mini box of raisins, the small person stops

everything, stands up, drops whatever he or she was holding, and grabs the tiny box in small fingers. With a nice, round, fat stomach sticking way out, the small person looks down, concentrating on the tiny box of raisins, mouth-breathing noisily while a thin string of drool stretches down from her or his plump bottom lip. A tiny finger begins to pick at the flap of the thin cardboard tucked in at the top, or bottom, of the little box. No parent ever watches this though, because, as the heavy breathing and finger picking ensues, parents dive at their task. Mom or Dad runs to get the document from the printer, or takes the stinking garbage outside "all by themselves," or slugs back four big swallows of hot, strong coffee while staring out the kitchen window.

The raisin box is a game changer. Imagine the small hellion picking out and eating at least twelve raisins from the box, individually, one fabulous pick-and-eat at a time! One swoons at the possibilities. If you ever see a parent buying a package of small boxes of raisins for some ridiculous price and think to yourself, *Fool!* well, the joke's on you.

Now, back to the Coping Strategy.

Arrange all gathered Diversion Tools on the counter or table, along with the piece of paper and the pen that will be required to take notes but suddenly, mysteriously do not exist *anywhere* in the place where you live, causing the entire Strategy to disintegrate to shambles. Warm up a bit, stretch, take your phone (laptop, garden tool, hair-colouring kit, etc.) slowly in your hand, and turn your back to your child. Breathe slowly. Act cool, as though you are definitely not doing anything.

Make the call or try to do the thing.

Your child will immediately sense that cell phone signals have been activated in her proximity, or that your brain synapses are suddenly firing with formed intent. She will instantly need you, desperately. Present her with the orphaned remote control, stand nearby (don't run away yet), and talk/act casually, keeping your voice as normal as possible. If your toddler wanders off, you are obliged to follow him, but do so at a distance, without heightened interest, like a predator with a full stomach.

Introduce further Diversion Tools, *only as necessary*: eggbeater, plastic bowl of prune pieces, rubber hot water bottle, or tape measure, standing close and stroking her hair. Keep going! Use the presourced piece of paper and pen to take notes if you must, but without making them seem interesting.

If absolutely necessary, deploy the tiny box of raisins. Immediately inform your boss/lawyer/friend who planned a call because she "thinks you're not coping well" that you have ten minutes available before you must go.

See? Easy. Gem of a plan, am I right? You're welcome.

> "Dad! . . . see how long I weigh? . . . that's pretty
> old, isn't it? . . . 40."
> —Levi, 4, holding a tape measure up
> against himself

SEPARATION

Even the most confident or defiant of young children are in great need of you. You're reminded of this whenever, randomly or routinely, your child experiences a frenzy of deeply charged, emotionally wrenching terror at being separated from you. These experiences end with you in a lather of sweat, feeling about the same as if you'd just been attacked at a bus stop by an emotionally needy child wrestling champion.

I thought I'd dodged that bullet, our eldest three children having so far tootled off fairly happily to preschool, or been fine with being left with babysitters and such. Madeline, quiet but not shy, particularly *loved* going out to things, as though keen to break free from me and her sibs to see what the world had to offer. Mads marched into preschool without looking back, eyes dancing with excitement. She eagerly beetled into a little gymnastics class, begged to take part in a preschoolers' ballet session at the community centre, loved it when babysitters came for the evening. Madeline was always ready for outside adventure, never wavering from that position.

Then out of the blue, Emily began having separation stress, for a few weeks of kindergarten, and later again in Grade 2. Those school mornings began with a quiet but observable escalating anxiousness in Emily, my little girl with missing front teeth, a hooded pink raincoat, a too-large backpack, and a death grip on my hand.

Emily's small, pleading *Mom, I'm just not ready again to go to school anymore*, made me need *my* mother.

Our arrival in the classroom involved silent, eye-contact communication with the teacher over Em's head, a lot of arm clutching—hers of mine—serious teacher intervention, and my frenetic escape, hustling toddler Madeline along, with kindergartener Adam miraculously cooperating, seemingly terrified that *he'd* have to stay if she didn't. It was a heart-wrenching way to start each day.

Just as I was getting seriously worried about this, she stopped, just like that.

Years later, our youngest child, Veronica, was, from the get-go, decidedly opposed to being separated from me. For the first couple of months of three-year-old preschool, at every morning drop-off, Veronica fought like a juvenile chimpanzee being torn from her pack. The darling young preschool teachers almost had to leg-wrestle Veronica to keep her in the room, her desperate face and frantic voice pleading with me as the door swung shut. It was awful. This was my sixth child, and I cried in the car in the parking lot a few times, wondering whether I should abandon this madness. We persevered. Weeks later, it was a breezy, *Bye, Mom!* over her shoulder as Veronica ran to the greeting circle.

These things are excruciating, and normal. Don't make them worse by torturing yourself with self-doubt—kids just need to do stuff like this sometimes. That's a frequent dynamic in coping with your child's developmental journey: just as *you* begin to fixate on how to solve a problem, he or she moves on. Certainly, keep your eye on a situation, but be open to the idea that most often things need time.

> "They call me Boo Bear."
> —Veronica, 4, waiting with me as I stood chatting with the elementary school principal, contributing small talk during a lull in the conversation

WHAT IT FEELS LIKE

SWEETNESS

Having young children is, after all is said and done, the sweetest of sweet things you will ever experience.

The same dainty elf, or chunky monster, who only moments ago made you wish you'd never had children, will bring about a sweetness of moment so delicious you almost can't bear it, thus ensuring his survival, and yours too.

He will climb up onto your lap, his feet pressing too hard into your flesh, somehow pulling your hair at the same time. He'll be restless, like a puppy finding his place, then settle in, heaving himself against you. He will do something quite unexpected, like stare at you and reach up to stroke your face softly, or fully expected, like turn his face toward you and wipe his nose on your shirt. His hair will be slightly damp, like someone who's been exercising heavily, because he has been, his hands sticky without discernable reason. Maybe he will begin rocking back and forth a bit, or maybe it's you who rocks, and he will get heavier. He will shift and lurch, perhaps smashing his head against your chin. Then he will sink into you, his body melding against yours, and in a moment, be asleep. The monster tamed will now be an angel asleep on your chest, so beautiful and new you can barely stand it, or believe he is yours. The fact that he put your phone in the toilet a few hours ago will start to feel like it matters less than it originally did.

His cheeks, plump and round, will squish up, pressed from the side against you, his lips slack and soft. Eyelashes, fine and long, striking you as oddly out of place on a small tank of a male human being, sweep down and lay against the translucent skin under his closed eyes. You'll stroke his small, solid, heavy body, his feet dangling on each side of you, bare because he's always taking his socks and shoes off, his fat hands curled limp against your sides. The day and your life dangle there too, a few long moments of bliss, the bliss that keeps parents of toddlers going through Crazy Town.

This is peace. Observe it, too great a moment to be overlooked. Breathe it in.

Nobody honest ever said this would be easy. It's not. It is hard. I have a memory of schlepping along with a stroller in the company of my young children when an older lady, passing on the sidewalk, stopped me to say, "Oh my, you lucky thing! These are the most beautiful years!"

"THESE?!?" I answered in a panic. "*These* are??"

There is no denying: young children can make you nuts. Remember though: the fact that it's terribly hard doesn't mean you're not doing it right. It just means it's hard.

I want to encourage you. You *do* know what you're doing, and you can ask others about the stuff you don't know. I'm with good ol' Dr. Benjamin Spock, a pediatrician who, in 1946, wrote a world-changing, now-classic parenting book called *The Common Sense Book of Baby and Child Care*, in which he said:

> "Trust yourself. You know more than you
> think you do."

Amen, brother. Yes, you do.

Try to take it as it comes. Wonder at the insanity, and the joys, treasuring "all these things and pondering them" in your heart, so you can gaze and wonder at them again years from now, through the rosy glass of memory. Beauty is found there, within the madness. Taking time to ponder it is both fruit of your labour and fuel for it. Fuel for, perhaps, cleaning up projectile vomit after your toddler eats an entire bag of slightly unripe plums she managed to reach from the edge of the counter, again, like a dog might.

Ah, the paradox of life with young children, the mysteriously beautiful jammed against the painfully concrete. Try to notice it all. Perhaps you think me overly sentimental. If so, I come right back at you: if you're not sentimental about your magical young child climbing all over you and your life, what is it you are planning to be sentimental about?

DANGEROUS FISHING

"Uh, Mom? I'm having some trouble here."

My preschool son's voice warbled, his tone signalling both worry and a difficulty. Its intensity did not indicate a dire emergency but rather a predicament, one not easily resolved by a three-year-old.

"Mom? . . . Can you help me?" His voice was higher now with the strain of increasing alarm. I stepped down from farther up on the beach we were both on, preparing from experience to expect the unexpected.

I was not disappointed.

His difficulty was immediately apparent. He stood as though straddling a canoe, with his feet rolled out onto their very outmost edges. His dear little face was a picture of forced optimism, a feigned smile of bravery wavering to reveal his building anxiety. There was nothing subtle about the source of this anxiety because there was a fishing rod down the front of his swim shorts.

I mean to say, to provide a more accurate picture of things, that the entire handle and working parts of a fishing rod, though not visible, were immersed completely in his shorts. The end of the rod projected up sharply to a point high above his head, forming an unusual exclamation point. We gravely surveyed the situation together, as he shook his head in disbelief at the misfortune that had befallen him.

He shuffled toward me like an old cowboy, and I gave a gentle test tug on the rod, shifting him off balance. He gripped my arm in panic, warning, "Mom! There's some hurting parts!" A gentle test tug of the swim trunks also resulted in the same loss of balance and grip of panic. Even the roomiest of shorts become snug, or downright compressive, when a large space is taken up at the front. Anyone who has gained a lot of weight, or been six months pregnant, or had a fishing rod stuck down the front of their pants knows this.

We had a problem. Within the little room available for inspection, we both viewed the combination of fishing rod parts and fleshy human parts in close arrangement at the front of the shorts.

I discovered I was not familiar with fishing rod parts.

Further examination and some minor adjustments revealed that the fishing rod parts included a ball encircled by a wire half loop thing, a small pointy plastic ledge piece identified by my son as "the hurting part," a handle that turned, and, of course, some fishing line. I decided that one simply had to envision all these parts (human and fishing rod) as some sort of movable puzzle, like a Rubik's Cube but different.

Adding my hand to the limited space available in the front of his swim shorts, I slowly executed a series of precision maneuvers, a secret agent assigned to curious domestic mishaps. With a half turn of this, a slight shift of that, and the rotation

*or lifting of various spherical parts, eventually the puzzle was
solved. With a slow twisting and rotation of the handle, the
fishing rod drew a sweeping arc over our heads, a shooting star,
down toward the sand as it was freed from the swim trunks.*

*I laid the rod on the beach, and we stared at it, two spies
having just defused a bomb. My son squatted down fully the
way young children do, his face still sombre, leaning forward,
his hands holding his knees. He studied the fishing rod handle
that only moments before had been trapped in his shorts. He
contemplatively tapped the otherwise unidentified pointy ledge
piece, saying quietly, "This is the hurting part."*

*All at once the darkness of concern lifted from his face,
like a window shade going up, returning him once again to his
sweet, small boy resting state of buoyant happiness.*

*He leaned close, smiling as my conspirator. With obvious
satisfaction he said, "Whoa, Mom. THAT was dangerous!"*

Indeed. Thank God there was no hook involved.

Be careful everyone. It's dangerous out there.

HELP THAT IS NO HELP

As soon as they can barely walk, and even as crawlers, your
young children will want to help you, whether you like it or
not. Help click buckles, pour stuff, get dressed, stir things,
open doors. None of this will help, at all, not for ages. Their
help will slow you down, make a mess, maybe hurt your back,
and generally be of no assistance whatsoever. But that's not the
point, as you might guess. You nod, and smile, and say yes, and
get small people to "help you," not because you are a masochist
for frustration but because you desire that she or he become a
competent human. Also, because, though a hindrance, it's also
epically cute.

Being helpful, capable, and aware of what needs to be done
and able to do it are extremely gratifying for a person, probably

one of the greatest drivers of true self-esteem there is (zero references to support this, only logic and experience). Competent people get shit done and contribute to the well-being of others, and usually feel pretty good about it.

How do people learn to be competent and reliable? In many ways of course, but a lot of it begins when they are two years old and you hand them the package of toilet paper to carry.

They love this! Loud mouth-breathing, complete with weight lifters' exhalations, accompanies the flat-feet stomping along of their little Velcro'd shoes, their small, strong hands tightly gripping the sides of the package as they peek around the reportedly downy-soft contents, making their way along, all with the proudest look of satisfaction on their faces. *That* is why you get them to help you stir the pancake mix (and spill it), sweep the floor (and make no difference), get your phone from your bedroom (actually helpful, because you are competent but feel lazy sometimes), and bring their dish to the sink (and maybe break it).

Your moment of glory for all this effort will come years later, when your visiting mother is trying to pull her suitcase from the trunk of a car and that same toddler, who is now a teenager, sees your mom struggling. Your teen daughter strides over and hauls the suitcase out of the car for her grandma. You give yourself a high-five in your head, your turn to have the proud look of satisfaction on your face. That satisfaction will be hard earned, you having endured about four years of the young-child version of that teenager "helping you," and, even more exhausting, from the following years spent relentlessly insisting that his or her help continue.

And that's the goal: you want your child to gradually go from helping you to helping others. A family—whether there's two or three of you, or eight—presents plenty of opportunity to learn to help, to be of service, "to wash one another's feet." The goal for children (and adults) is to move from being obliged to help all the way over to choosing to help. Choosing to help is one of the greatest of freedoms a person ever gets to exercise.

It's ruthless though, man, ruthless, the consistency demanded of you as a parent of a young child. Paradox again: your "helper," totally adorable and entirely frustrating, equally and at the same time.

"Dooing? Dooing? Doooing?"
—Levi, 2, asking, "What are you doing?"
many, many many times in a row

Sixteen times once.

I counted.

ROUTINE, O ROUTINE

In the world of parenting, routine falls squarely in the enormous category of things that are not for us. Like Barney, the big, purple dinosaur popular a solid generation ago (look him up, young parents). Not for us.

Children love routine. They get routine. They know it, learn to predict it, participate in it, even direct it. It makes them feel secure and knowledgeable and safe. We parents live out that routine despairing at the wearing sameness of it all. As we sing "Wheels on the Bus," or set out the same quiet, crafty things for the umpteenth day in a row, or read the same storybook—again, we feel our IQ plummeting, our psyche shriveling, puny and whimpering in the corner, perhaps questioning whether psychedelic drugs might be a good idea (probably not, in case you're seriously wondering—you have a child in your care).

Late in the game, I must have hit the wall entirely with the whole "Wheels on the Bus" thing; Veronica's "All About Me" poster in kindergarten, on display in the school hallway, stated her "favourite music" was the Red Hot Chili Peppers. We must have switched it up quite a bit at the end.

Try to pretend that the mind-numbing routines serve you too, because, in many ways, they do.

I learned over time that when I felt overwhelmed, as was often the case, I would feel better if I just "did something," one small, practical, simple routine. Do the dishes. Throw in a load of laundry. Wipe the counters. The small act created momentum.

Family routine furthers that momentum. Routine reduces the Herculean effort it takes to initiate "what's next" with kids, which happens multiple times a day, for example, morning, afternoon, and evening. Things like nap routines (for the kids) keep the peace and create some order, a protected window of sanity and recuperation for the young child and the caregiver.

I protected naps like a drill sergeant, as if my life depended upon them, because it did. A bohemian lifestyle of freewheeling spontaneity, though alluring, did not lend itself to the gig we had going on. Or my personality. Or both. The routine of afternoon naps *every single day* for young children hit the "Pause" button for us all, giving us a whole new run at the same day. Once the napping years were over, my preschoolers in turn had an afternoon routine of playing in the kitchen sink filled with warm, soapy water, standing on a chair, wearing an apron, talking to themselves, playing with ladles and cups and sieves and such, like an hour of free babysitting.

Routine helps keep the big old ball of life rolling—because everyone, including the kids themselves, knows "what's next."

When Veronica was young, by midday every day, she knew what was next: cheese melted on a tortilla, cut into wedges, with apple slices. She wanted that exact same lunch for two entire years, from two until four years old. I mean *exact* same. Every day, for twenty-four months. Why did that bother me at first? I would persist in offering other, albeit limited, options. It took me a solid few months to realize that Veronica was directing an important routine, important to her. Who cares? Let the kid decide! Her lunch was healthy . . . and we always knew what she wanted! (FYI, she is a highly adaptable, self-motivated young adult person now.) Initially, I resisted her preference for this sameness. *Really? You want the same thing?! Every day??*

Yes. "T for tortilla," she would say. Routine.

You know the drill:
same bear, same bath toy,
same shirt, same place to put their shoes, same bowl,
same song, same puzzle, same storybook, same
bobbly rocking duck at the park.
Same.

One routine that was fantastic for me was the routine of Marcel getting home evenings and immediately taking on "Animate," as we called it, the full-on-mayhem bedtime mega-routine upstairs, while I did "Inanimate," the messy but blissfully serene kitchen cleanup routine, somewhat removed from the jumping, hollering, and running situation heard overhead. The upstairs thing made you sweat; the kitchen one just took some time. As part of Animate, on weekday evenings, the kids would lay out their "next day clothes" on the floor, beside their mattress/bed, in the shape of a person (extra fun). They had to be wearing the person-shaped clothing *before* they ate breakfast the next morning. That was a routine . . . aimed simply at getting out the door. I'd convinced my sheltered children that the clothes routine was a game.

There is something important for young children in routine. Just remember: not for you. (Also, say no to drugs.) Routine provides rhythm and structure for chaos to occur within. Routines become our instinct. We'd probably follow routines during times of catastrophe, or disaster, and that would help us. Our family is a small tribe, and we know what we do.

Some routine is pleasant, reassuring, becoming a memory shared by both parent and child—if we didn't do it so many bloody times we probably wouldn't remember it at all. A lot about these years becomes an indistinct blur in retrospect. Routine guides us, and is good for kids, so on we go.

CRAZY IS NORMAL

Extremely young children are never being bad. They can't be. They're not conniving yet; they are without malice. They're just crazy, that's all. Kids from, say, one year old to two or two and a half are simply a menace to themselves and society; there's nothing to be done about it. Our job is to just keep them safe and not go insane, that's it. Your young child will engage in multiple patience-taxing, near-death activities per day: standard-issue behaviour for the walking-baby/young-toddler crowd. They just forge ahead, livin' their best life, and if they happen to be a live-wire anarchist by nature, it's a wild ride.

I recorded a week's worth of Eva's activities at age one, specifically, thirteen months old (new parents love using this "month specificity" as a badge of honour indicating exactly how long parent and child have survived together so far). I share this with you for the same reason I recorded it for myself: to make you feel better if your very young child is driving you berserk.

ONE-WEEK PERIOD WITH A ONE-YEAR-OLD: APRIL 2000

- Monday, April 3: aspirated, occluding her airway, going unconscious under kitchen table while eating a carrot.
- Tuesday, April 4: ate compost from the compost bucket, kept in a childproof, safety-locked cupboard.
- Wednesday, April 5: undid her own high chair straps, climbed up and fell out, caught by five-and-a-half-year-old Adam.
- Thursday, April 6: pulled a teapot out of cupboard and broke it, got road rash on chin and hands from a wipeout running at school, ate a live ladybug and cried when it was taken out of her mouth, rubbed cooked spinach all over face during supper, ate a chomp of soap during bath time with four-year-old Madeline, and spit continuously for remainder of bath. A busy day but none of it life threatening, so that was good.

Also in same week:

- Crawled behind couch, pulled cord of lamp.
- Pried plastic "safety plug" from electrical outlet, sucked it, tried to re-insert.
- Pulled bottles of wine out of metal wine rack on floor, one thousand times, until I finally moved the rack. (*Hey, why's the wine in the laundry?*)

You get the idea.

Dear Parents of Young Children and Non-Parents: for your information and reassurance, the behaviour described above is not "hyper" at all. It is not extreme. This is what normal looks like when a child is an active, walking, thirteen-month-old. You're probably better at preventing danger than I seemed to be, but overall, yes, it's this crazy. Your life is bonkers, and that is perfectly normal. No need to worry (as if we ever "need" to).

As further encouragement, I wish to inform you that the very child I describe above, some twenty-plus years later, is not insane and, in fact, is quite reasonable. That might be helpful for you to know.

I'm trying to make time with young children sound amusing and fun, which it absolutely is but also often, honestly, is not. It can be frustrating as hell and make you rageful, which causes you a kind of internal conflict, because you realize that's stupid. There's no one to rage at here. Young children just show us how much of life is out of our control, in everyday small things and epic big things too. We pursue and choose and influence things in our lives as best we can, but mostly, vast terrain of our existence is entirely out of our control. Children are a window into that.

THE CARROT

The carrot incident appears on a list intended to playfully illustrate a toddler's busyness. Truthfully, it was a sickening thing, for reasons peripheral even to its main awfulness. Days like those happen in life lived with small children, ones with gut-punching experiences that leave a parent distraught.

One-year-old Eva was a nightmare at mealtimes, shouting demands from her high chair, throwing food, and struggling with her straps to break free, managing to be extremely disruptive for a very small person. This was wearing on her siblings as well as her parents, particularly our eldest, Emily, who was seven years old at the time. It was like dining daily in the company of a restrained miniature madwoman.

To decrease the disruption, I released Eva from her

high-chair prison to crawl and walk around while we finished eating in some peace. As Eva was annoying people from under the table, I did not see Emily pass Eva a carrot stick from her own plate, hoping to occupy her with something for a few moments.

What I did notice, presumably minutes later, was Eva crouched under the table, motionless, as she never was, in the recognizable posture of someone who is choking. I scrambled under the table and grabbed her just as she slumped over, unconscious. I began doing first aid, back blows to clear whatever was obstructing her airway. No result. Nothing. Without thinking, I knelt under the table and switched her limp body to the "head down for baby" position taught in first aid courses and began hitting her midback between her little shoulder blades with the flat of my hand. Hard. Really hard. I hit repeatedly, with cold, rising panic.

With one of the blows, something shot out of her mouth, followed immediately by a wheezy pull of air into her lungs. Moments later, Eva regained consciousness, coming to in my arms as I sat on the floor, where a small piece of carrot now lay under the table, surrounded by Emily, four-year-old Madeline, and Adam, still five. We all began crying, Adam quietly, scared, Madeline loudly, and poor Emily inconsolably.

I felt sick about Eva, subdued for once in her young life, clinging to me crying, but worse, in a different way, about Emily, sobbing beside me on all fours.

Emily would never, ever, have given her little sister a carrot as "food." Never. This "big sister" kid was more aware of baby care and safety than most adults are, conscientious beyond her years. More than once Emily had reached over an adult who'd given one of her baby siblings a set of car keys as a toy and, knowing the baby would suck on the keys, taken them away from the baby. At four or five years old, Emily would hand the keys, or other dirty, potentially unsafe item, back to the adult giver, saying mildly, "These have a lot of germs." A polite, attentive child by nature, she did not protect the adult's feelings; she did what was needed.

I knew exactly what had happened. In that moment, Emily had handed the carrot to Eva as "toy," not food, as a natural diversion tool of the Coping Strategy. But Eva had choked on the carrot as food.

I hugged and kissed and rocked Eva, and consoled Emily, and all of them, under the kitchen table, which helped me to hold off my own meltdown, to push away losing it as badly as I felt it building inside me. Somehow we got through the evening, me sitting on the bathroom floor beside the tub, staring at them during an extraordinarily long bath playtime during which Eva was as rambunctious as ever.

After all were in bed, Emily and I lay together in hers, wrapped around each other, me stroking her hair and kissing her, sweet thing. She was haunted, knowing full well what could have happened if the lodged piece of carrot had not cleared out. To quote her distressed, heart-wrenching whisper:

. . . *and it would have been all my fault!!*

No baby, not your fault.

Not at all. Probably my fault. Or maybe not even. This uncertain state of things, of things that can happen, of bad luck and good luck, of a moment's difference, a split second of timing that changes everything forever for people all the time, all the time. We cannot keep it at bay, cannot prevent it. We think we can, but we can't. And my sweet little seven-year-old was slammed by a first bitter taste of that reality that day, by a carrot—the savageness of human existence stark against the loveliness of her young being, side by side, pressed up hard against each other.

That's what made my heart break as I lay in my own bed and cried for real that night, waiting for sleep to carry me away from raw terror and sick relief, undeserved gratefulness and mysterious, yearning sadness. Empty and full.

This too is what it feels like having young children.

IT'S BORING

Life with young children is often boring.

If you've never thought that, you don't need to read this next bit.

That seems a shocking thing to say right after revealing how deep the experience goes, but it's both things, deep and boring, at the same time. Being with your young child for days is deadly monotonous. There's no getting around that. Small kids are delightful living explosions of creativity and development. But they do not speak in full sentences of any language, particularly the one you speak. Simplicity and routine bear down upon you, numbing your brain with their predictability. Life with young children is, inexplicably, simultaneously unbearably structured and entirely out of control. When I hear someone wax on about how they "love every minute" spent with their child, I always think, *Wow, you must not spend much time with her.*

Ideally a person could get Zen, all at one with being, live in the moment, yada yada. But an absence of impressive, adult-level problems to solve is wearing in a particular way, unless you consider a toddler removing her pants, and her diaper, in a store, demanding to "go pee *now*," an adult-level problem.

Long segments of days spent with young children feel bereft of purpose or achievement. In our go-go, status-oriented culture, I many times felt lost and left behind while caring for my little children. A person off work *is* left behind by the adult world, he or she just is. You've jumped off a treadmill set on High into a parallel foreign universe. There you find yourself, trying to get car keys out of the moving parts of a hideous clown toy, instead of being at work. Or maybe you don't make it to work, because car keys.

I totally get parents who've said to me, "I love my work. I'd go insane if I stayed home with my kids." Fair. Or ones who state flatly, "I don't have a choice, I have to work," reminding me how inordinately lucky I am to be able to be with my kids. Still, I understand parents who say, "You know what? I'm over-qualified to do this." That's true too. I mean, go to the park? *Again?* Another discussion of how poo gets made? With some-one who has a fifteen-word vocabulary? I hear ya.

So I'm back to that both thing again, a "both" of boring and beautiful. We often seem to need more time at work, or less, want more time with children, or less.

It's weird though, much easier now, and benign, exam-ining those early parenting years from a distant perspective. FYI, businesspeople describe this perspective as a view "from thirty thousand feet," in case they invented that term while you were off on parental leave, wrestling small children. I have no idea why that specific height, just far up, I guess.

From that frightening vantage: the young-child period is only a few years of your whole life gig. Your child is only little for a little while, this son or daughter of yours, becoming a most precious part of your existence on planet Earth. Being with your young kids is a big deal when considered from that viewpoint. It's just that what it gives you is found in a com-pletely separate category from what you get from work, includ-ing the money. (Yeah, there's no money.)

Being with your young child is found in a different bucket, measured in a completely different way, and it addresses an en-tirely different issue. Time spent with your young child, when-ever that happens, and even when it's boring, is an investment in something you can't see yet, in your child of course, but mysteriously in yourself too, in your own life. It's an invest-ment in long-term gains, difficult to see properly now, and hard to measure, but real.

This is a long game. The little-kid years are like boot camp,

I know. Try to think of them as an arduous segment of a long hike, a steep, rocky section, leading up to a lookout spot where you have a breathtaking view you've never seen before. That *is* what's happening. You are hacking away through thick underbrush right now, but push on (there's more heavy hacking to come, never mind that right now).

Regardless of how much you're at work, or at home, you need time with friends, adult ones, the occasional afternoon off, opportunities to walk fast, or blast music alone in the car. Perhaps a stiff drink, but, you know, not too many, too often.

I get my aunty now, who used to go stand outside and smoke. I gotcha, gal.

"Mom, it takes forty cups of maple sap to make one cup of syrup."
—Adam, 4, having a cuddle/nap with his pregnant mother, after a lengthy silence

"Really," my dazzling response.

"But you can't take off too much sap, or you'll harm the tree."

"Oh. I see."

Another long silence, then:
"What does 'harm the tree' mean?"

That explained, and following another long stretch of quiet, he asks:
"What's sap?"

HARD STUFF

WORK AND CHILDCARE

I've been avoiding something. Up to this point, I've only brushed against a gargantuan issue of having young children: childcare. Work and childcare. My management of these issues has been a debacle. I don't have much to offer, except to say it's difficult to figure out. Maybe we could stay there for a moment, stay with that a sec.

It's difficult.

It's a gong show, the years of finding care for your children, wrought with hassle and heartache, scheduling and complexities, and sometimes, apparently, a fabulous sweet spot. I never found the sweet spot myself, but I've observed many people who have, through their own ingenuity, persistence, and resolve. Impressive, really.

As a parent I had three different part-time jobs over eight years, using four different modes of childcare, and then gave up, so I am a nightmare. I had quite a few babies, so there is that too.

I've collected lots of good ideas along the way though. I always ask parents about their childcare solutions; their answers intrigue me, so cultural and personal, as varied as children, it seems. We should keep a worldwide database of these solutions . . . but of course, we already know the most common solution is care by extended family. But that doesn't work everywhere, for everyone. Parents seek reliable, licensed, and hopefully subsidized daycares, for sound reasons I'm about to demonstrate. Yet sometimes those don't quite work for everyone either.

FIRST JOB, FIRST BABY

I remember the small, family-run home daycare we used when I returned to work after our first child. The middle-aged Greek lady who ran it came highly recommended by a trustworthy coworker, a smart woman. That was all I needed to go look. I visited the daycare, located right near my work, with our daughter, looked around, asked one hundred pedantic questions, fretted, and signed up.

During one of my earliest days back at work, I called the daycare during a break, to check in. I'd been doing well, but moments into the call, I was hit, hard, a visceral punch to my stomach, by an unexpected sound.

I heard my twelve-month-old daughter yattering in the background.

Until that exact moment I had never heard Emily in that way, away from me, somewhere else. I could picture her there, in the tidy, worn apartment, its two high chairs neatly in line with a booster seat at the end of a small dining table, its second bedroom lined with three playpens, the living room "play area" cordoned off with a husband watching TV in the middle of it all. I felt panicked being away from my child, with her being away from me, at a rando essential-stranger's home. I stood tense, distressed, considering how I could leave, maybe even quit, on the spot, to run directly to the apartment and my daughter.

The kindly woman sensed my panic, having heard the same in others, bless her, likely many times before. In a conversational tone, she began describing the ordinary, factual details of what Emily was doing, what she'd eaten and chosen not to eat, how long she'd napped and what position she had slept in, how many diaper changes she'd had, the toy she was playing with as we spoke, all the while with Emily's little voice babbling in the background. Hearing the simple details of my daughter's routine, that deadly routine, reassured me, calmed me down. The practicality of it was real, grounding; it made me feel better.

It got easier. I liked work. I was good at it, and they paid me.

Otherwise, the thing I remember from that period was the underground parking garage I used for drop-off and pickup, and the long, steep, concrete stairwell we took out from the parking garage. (Good grief, was there no elevator??) One of the most physically demanding maneuvers I've ever performed in my life regularly took place in that setting.

On my workdays, Marcel rode his bike to work, frightfully early, and I took our vehicle, which, at the time, was a two-door Jeep type of thing, with front seats that folded to access the back . . . where the car seat was. Imagine lifting, from a crouched position, the dead weight of a sleeping child, like a twenty-two-pound sack of flour, while hunched in the inadequate space between a secured car seat and the folded front seat. Not an outrageous weight, I grant you. Now imagine that the same sack of flour suddenly sprouts appendages and begins fighting you, aggressively, with every fiber of its sack-of-flour being, because that's essentially what often happened.

I remember pausing back there, hunched over the car seat, like Gollum over his "precious," with approximately the same hairstyle, my feet jammed outward at alarming angles required to fit within the freakin' narrow available space, gathering my strength to lift an appendaged, struggling Emily. I was sweating, tired, worn out, and on my way to work. Later that same day—and later the next year, with a huge pregnant belly added to the mix—I performed this maneuver in reverse, after my workday: an endurance event that made running an ultramarathon in a desert sound tranquil, even relaxing. I'd wish we could just lie on down there together in the back seat, in the cool of the concrete parking garage, snuggle up, and go to sleep. If I could get just a few solid hours of sleep back there, tucked in behind the folded seats, then I'd really be full of energy to do this!

Was this childcare plan any kind of good solution? Who knows. The thing is, it seemed so at the time, and it worked for almost two years, which seemed pretty good at the time too.

Yes, we did eventually get a different car. Thanks for suggesting that. Good idea.

SECOND JOB, BEFORE THIRD BABY

A couple of years later, after my parental leave "time off" (lol) following the birth of our second person, Adam, I was back at work, at a different part-time job. I remember riding my bike to work. Our part-time babysitter, who came to our house, needed to use our "new-to-us" car, with its car seats installed, to do something with the two kids. What was it? Preschool for Emily, I guess? Why did we do that? I think I thought preschool was necessary, which it sort of is and also isn't.

I cycled along to work feeling sick. I was early-pregnant with our third child at the time, nauseated with the usual persistent morning sickness. I rode both waves of nausea and my bicycle along until, my toes curled over the end of the surfboard/pedals, I felt a wave rising that I could not stay on the leading edge of. I stopped at the side of the road, leaned over well away from my bike, vomited my breakfast on the roadside, and instantly felt better. I got back on and kept riding.

In that moment I was Marge in the movie *Fargo,* bent over with morning sickness at a crime scene in the barren frozenness of winter in North Dakota, though, in my case, it was a leafy autumn morning, I was wearing a bike helmet instead of a fantastic, fur-lined police detective's hat, and no one brought me a coffee.

The looks on the faces of other cyclists as they rode past were pure gold. I should have called out:

"I'm okay! Just hungover!"

Or,

"What? You've never seen a white, suburban housewife-type projectile-vomiting from a bike before?!"

Was this childcare plan any kind of good solution? It seemed so at the time and worked for, well, six or seven more months, until the birth of sweet Madeline, and then for a couple years again after my "time off" with baby Mads and toddler Adam and preschooler/kindergartener Em.

Stop. Reinvent. Start over.

THIRD JOB, BEFORE FIFTH BABY

A few years later, after Eva was born, at another job, in a new setting, with a different childcare plan, I was covering for someone who'd just left on maternity leave . . . while I was pregnant. (You can't make this stuff up. I know—think of it as a *Saturday Night Live* skit.) The office manager at one of the facilities I was covering stared at me flatly as I waddled up to her station. With a deadpan face, devoid of all humour, without a tinge of irony, she said, "You don't look any better than the person who just left."

Hmmpht, be a poo-head, I thought, indicating I was still spending a lot of time with young children, unable to pull off an adult diss even in my own head.

I remember being back at the Community Home Care

offices at the end of my workdays, after multiple facility stops, needing to "chart," meaning document what I'd done, for the record and for the next staff person who came along. I had a hard-stop time for my childcare person, an absolute deadline, which did not allow me for some reason, to arrive home even a few minutes late. At all. (Why was this? Why did I agree to it?) I remember being stressed to the max, "charting my ass off," as a lovely coworker called it, in order to tear across the city (in a car this time, not on a bicycle, thank God) to arrive in time, before the appointed deadline. Arrive home, that is, to a wall of need waiting there, greeting, settling, and making supper for Emily, almost eight years old and Adam, then six, both in school; Madeline, four, in preschool; and Eva, eighteen months.

Was this childcare plan any kind of good solution?

No.

Finally, now, no. It was not. I could not keep doing this. It was impossible somehow, this juggling, this trying to figure it out, this being torn all the time. I felt a social pressure to keep working clamoring at me somehow, yet I would quit. I would just be with my kids. That's what I wanted.

My decision to quit, to stop working, disappointed me though. Or, should I say, seemed as though it was disappointing . . . someone. Who? Maybe me, yes. *You're not working?* felt like the identifying of my failure, my abandonment of all that the adult world weighs as important or impressive. My career was never prestigious, but it was something. Hardworking women and smart women go to work. And now I would not be one of them. Now I'd be called a "housewife," whatever that was. Eww. Despresso. Or, not much better, a "stay-at-home mom." Really? What is that? I hardly ever stayed at home all day. Besides, the term sounded terrible, like a command.

Could I not just be called a "mother"? Is that not enough? Everyone: *So do you work?*

Me: *No. Fuck off.*

You: *Yeah . . . uh, but—you're the one who kept having babies . . .*

Ah, yes, you've got a point there. True that: babies galore, all those babies I wanted, and was lucky enough to have. *And . . . I,* because of Marcel and his work, *had the luxury of a financial choice about working*! What on earth—who gets that?

I wanted to be the one who was with them, with my kids, and, being incredibly lucky, I could. So I did. The pull of my children was greater than other pulls in me. The decision to quit working felt like failure, even to me, and strangely, also felt like the right thing, for me.

There it was, confusing as hell. Now people would think I like doing papier-mâché.

I admire the hell out of strong women everywhere who keep going, juggling kids and work, pressing on in demanding lives of steady jobs, because they have to and/or because of the goals of achievement, and creativity, and paycheques, and the meaning found in bringing innovation and smarts and leadership to the work they do. Go, ladies!! You keep your families and the world going with the work you do. Props to you, as the kids say. You are impressive; we need you. I am in many ways jealous of you, which is dumb, I admit. I applaud the contributions you make through your work.

But I had to decide. What I was doing was falling apart.

Back in those days, women living these different paths were seen somehow as separate from one another, in "camps," ones that did not allow for acknowledging the ways in which we were the same. The broad discourse back then, along with many disheartening exchanges I experienced, presented a view that my decision in that draw to be with my children was some obedient submission to subservient domesticity socialized upon me, or the result of being "pushed home" by a domineering patriarchy, or a cop-out.

I have two words for anyone holding those opinions: fight me.

I would rather physically fight you than accept your premise that I was without agency in one of the hardest decisions I've ever made. Seriously. Let's go ... though, uh ... would it be okay to ask you not to punch me straight in the face? I'm pretty sure I couldn't handle that. All else could be a go though. Maybe I actually mean "wrestle." We could wrestle. Fair warning: I'm stronger than I look.

Young parents today seem to be kinder to one other on this topic than perhaps my generation was. They seem to better accept and acknowledge the unique pushes and pulls in all this, and the differing outcomes woven by those pushes and pulls. Still, there appears to be no one solution that frees mothers and fathers from all doubt.

Ach, never mind. This is too much blah blah blah. My situation is not yours, and mine is rare, almost unheard of. We all seek a childcare solution that's good for our own situation. Please, *please*, though, let's stop pretending the answer will ever be easy, because it won't. We do not all want the same thing, and our children elicit a hunger in us for them that we underestimate before we get there.

A crucial question in all this, dear mothers and fathers everywhere, seems to be, in the broadest sense, *What can you afford?*

What can you afford in life because of your work? What does work afford you? How much can you afford if you work less? What kind of childcare can you afford? How much can you afford to be away from your work? Away from your child? Can you afford to get extended family involved? How much can you, specifically you, afford to miss ... at work? And at home?

These are complicated questions. Consult your finances, your head, your spouse/partner, your heart, and your gut— not necessarily in that order. Mind you, this is coming from

someone who tapped out, because I had the outrageous freedom to do so, and the desire. I am unqualified to comment on
work life, or career, or work/life balance, or childcare, any of
that. Ask the clever people who've figured out a childcare plan
they can afford, in every sense, and see if one of those plans fits
with you and your family.

You're all better at this than I have been.

I'll boil it down to one simple reflection: It is a mistake to
leave your gut and your heart out of this decision. That's all.
No easy answers. Lots of good ones though.

> Me, in bathroom, vomiting in late afternoon
> with "morning sickness" in early pregnancy.
>
> Child, throws open door, asks cheerfully, "Hi
> Mom . . . What's for supper??"

KIDS GET SICK

THE "HOLIDAY"

Young kids get sick. A lot.

Illness is part of life with young children. In our house,
someone was sick every few weeks, or so it seemed. There was
thrush, rashes, days and nights of teething, ordinary colds
and terrible ones, ear infections, chicken pox (our first three
kids, at the same time), flu, pertussis or "whooping cough" (not
common but still happens, we found out), fevers of no apparent cause, hallucinations due to fevers of no apparent cause,
and more. There are curious illnesses, such as hand, foot, and
mouth disease, which sounds like something veterinarians
should deal with, not human parents.

Non-parent (side-eyeing alarming tubes of
pale green snot pouring from each nostril of
your young child): "Wow . . . your kid has a
bad cold, huh?"

You (severe dark circles under your eyes,
listlessly glancing about, wondering where
the ever-present jumbo box of tissues went):
"Yeah."

This stands to reason. Children produce, and generally
spread around, copious volumes of saliva, and are constantly
putting things in their mouths. Germ Central.

Oh, and if this real talk about illness and bodily fluids, spit,
snot, and such strikes you as off-putting? Bear this in mind: *all
parents* used to feel the same way a number of years back, specifically the exact number of years back as the age of their eldest child. Kids have a way of getting one accustomed to gross
things. You may suddenly find yourself reflexively catching hot
vomit, midair, in your bare hands, pausing, and running off
with it. In your bare hands.

Our family once went on a "holiday" that could go down in
history books as The Worst Ever. Marcel was away, and I decided to branch out and "do something fun": take the kids to a
small hot springs resort not far from the city for the weekend.
We'd swim, soak in the warm pools, lay on the beds of our two
adjoining rooms, eat junk food and fun snacks out of a cooler,
and watch movies on the hotel television.

None of those things happened, not a one. The bathing
suits were never even taken out of the bags.

We checked in, then excitedly hurried to our room, me with
toddler by the hand, the four- and five-year-olds scampering

along, following the jubilant eight-, ten-, and twelve-year-olds leading the way, each hauling a small sports bag of stuff. Upon arriving at the adjoining rooms, as they ran around arguing about who'd sleep on which side of which bed, turning on and off all the lights, opening the curtains and the sliding door to a balcony, I began having a queasy feeling in my stomach. Soon looks on the faces of a couple of the kids told the same story.

Soon after that, evidence supporting the reason for this queasiness revealed itself, violently.

A group barf-o-rama began.

I don't want to traumatize you with specific details of the shared family memory of those few days. Perhaps it's sufficient to say that I quickly "ordered up" four or five more blue plastic recycling bins, a stack of new bed linens and towels, and some oversized orange plastic garbage bags. By midnight of that Friday evening, I had hotel housekeeping on speed dial, and I was on a first-name basis with the staff, as though I was a member of their team myself, or they a member of mine, partners in management of an appalling situation. I was "on shift" the whole weekend, an inside operative, ordering in spray bottles of their disinfectant, rubber gloves I eventually gave up on using, professional cloth rags, more sheets and towels and such, all received through the delivery portal of a barely cracked hotel room door.

All weekend I dropped tied bags outside the delivery portal, or clutched items and pulled them in. The only room-service delivery brought to us that weekend consisted of dry toast, saltine crackers, apple juice, and ice.

Not a single one of our seven-person group left our adjoining two rooms once, from Friday afternoon until Sunday midday. It was horrible: some people had to wear diapers who did not normally wear diapers. My sad children, with woeful, teary eyes, took turns saying variations of, "Mommy, I don't like throwing up."

Or running to the toilet. Or both.

They were such troupers, all so brave and good. I was sick too, so they often had to manage on their own, or by helping one another, like one of those survival reality shows. It was absurd, like a fever dream that was real. Yet there was nothing to be done about it.

I remember a moment of distinctly thinking, *I can't believe this,* which, for me, was saying a lot. I had not imagined parenting would involve weakly propping myself on one elbow on a hotel bed, vomiting into a recycling bin, and then, seeing my four-year-old son stir beside me to rise up as well, simultaneously reaching over him with my free hand to grab another recycling bin from the floor, to get it under his face in time. (See? "Observe.") I did not see this coming.

I was an action hero in a low-budget, seriously weird horror film. It was surreal, and bizarre, even to me. Changing diapers, washing my hands, lying down, refilling cups with ice water, rinsing and disinfecting recycling bins, throwing up, lying down, assisting someone else throwing up, washing my hands, changing the TV channel, changing the sheets, rinsing clothes in the toilet, bagging linens in hazmat bags (which we advanced to over the weekend), getting a child to run to the *other* toilet while someone was busy using *this* toilet, washing my hands, lying down, holding a crying child, handing out crackers, putting bags out the portal, providing toast, lying down, throwing up.

By a late checkout time on Sunday we'd turned the corner. After a seven-person, thirty-three-hour "twenty-four-hour flu," we were ready to make the two-hour drive home. We emerged, a funeral dirge march of wan "travelers" setting out on our voyage home, bearing our belongings, which now included hazardous-material garbage bags filled with our own now-burnable laundry. The hotel staff waved goodbye in a forced-friendly manner acquired through rigorous hospitality-industry training, then proceeded immediately, I assume, to fumigate and industrially disinfect every inch of the rooms we had inhabited.

Is any of this making you feel better about your life? I hope so. That experience has to be good for something. Looking back, I realize now that this "holiday" was the easiest possible way for that group illness to happen. It would've been much worse at home. There's no fairy-godmother housekeeping service at home, no room service, no four big beds within a few metres of one another, with two adjoining bathrooms, at home. I basically paid to be sick in a hotel, which, admittedly, is strange but, it turns out, a spectacularly efficient place for a group of people to be sick! A best-case scenario of sorts.

Anyone: "Hey! How fun was that?! Getting away with the kids for the weekend?"

Me (turn silently, walk away)

THE HOME WARD

Group illnesses, when the kids were all sick at the same time, resulted in a surprisingly restful few days of calm and rare quiet. (If you're thinking, *My God, what the hell's wrong with these people? This woman can describe* multiple occasions *of group illness??* Yes. Yes, I can. That is my point.)

No child wants to be alone in his or her room, away from you, when feeling sick. They want to "be with everybody," a state that is likely a causal factor of group illness in the first place. Children love *being together* all the time, when they are young anyway. (Later, not so much.)

To facilitate this "being together," I'd make up little beds on the floor for whoever was sick, around our family room next to the back door, using old sleeping bags or folded comforters or play blankets, covered by a sheet if they were sweaty, along with each person's bedroom pillow. These illnesses must have been caused by specialized kid-only germs, as I rarely got sick along with them.

There we'd be, me and my boutique ward of young patients lying on makeshift cots. They'd be wearing only T-shirts with their underwear, or pajama bottoms, or diapers, often without covers because of fevers. Dora the Explorer or Bob the Builder plastic drink bottles of ice water or apple juice by their sides, cold, damp facecloths across their foreheads, barf receptacles positioned nearby if that were the nature of their illness—not blue recycling bins this time, mind you, but white, plastic "ice-cream buckets," as we called them.

There exist numerous accurate memes on this topic, the curious development and identity of "throw-up buckets" within a family. As my niece said recently, as a young adult: "How is it we used the same bowl to eat movie popcorn out of, that we used to throw up into?"

Through those early years, we purchased outrageous quantities of ice cream: low-quality, cheap, crappy ice cream that comes in those white, plastic, handled buckets. Neapolitan. Ugh, hideous stuff, eaten literally by the gallon. Subconsciously, I was also purchasing this in order to have more buckets in the house. We used the buckets for car washing and rando-organizing, as freezer containers, for "toy collections," and, yes, as barf buckets. Fantastic. It's a wonder any of us continue to like ice cream, but we do—though better stuff now.

Slow mornings or afternoons spent with kids-sick-at-home were tranquil, the usual household sportsmanship of living stilled. My children dozed between rounds of Tylenol, or after a bowl of applesauce, looking at books or listening to kiddie music, with sun streaming in if we were lucky. It was oddly relaxing. Peaceful. No sports, no homework, no running around—them nor me. I knew they were beginning to feel better when some play began breaking out, when one or two got up and wandered off, when bickering started up, and the eternal inquiry of *What's for supper?* began again. Life as usual.

HOSPITAL VISITS

We only had a few visits to hospital with our sick young kids, thank goodness.

Sweet little Veronica, at three and a half years old, became very sick with a terribly high fever. Fevers are tricky things in young children, wildly variant in meaning and severity, difficult to evaluate properly with a feverish child lying in your arms. Sometimes you sense a difference though (trust yourself). Veronica was a limp rag doll, eyes glassy, cheeks red, burning, burning hot.

We spent a few hours with her at a nearby community hospital, for chest X-rays and tests, then were sent to Children's Hospital for further attention. She was weak, slumped up on a stretcher in their Emergency, little face flushed, breathing hard, an IV in place, burning hot. She called out loudly, between rapid breaths and through the noisy, humidified oxygen mask covering her mouth and nose:

"I better not go to preschool tomorrow, Mom."

Okay darlin'.

Actually, the word she said was *pwe-skool*, which made it even more darling. She mentioned later, all casual-like, making conversation with me at her bedside, "Mom, . . . it's no fun being sick," in case I wasn't aware of this fact. Amen, sister. We returned home late in the night. The whole family greeted Veronica's return excitedly the next morning, and she regaled them with details of her hospital stay.

"When the doctor came back in, again, to give me *another*

needle, I just FWEAKED out!!" Indeed she did. It took three people to hold her down.

Which reminds me of the time we had to take Madeline to Emerg to be examined, for the same thing, around the same age (illustrating, again, kids get fevers a lot). My parents happened to be visiting at the time, and my dad came with me, to make driving and parking with a sick kid easier. We too had to help hold Madeline down, while the lab technician drew blood for testing. My dad said quietly, to no one in particular:

"They poke the child and the mother cries."

As we helped pin Madeline down, and they poked and prodded her with the needle, to get the vein, her eyes widened with panic and fear. She tried to pull, then push, away, started to cry, and grabbed for me. Tears began rolling down my cheeks. Seeing her this way made me feel as vulnerable as she did. It's like that, this journey along the path of parenting: you feel for your children.

Actually . . . it's more than that. You feel what they are feeling. You feel it hurting them. And that same dynamic just keeps happening, presenting itself over and over, in countless situations, as they grow up and in the years to come, of you feeling their hurt. Sorrow and love entwine.

Me, encouragingly, holding tissue over her nose: "Blow, Madeline!"

—Madeline, 2, inhaling epically, smiling around her soother somehow, pumping both arms in full arcs with each blow

MELLOWING

THE SHOE PILE

These harsh, demanding experiences of parent-life cause a shift in a mom's or dad's perspective, bringing about a broadening, a mellowing of sorts in us. We become more adaptable, more accepting, better prepared. This growth and mellowing has both upsides and downsides.

An upside is that you experience less angst about things over time, less worry. You have more headspace to be in the moment and enjoy it. Many a night when our youngest, Veronica, was a baby, I'd find myself holding and rocking her in the wee hours, her warm little body on my chest, her silky hair soft against my skin, her sweet face turned up toward mine.

I'd stay there awhile—I wasn't in a hurry. Hell, I'd even sing if I felt like it. I like singing. I'd sing whole songs, not baby songs, but whatever I felt like. Fleetwood Mac and Neil Young were always good. I mean, was I going to be "less tired" by rushing off immediately versus hanging out, rocking and singing a while, feeling my voice through her little body, enjoying both her and the moment? Of course, sometimes I would hurry off to file her into her bassinet, but I didn't feel anxiously compelled to do so, as I had with my first children. (I'm not suggesting you have ten babies to get really relaxed, just making an observation.)

Months earlier, while I was in labour with Veronica and things were going really slow, Marcel left and took Adam to the orthodontist. We knew we had enough time, and rescheduling that appointment was about to become much more difficult. And that was all okay.

Over time, my parenting experience has allowed me, unexpectedly, to slow down, not hurry up. I'm better able to let go and "just be" more often, as I was never readily able to do before. I grant you, some of this progress is likely in good part simply fatigue, but a letting go nonetheless, helpful to me as a person.

Now, a downside to all this mellowing and attendant relaxation is that one can become too relaxed, or too relaxed for cultural norms, that is. Excessive relaxation can lead to certain habits, ones that pretty much fulfill every stereotype of the inattentive, neglectful parent of a large family. I could see that happening in myself and was never quite sure whether to find it amusing or embarrassing, or both.

I'll give you an example, an unimportant one because it doesn't involve the children, just the house. This unimportant development became symbolic for me.

I liked shoes being lined up neatly at the front door. By nature, I preferred that. Put away in a closet? Even better. For a great number of years, I arranged shoes neatly by the front door, and tried to get the kids to do the same.

The shoe-neatness issue began to burn up a lot of energy. A child would come tearing in from outdoors, flipping off her muddy, slip-on shoes that were actually her sister's, run to have a pee, then slide into a pair of boots to tear back out . . . Were we actually going to stop and talk about the muddy shoes that were just flung about? If so, when? Then? Later??

Wet soccer cleats left upside down to dry over a heat vent

simply made sense. Shoes lying around for half an hour, because someone was about to leave in them again soon, also made sense. Time and effort spent finding those individuals who were *not* leaving soon, to put *their shoes* away, really did not make sense, especially when compared to, say, making supper. Were we really going to have a system in place to make all footwear disappear, unseen, between dozens of usages per day? The goal of shoe-neatness began to seem unreasonable.

I decided we would stop the shoe-arrangement thing. I would learn to not care. And after a while, I didn't. Shoes at the door did not matter anymore.

Over the years that followed, when someone arrived at the house, I would notice them glance at the pile of footwear scattered around the door, as though we were hosting a poorly staged rummage sale of used runners/slides/cleats/boots in our front hall. I could tell that visitors thought I didn't notice things like that. Their glance would momentarily make me see that jangled mess anew, eliciting in me still a tiny pang of yearning for neatness. But mostly, the shoe pile was okay. I knew that leaving the mess was the best thing to do.

EVERYTHING BEAUTIFUL

Shoe-pile acceptance was an obscure, limited area of personal growth for me, yet it set the stage for more important ones.

With my first babies I cooked carrots, pureed them, froze them in ice cube trays into earnest little squares stored in containers in the freezer, as I'd read about in a magazine. Later we fed Madeline and Eva pureed veggies sold in the little jars. When Levi and Veronica were babies, they ate a lot of whatever the rest of us were eating, cut up small and mashed all together. It was healthy, just less . . . I don't know, . . . prepared? proper? special? Insta-worthy? By then I was even willing to pass a toddler a French fry in the car.

What? Shocking, yes. I'm not suggesting you do this; I am just admitting that I did. Atrocious nutrition, I admit. In my defense, I will quickly add that I knew a French fry munched on by a toddler disintegrates into mush that's easily swallowed. Still, bad idea. Guilty. Sorry, my dear children: I got too damn relaxed. To everyone, everywhere, outraged and scandalized that I would hand my preschooler a French fry in the car: my deepest apologies. My bad.

And yet.

Yet. Trying to fulfill a standard that everything be "perfect" for your children is a killer to achieve, harder still to measure. Is that even a good idea? Perfection as a goal?

Viewed from my oldster-parent outlook, the "nonexcellence" and risks associated with less-than-stellar parenting practices are fabulously offset by the bonus of raising a child in a less anxious, less pressured or fearful manner.

By all means, wash hands and use clean dishes. But a child will not melt if she gets some actual dirt in her mouth (it happens, kids are weird). Of course, keep activities generally safe, but if they start jumping off the picnic table (seat bench for little children, tabletop for bigger ones), the world will not stop turning. Of course you care about your child's education and psychological well-being, but twenty minutes of kiddie-show screen time occasionally will not throw his entire childhood off course. A healthy diet is essential, absolutely, but a child is not a fragile chemistry set that will self-destruct after taking in a few potato chips. Things don't have to be perfect.

When Eva was a toddler, she wore yellow gum boots. Every day. For eighteen months. More than half the time somehow on the wrong feet. Despite all the tripping, this was the best thing for us to do. And it was fine.

I allowed our kids to watch TV weekday afternoons from 4:30 to 5:30 p.m. They'd sit staring at the clock like prisoners waiting to be let out into the yard. So would I. During their TV time, I enjoyed the quiet, made supper, chatted on the phone, got a couple of things done. I then prepared myself for the inevitable meltdown that comes, then passes, whenever media is turned off, requiring children to change brain-gears and interact with the real world once again. Still, during that hour, we all had a little break.

There were times it took the Tooth Fairy a full couple of weeks to get to our house, with a creepy-cute lil' tooth just a-waiting under the pillow for days. Not a crisis. Everyone survived.

We parents don't want to convey that the world is a place to worry about everything, a place where perfection must be achieved—a belief that is a debilitating burden. The risks of constant worry and stress far outweigh many other risks. Life is generous. We want our children to know that.

Maybe we can relax, mellow out a bit, and transfer that same energy toward pointing out everything beautiful, as much as we can think of, all around us every day (which may not include the state of the front hall). Be into "noticing nature," whatever that looks like around you: buds on trees as you walk to the subway, sunsets from the bedroom window, new snow on the ground as you head out the door. Point out the elderly couple helping each other across the street. Sounds corny, but I am dead serious. Sterilizing water bottles, and prioritizing learning goals, and fretting about badly scraped knees are important in some ways. But scrapes heal, and learning happens with time, and the world abounds with beauty and reassurance; we want our children to know that.

My children will confirm that my standard, immediate response to a young child's tumble or minor injury became, and still is, "Oops! Quick—give it a rub!" And they do, little children rubbing their own "owie" to make themselves better. Because everything is okay.

Hopefully you get my point. Try to roll with it. Squeeze as

much enjoyment as you can out of these young-children days. Many are just plain hard, but the whole thing *is* passing by. Try to relax . . . without giving your kids French fries in the car (that's too relaxed). Point out the beautiful in every day, but don't beat yourself up if you yell at them once in a while to put their crap away. Sometimes that's just necessary.

Whoa, I'd better stop. This may not be helping.

This might be a good place to wrap this up completely, to finish out this chapter on parenting young children. It's chaotic and confusing, a little person so heart-stoppingly adorable and sweet, without guile, or not much, who's quiet and methodical sometimes but, at others, can frustrate you to near insanity, causing disorder and exhaustion previously beyond your wildest imaginings—and make your heart sing with pure joy, and swell with wonder and a love also previously beyond your wildest imaginings. All that.

If you have a young child in your life, observe everything with the intent of a biographer, focused on the details, the particulars, the scenes of your life. One day, you will be that biographer, recounting the blur of hazy, precious days you spent with your very own small person.

HAPPINESS

This is a good time, early in parenting, to mention that happiness is not a separate chapter, even though it appears to be one here.

Happiness is sprinkled everywhere, woven throughout, found in every chapter of parenting life, even in the messiest and worst bits. There's something helpful, maybe even essential, in understanding from the get-go that seeking happiness in your parenting doesn't work. Happiness comes and finds you.

Happiness shows up, a divine reward it seems, just for noticing the beauty of a moment, especially after contending with something. Happiness is a side deal. Don't grab at happiness, or she will evade you. This dynamic is similar to that of a professional hockey player in a scoring slump, said to be "holding the stick too tight," trying too hard, rather than playing with abandon, immersed in the game. Things don't usually work as well when you're holding on too tight.

Same goes for trying too hard for happiness—though if you hand me a fresh orange juice mimosa to sip on a glorious morning as I loll about in a king-sized bed with a view from a fancy hotel room, I am confident I could cobble together a decent amount of happiness, on demand, as it were.

But in the day-to-day as a parent? Happiness just shows up, an unexpected guest, a soothing balm to keep you going, randomly, "in spite of." You never quite know where or when she will arrive, but scrambling about looking for happiness scares her away and makes us puny, and also boring.

Looking outward, and all around, opens things up, creates opportunity—often simple, sometimes huge, usually for others. It's generally then, when we're busy, engaged in the world, that happiness saunters quietly alongside and slips her steady, warm hand into ours and shows us beauty. She's an elusive gal, happiness. She arrives unbidden. Don't look directly at her when she does come along: keep looking at the thing you are doing, and she will lean against you there, keeping you company.

For a parent, happiness comes when your baby is nestled in your neck, breathing softly, warm, and you decide to sit awhile. Happiness appears when your children are young, as you look up, realizing that each is fully occupied in something of their own choosing, and the room is peaceful, quiet. Happiness, as a deep joy, joins you when you watch your child do something you know he is afraid to do, and it works out this time, and he looks right at you, and his face tells you how he feels. Happiness comes while you listen to your father tell your attentive teenager a funny story, and in the telling, your dad is crying with laughter recounting the outrageous, and you watch your teen delight in his grandfather's merriment. For parents of larger families, it's being gathered at supper with everyone talking loudly, multiple exchanges taking place simultaneously; you and your spouse make eye contact and smile at each other because you both know how much the other loves this. And happiness sits down quietly too.

I remember being on a road trip once, years ago, on my

own with all our kids (so not really on my own) as Marcel wasn't able to come. I decided to travel at night because I thought it would be easier.

It was.

Hours in, we were flying along in the dark on a wide, open highway that cut through the mountains, almost no other cars in sight, our big old Suburban heavy on the road. The kids were all asleep except the oldest two, awake and leaning their heads against a balled-up jacket or baby blanket on a window or car seat, staring out, lost in sleepy thought. It was completely quiet except for the deep hum of the engine and the whoosh of the car driving along. The dark sky was clear, the moon out, bright, illuminating the entire valley. The road rolled far ahead into the distance, a ribbon of moonlight winding its way through the valley of jagged softness, of dark-green trees carpeting the sloping steepness surrounding us.

I felt settled, deeply content, as I drove along. All was right in the world. Everything was fine, the havoc of life stilled. I was with my people, a capsule of quiet contentedness and slumber, flying along together in the dark. The moment was complete. I felt deeply happy.

You could argue I was delirious, from lack of sleep and too much coffee, high on the simple joy of having three kids out cold in car seats at the same time. All that may have been true, I grant you. Still, I felt totally happy and I will take it. As it comes.

As an aside, if at that moment flashing lights and the wailing siren of a police car were to have appeared in said happy darkness, there was no damn way I'd have stopped. Sorry, Officer, but a high-speed, cross-country chase it would have been. The stars had aligned, all were settled, and I was not stopping—for anything. Besides, I was crazy enough in those days to have any charge thrown out, by pleading insanity, *no problem.*

The trick, it seems, is to be looking outward, doing your thing, engaged, attuned for these gifted moments. Watch for them like a friggin' hawk, lest they appear and pass you by unnoticed. Life is short. Pay close attention and notice when happiness comes looking for you. Prepare to be surprised by her timing.

CHILDREN

A CHILD

A child runs in full squat surprisingly fast.
Strange full range.
Scoots to push a tricycle, skateboard, a
    bike, on the move, and hops on.
Go.

A child sparkles with delight when he
    understands what is funny.
Glee be free!
Possibilities dance across his face, body
    tense in anticipation of the mirth.
Joy.

A child sleeps in total abandonment to
    letting go.
Sleep deep.
In a ball, face tucked against the pillow,
    hands curled, or
Flopped spread-eagled on her back as on
    a dock in the sunshine of summer.
Dream.

A child eats with gusto, digs in without
    looking up.
Yum in my tum.
Chews intently, no pause of social obliga-
    tion, humming his approval.
Eat.

A child frowns with anger not attempted
    to conceal.
Mad not sad.
Crosses arms and stiffens, leaning away.
Outrage.

A child's humour holds taste for the ab-
    surd.
Weird not feared.
Tells of an airplane crashing through the
    roof to go to the toilet.
Hilarious.

A child's eyes follow yours to gauge fear.
You're not sure.
Comes close, takes your hand, stands
    wiggling one leg.
Need.

A child leans over a table in fixed concen-
    tration.
Print a stint.
Hands grip paper, pencil, and press with
    all their might.
Work.

A child inhales deeply, sucks in gut to
    form hollow void beneath his ribs.
Exhale laughing gale.
Thrill of a cannonball into the deep end to
    get you wet.
Ha!

A child collapses weak with boredom.
Chore in hardware store.
Runs in aisles because walking is boring
    and takes too long.
Blah.

A child says, "Watch this!"
"See? Watch me!"
Thinks a moment and does a random,
    kooky thing.
Look.

A child sits, arches her back to break the
    tension.
Reset you bet.
Stretches arms out and lets them drop,
    shifts bum, yawns widely then smiles.
Ready.

A child that was you.

And is your child too.

ODDITIES

ODD CREATURES

There's more to children than meets the eye.

We are deceived if we think them as nothing more than simple, sweet, and benign, trundling along through childhood. Children are complicated and intense, a mystery really, with their curious rituals, funny turns of phrase, passionate assertions of what is. My own teenage child put it well: "Kids are as concerned about things that matter to them as adults are about their own things; it's just a different set of things, that's all. But the amount it matters to them? That's the same."

Children are serious about themselves. My children despised being spoken to "like a baby" when they were young. They knew when someone was being condescending, and they were insulted. At six years old.

There is a lot to children. Much of the "a lot" is odd.

To avoid being too sentimental, too removed from reality as we discuss children, let's straight-up acknowledge that children can be extremely peculiar. They have what my teenagers called "crackhead energy," a terrible expression but one that captures a lot. Kids fixate on the strangest of things, then lock on, like a dog with a bone . . . a bone still covered with meat.

BEAD OR SEED?

Fixations begin young. Our fourth child was extremely young when she decided the world might need to be categorized into beads and seeds. Why? I have no idea.

Her siblings must have been messing around with one of those prefab craft sets we acquired as birthday gifts. You know the ones: "creative sets" with one hundred parts and "just fifty-seven!" excruciatingly specific instructions requiring dedicated parental involvement, aimed at making a tiny beaded bag. Naturally I was having no part of that and gave them the set "to do something with." Somewhere in that process, at around three years old, Eva learned what a bead was.

"Bead."

Soon thereafter she happened upon a seed, and called it a bead. This probably occurred during an activity about plants and seeds and such, at preschool, because nothing educational was happening with seeds at our house. She was corrected by preschool staff: "No, that's a seed."

"Seed."

What?! What is this variation of bead, this seed, being thrust upon my world? seemed to be her internal response. That "seed" correction apparently short-circuited entire tracts within her brain, causing her, for approximately one year, to question us unrelentingly on the identification of ALL small, roundish objects as beads or seeds, while displaying deep skepticism about the classification we assigned. I mean "all." Thank God we didn't inadvertently shell nuts around the same time.

For an entire year, throughout each day, the refrain of "Bead or seed??" was demanded unceasingly.

Child: "Bead or seed?"

Me: "Honey, it's not a bead or a seed, it's cereal.
It's a Shreddie."

Child (eyes me warily, slowly shoveling a
spoonful of Shreddies into her mouth)

I should have seen this coming, because this madness had
a precursor:

Is hot hot hot??? Or waaaaaarrrmm?? Just writing that
makes me crazy.

Earlier still in her young life, before she was two years
old, I'd foolishly gone above and beyond in teaching her about
some things being hot. I held her hand near a mug of tea, then
above its steaming top, saying, "It's hot hot hot." I amped it up
a bit, with an exaggerated expression of fear to accompany my
little three-word torture phrase: "Hot hot hot!"

Well. The categorization neurons began a-firing. She began
peppering me with "hot status" verifications.

I must have had strong coffee, or a full night's sleep, because when she pointed to some warmish food, toast or something, saying, "Hot hot hot," I unfortunately responded with
the veritable kiss of death.

"Oh no, sweetie, that's not *hot hot hot . . .* It's *waaarrrmmm*,"
I said, in a drawn-out manner, with a theatrical expression of
soothing comfort, like Florence Nightingale on her best day.
What's with the drama? Why?? I rue the day.

Locked. On.

For months, our twenty-two-month-old interjected into
every normally fractured "conversation" occurring in our
household the demand of *Is hot hot hot? Or waaarrrmmm?*

This might have been a reasonable question about a pot of boiling water, or a bowl of steaming soup—but try a hairbrush, a bowl of yogurt, a stroller strap, a toy metal dump truck, a ray of sun through the kitchen.

This was early crackhead energy at its prime. We had an unfathomable number of discussions that sounded as though we were both on crack, discussions that almost made me need to take some. (See? "Observe your life.")

IS THIS WATERPROOF?

This trajectory leads me to the pinnacle of all childhood fixation. I've discovered it: peak kookiness. It's found in the word *waterproof*, as in, *Is this waterproof?*

Children fixate all their potential for weirdness on the verification of whether or not something is waterproof. Or at least, all of ours did. I have engaged in one thousand outrageous "waterproof" discussions over the years.

This torture begins with the simple, beginner's classic "Is this watch waterproof?" This escalates rapidly to "Is this sneaker waterproof?" which soon veers to more-nuanced, entirely bizarre considerations. Advanced territory ventures into the realm of "Is this box of cereal waterproof?" or "Can a piano be waterproof?"

Nobody knows why this happens. (This statement is unconfirmed. Likely nobody knows, probably.)

As the glorious irony woven into human existence would have it, one of the most aggressive exchanges I have ever witnessed on this "waterproof" thing involved none other than my "Bead or seed?" child, delightfully as Interrogated rather than Interrogator.

Behold.

A child in a younger grade must have sensed a worthy foe in Eva, advanced by then through rungs of elementary school to, say, Grade 5. He was a little guy, maybe Grade 1 or 2, small for his age, a skinny, nondescript white boy with a messy long crew cut. Not messy-cool, just messy. But he was wily, it turns out. He walked straight up to Eva in the parking lot/playground after school, and stood in front of her, staring. Without a glance at me, or any introduction, or small talk, he got straight to the point.

Young Boy (gestures with a jerk of his chin toward the backpack she was wearing—like a crusty old cowboy in a vintage Western film, his eyes narrowed to slits that did not stray from hers): "Is that backpack waterproof?"

Eva: "Well, uh, yeah, it is. This kind's supposed to be pretty waterproof, I think."

Young Boy: "How do you know?"

Eva: "Mmm, it said so on the tags and stuff at the store. And it looks like the right kind of cloth." (points over her shoulder to the sheen of stiff fabric)

Young Boy: "WaterPROOF or water-RESISTANT?"

Eva: "Oh." (thinks a second) "Maybe more water-resistant. But it did say waterproof. Stuff inside would probably be okay in pouring rain." (staking ground a bit)

Young Boy: "Would water come in through the zippers?"

Eva: "In normal rain, probably not, no. No water through the zippers." (returning his stare) "It said it was waterproof." (claiming her position now)

Young Boy (steely-eyed): "Could you throw it in a stream?" (Narrator: Where the hell's the stream?)

Eva (steely-eyed): "Nobody throws their backpack in a stream, so it doesn't matter."

Young Boy: "But COULD you?"

Eva (bores into him with a look, turns on her heel, and walks away, done with this crackhead conversation. Young Boy looks at me. I walk away quickly too, wanting no part of this madness.)

My point? That was not actually a crackhead conversation. That was a perfectly normal, average conversation with a child. Kids can be kooky as all get-out. Pull you down a rabbit hole and hold you down there while they keep on digging, with breathtaking tenacity, seemingly not aimed at much. They must learn something terribly important with all that effort, yet any potential for meaning is obscured in the moment by the weirdness.

We undersell children if we view them as happy-go-lucky,

storybook lovelies. They are not. The next time you find your-self trapped in an absurd conversation with a child, think: *Is hot hot hot or waaarrrrmmm??* and *Bead or seed?* and *Is this waterproof?* This will help identify and sum up the situation before you, helping you stave off your own madness.

> "Speaking of private body parts, Mom, what's for supper?"
> —Adam, 3, making clever use of his favourite new expression *speaking of,* following a detailed conversation about penises and privacy

PARENTING, OLD SCHOOL

Much of what is "odd" in our family has been the parents, meaning us, Marcel and I, and our unusual, old-school par-enting style.

Case in point? Marcel took our children to the park *count-less* times, over many years. His philosophy held that his children needed him for certain things, for his presence, his occasional help to climb onto a rocking duck, for the push of a swing or reassurance after a tumble. But, in his estimation, his children did not need him to play—they could do that without him. He'd read the newspaper, or even a book, talk to work on his flip phone, or whatever. Marcel would glance up to see where they were, absentmindedly watch dads or moms kindly squeezing themselves through bright-red tube slides, or stag-gering across wobbly bridges for a while, then just go back to his paper, an unusual thing to do, even back then.

I asked him once if he ever thought he should, you know, run around a bit with the kids. He looked at me and said,

"No, I've never thought that," reminding me why I love this man.

I also had the good fortune of living out the oddity of my naturally old-school style with my children, of being straightforward and direct. I'd have found the earnest, appeasing style, of being nice all the time, terribly difficult. As it was, I felt completely free to answer, "No," when the answer was simply no. Offspring of parents who engaged their children in lengthy exchanges of collaborative negotiation could not understand my directness. I was a riddle to them.

One boy, a friend of Adam's, would grill me at after-school pickup as to whether Adam could go over to his house to play. Originally, he asked my son, but quickly learned that, weirdly, I seemed to hold the cards in this lack-of-consensus decision-making that went on in our family. He would beeline over to me.

Boy: "Can Adam come over today?"

Me: "No. Today doesn't work out." (I added that second part, to soften the no a bit . . . pretty nice of me.)

Boy: "What about tomorrow?"

Me: "Um, that has to be a no too."

Boy: "Why?"

Me: "Well, we have too many things on."

Boy: "What things?"

Me (softness suddenly dropped): "None of your business."

Boy:

I smiled, but probably like Cruella De Vil.

CHAOS/THINGS GONE WRONG

Children elicit chaos. No amount of planning or perfectionism or strategy will eliminate the chaos.

We'd be sitting in church with a toddler climbing about, in this case Levi, and he'd somehow manage to go flying out of the pew and hit the wall. No one reacted; he got up and climbed back in. Things like this were not unusual, in our family anyway.

An indication of the expected level of chaos in living with children?

We live in an earthquake zone, and one day, there was an earthquake in the ocean off the coast. We felt it, and it made the news, with reporters reminding everyone they should really make an earthquake survival kit.

I was in the kitchen by myself when the house began shaking, lights and dishes rattling, papers jiggling, chairs bumping, everything vibrating everywhere. Without hesitation, I yelled, "WHAT ARE YOU GUYS DOING?!" Apparently my expectation of the bedlam my children could create was easily gauged as the aftershocks of a 6.6 earthquake off the coast of the mainland.

LICE LIAISON

I harken back to the time I heard Marcel calling from the basement, or backyard, or wherever he was, "How long am I supposed to keep this lice stuff on my head? It's really burning."

This was hours after I knew he'd put it on, and the answer was ten minutes max. His hair and scalp were fried. Lice hair treatment is like turpentine for your head. We had a lice infestation in the family at the time, and Marcel was getting on a flight for a work trip that afternoon. He did not want to be "that guy," the one bringing lice on board the airplane. It is safe to say, with 100% certainty, zero lice boarded that plane on *his* head.

Before you get horrified and uppity about my mentioning, all casual-like, that we had an infestation of head lice, I wish to point this out as an absolutely ordinary example of chaos.

Lice.

And there you are. No plan. Lack of knowledge. Grossed out, but needing to respond. While regular life is happening around you, kid activities and school stuff, birthdays maybe and tax filing, you additionally, oh by the way, also need to stamp out an advanced infestation of lice on heads, and in beds and couches, coats, and maybe the car. Who knows? Not you. Or me. Such is an illustration of chaos in life with children.

Selling the house and moving seemed like it might be easier than getting rid of the lice.

Wash all soft items in hot water on heavy-duty cycle.

ALL soft items?? In the entire household? Really? Over what kind of time frame? Several months? A year?

Dry-clean items that cannot be washed.

Um . . .

If it's not possible to wash items, such as stuffed toys and pillows, seal them tightly in plastic and store in a freezer.

What the hell kind of freezer do they think I have? An industrial walk-in, like some fish-packing plant?

Then there's children, and their hair, and soon yours too. A parent dealing with lice faces an onslaught of lightning-fast, crawly pests whose numerous eggs stick like glue to individual strands of hair, leaving itching, thus scratched and bleeding, scalps. Initially, parents may face this with the best of intentions, wanting to "take a natural approach, which is environmentally friendly and sustainable!"

But just as cleaning a putrid shower with "only vinegar!" is often abandoned in exchange for the firepower of Toxic Chemicals, the same goes with desperate lice situations—thus my husband and his fried head. (I learned, eventually, that drowning lice in cheap conditioner every couple of days and combing the whole mess out with the finest of special lice combs works better than anything else. Knowledge borne of pain, people. You're welcome.)

The kids' school developed a yo-yo cycle of recurring lice infestations, which resulted in the formation of a new, hard-sell "parent-volunteer opportunity": the Lice Check Team. Why call it anything fancy? The kids all knew what this team was up to.

Levi announced at supper one evening, "I LOVE lice checks at school! The ladies"—if all the volunteers for this hideous task were women, I'm sorry my son persisted in calling you "the ladies," and thank you for your service—"wear gloves, and lift up through your hair . . . and gently move it all around . . . It feels *SO nice*, it's awesome!" Sort of a lice-screening/spa experience, then. An upside! Chaos and good together, sort of.

We had somewhat bigger things go wrong too, the vast majority not earth shattering, or life changing, for which I am grateful. I purposefully express this "things go wrong" theme to help you feel better about life with your children. Problems are normal—even to be expected.

"Mom, I threw up."
—all children, any age, randomly, any old
time of day

THE GREAT PASSPORT FIASCO

Our family had a problem with our passports once.

We'd never been to Disneyland. That statement seems to invite visceral reactions from either extreme of the spectrum, so let's just move on. Our youngest was old enough to cope with the whole environment, know what was happening, enjoy it . . . and remember it, and the older ones humoured us, because going anywhere, regardless of where, would surely provide some fun, despite their pretending they expected not to have any.

We live in Canada, so traveling to Disneyland was an international cross-border adventure. The early evening before our departure, I was preparing a bag of flight stuff (so organized, right?). I pulled out our file of family passports, flipping through them as I placed each in the bag. I froze.

One was expired.

I checked the date three or four times, staring at it a lengthy period for full verification. Definitely expired. Expired. Heart pounding, I did the same with all of them and made the sinking discovery that three passports had expired, the three youngest children's. I stood motionless awhile, inert, before finding Marcel to quietly show him. We stared at each other.

Without passports, we were, in fact, going nowhere.

How could this happen, you ask? If one acquires multiple passports on a rolling basis, they expire on a rolling basis as well, something you don't think about while you are busy, say, living. "Routine checking of passports" happens right between reviewing all insurance policies, getting your core strong, and changing furnace filters to avoid having them look like heavy felt pads when the furnace guy comes. So yeah, never.

Marcel and I created an alternative plan to comfort ourselves. It hadn't been long since Canadians could travel to the US with any form of government-issued photo ID. "We'll do that!" we convinced each other, in a shared delusional state, conveniently overlooking the fact that none of our eight-, ten-, or eleven-year-olds possessed any other photo ID.

What else to do? We'd planned for, and talked up, this trip for months, had even presented it as a group Christmas gift.

Down deep, we knew any solution to this problem would require somehow getting new passports. As Step One, without knowing what Step Two or Three could possibly be, I breezily told the younger kids we needed to go get new photographs . . . for their passports. Then. At 6:45 p.m.

Reading situations by feel, not words, as children do, they knew something was wrong. This was made painfully obvious by their new photos. Later, muuuuuch later, these photos are hilarious. Sort of. Though, also, still terrible.

As you well know, a passport photograph must display a neutral facial expression: no smiling allowed. Well, zero risk of that pesky smiling problem this time around! No cheery child to coach into an unnatural state of not-smiling, no siree Bob! The kids' faces in these photos are so, so sad, it's unbelievable. Saddest. Photos. Ever. You feel sad just looking at them. Full pre-cry mode. Ugh, awful.

Later still that evening, armed with sad-sad passport photos and three completed multipage passport renewal forms, I went to a friend's home to have him sign the photos and forms as "guarantor" for the applications . . . without any "guarantor" as to why I was doing so. It was a strange activity, later that night, packing for a trip we were most likely not going on. Marcel and I considered, for about five seconds, the possibility that one of us go ahead with the three older kids, in order to not "waste the trip." But no.

Before 7:00 a.m. the next morning we were on our way to the airport in our big ol' vehicle, feigned smiles of optimism plastered to our faces, our older kids looking wary, and our younger ones looking sad-sad. I had in my bag, all casual-like, three completed passport renewal forms along with signed sad photos, original birth certificates, and government health care cards, without knowing why. As one does.

At the check-in kiosk, we acted surprised that three of eight passports were not accepted.

Both Parents: "Hmm, that's weird!" (I cannot explain what the feigning part of the fiasco was aimed at. No idea why we did this. Fully illogical in every way.)

Same-same with the airline ticketing agent at the counter. "Hmm, that's weird!"

"But these have *expired!*" the ticket agent explained repeatedly, holding up three passports, with a pained look on her face, glancing at the sad-sad faces gathered around her. (PSA: airlines do not disobey international travel and immigration rules because you look sad, just so you know.)

We offered a couple of invalid options as alternate plans, and, uh, no, these did not help either. By then we all looked despondent and she looked distressed, with our pile of documentation for eight flights to Anaheim, California, piled on the counter between us. She knew where we were going.

We stood waiting, no one saying a word. Then she hesitated. You could see it on her face. Compassion is a beautiful thing. In all situations of duress, wait as long as humanly possible for The Hesitation of the Other; it is always the beginning of something good.

Compassionate Ticket Agent: "I could cancel all these flights and book you onto the exact same flight tomorrow morning? That would give you time to get new passports."

Sad Family: "Really?!" (truly surprised, no faking necessary). "They won't issue passports to normal people that quickly." This wasn't a diplomatic corps needing rapid dispatch to manage an international crisis; these were three ordinary kids trying to get to Disneyland.

Compassionate Ticket Agent: "Actually, they don't seem to care why you're travelling. Just present your airline tickets for travel tomorrow and say you're in urgent need of passports. I'll reissue new tickets—they might just do it."

Now I wanted to cry. What makes some people care and other people not care at all? We parents need to pay attention to whatever makes that difference, and breed it, or teach it, or demonstrate it, or however that works.

We stood frozen a moment, Marcel and I looking at each other, before flying into action, as solid couples who've been together a long time do, without needing to talk about it. Marcel grabbed sixteen-year-old Adam, totally jazzed now by an actual, real-life adventure instead of Disneyland. They took off, carrying and pulling our luggage with them, to get our car from long-term parking. Marcel called, "I'll pull up out front," gesturing to the drop-off area outside the nearby entry doors.

I stayed with everyone else, waiting for the ticket re-booking. Our agent eventually nodded: we were good to go. The kids and I ran, for no reason really, to wait outside, me holding the hand of eight-year-old Veronica, who was laughing like a maniac now. Some time later, our vehicle pulled into the no-stopping zone just outside the terminal, flashers on. Marcel and Adam hopped out. Marcel passed me the car keys; I handed him all the passport paperwork and documents. He waved down a cab, and he and Adam started climbing in, ready to speed off to the passport office in the downtown core of the city.

But wait! "Don't go!!" I called.

I waved at Marcel in the taxi to stay, so he stepped out and held the cab there, while "supervising" the illegally parked car full of children. While Marcel cajoled Traffic Security Man, I sprinted back to Compassionate Ticket Agent, realizing that we didn't have any proof of our new tickets for the next morning. She printed the ticket info, tearing the paper as she pulled it from the printer. I ran back to the car (adults rarely run in public wearing normal street clothes, I was reminded by the looks in my direction).

Finally, I waved to Marcel, and the taxi tore off. Adam told us later that "Dad handed the driver some cash and said, 'Get there fast,' like in a movie." I climbed into our car, waved at Traffic Security Man, who wanted to kill us, and drove the now-hopeful remaining team home. To wait.

I left our luggage in the car. We waited.

Almost three hours later, a phone call: the passport office needed proof of the new flights.

Hell yeah! Like Agent Landy in *The Bourne Ultimatum*, I faxed, not incriminating classified Treadstone papers but, rather, the torn, ticket-booking confirmation to the passport office. (Yes, "fax." It's a thing, a prehistoric, pre-internet communication device. Look it up.) And waited. And waited.

Marcel phoned. For a rush fee, the passport office would process three new passports by 4:00 p.m. that same day.

We all met Marcel and Adam, bearing three brand-new Canadian passports, at five o'clock at a family restaurant between home and downtown, since there was no food in our house, as we'd planned not to be there. I had two glasses of wine. I felt like going to bed and sleeping for a week. Instead we went to bed and got up early and did the exact same morning on repeat, like those movies where the day repeats itself.

This time, all the passports worked at the check-in kiosk.

We rushed over to Compassionate Ticket Agent, on duty once again, to greet her like the cherished old friend she was. There was jubilant chatter and laughter, and I think a couple of the kids even hugged her. The freshly documented travelers vibrated with excitement, with Veronica jumping up and down on the spot. Everyone was happy. At this moment, Disneyland was already the Happiest Place on Earth, and we weren't even there yet.

As we boarded our "new flight"—Marcel and I exhausted, all of us on our way to Disneyland—the only sad faces to be found anywhere were on photographs of three new passports in the family travel bag.

LEARNING

SIBLING CONSIDERATIONS

We haven't talked about siblings yet. What a thing. Siblings, who have an enormous influence in your life that no one can predict, least of all the siblings themselves. Your brother or sister is just livin' his or her best life and, well, there you are too. Certain dynamics occur, whether there are two children in a family or a bunch. One of those dynamics is fighting.

I didn't handle our kids' fighting all that well.

"Fighting." You know what I mean. *Bickering. Poking. Framing. Arguing. Tattling. Picking. Harassing. Teasing. Exaggerating. Vexing. Instigating. Feigning* All that, the usual. You'd think the mom of a larger family would be chill about sibling fighting, as the background soundtrack to family life. I did tune it out to a point, something that looks like neglect but is not.

"Tuning out" is, in fact, an indispensable parenting tool: to ignore.

Let the kids work it out. Keep one ear open and see where things land, listening for meanness that needs to be stopped in its tracks. Yet garden-variety, mundane, mind-numbing bickering? It's par for the course. It doesn't require swooping in, peacekeeping parental intervention at every turn.

Mostly, that is.

Unpredictably to my kids, and also to me at times, I would snap, and not swoop in, but hurl myself in. Not good.

I'd transform, instantly, into a burnt-out, hardened woman in a black-and-white documentary on the Great Depression, wearing a faded cotton housedress that hung lifelessly on my suddenly bony frame (not real), with chapped hands and a barefoot baby on my hip (real), pregnant (possibly real), a tea towel slung over my shoulder (likely real), as a dust ball rolled by (definitely real):

"You kids git!! Git in the houSE! . . . NOW!!"

"BE QUIIiiiiET!!"

"Stoppit! Right NOW!"

"CUT IT OUT! I've HAD IT. That's IT!"

Yes, I screamed at them . . . "to be quiet." Yes, I was able to do that without inner conflict or shame. Amazing, I know.

None of this is good. I wanted the fighting to stop, that's all. Hunched, all angry and salamander-like, I'd hiss offenders' names in series, in a manner terrifying to everyone, more a monster/horror film now than the depression doc. Marcel would look horrified when I did this and mention quietly that the neighbours could probably hear, which would bring about a tirade of another kind, suddenly a war-correspondent/reporter vibe, I'd say. Again, I am not recommending any of this; I'm just saying I did it. All terrible. But then, I've told you about chasing-children-in-anger, so you already knew that yelling-at-kids would be a thing.

If my outbursts were excessively bad, I'd regroup, and in a quiet moment apologize to my child(ren) sincerely for my bad behaviour . . . and begin again with fresh resolve to be nice/not a nightmare. Tomorrow is another day! Parenting is not determined in one bad day . . . unless, I suppose, you have one *HELL* of a bad day, Greek-tragedy style. Don't do that.

In a curious and lovely twist of human development, your

child might possibly learn more from your losing it, then apologizing to him, than he ever would from you acting properly in the first place. Weird but possibly true. Maybe.

Another ill-gotten positive that came from my rabid over-reacting? My children would band together *immediately*, all on the same side. Mom was going cray-cray and they needed to absorb this force as a unit, their dispute resolved, forgotten, or deferred.

That's the thing about siblings: they're in it together, for good and for bad, whether they want to be or not. Nobody knows you like a sibling, which is why they are deadly accurate in pushing your buttons. Hell, they invented half your buttons. A sibling offers endless opportunities for "self-correction," showing us to ourselves with excruciating accuracy.

One of my all-time favourite exchanges between my children occurred when they were still fairly young, as we were getting ready to head out the door. One child did something, I don't remember what (indicating that it wasn't over-the-top terrible, but rather something annoying—infuriatingly annoying). I was about to deliver the typical, bland "be nice" admonishment, which would render me the ubiquitous, meaningless adult voice found in Charlie Brown movies of the past (worth looking up), when this magic occurred:

Sibling One (does annoying thing . . . steps in front of someone to block their way, pokes them in the side, eyerolls at a story being told, or the like)

Sibling Two: "Cut it out." (Where'd she learn that?)

One: "I don't have to."

Two: "It's annoying. People don't like that."

One: "I'll do it if I want to."

Two (plainly, as statement of fact): "Yeah, okay, do it if you want. But people will hate you."

All Other Sibs (nod in agreement, silently concurring)

Facts, dude: people will hate you. Best advice ever. I did not say a word.

Siblings have a hold on each other, for ill but also for good. I'd be negotiating ineffectively with a toddler-terrorist scream-ing bloody murder and resisting all trickery of being duped into cooperation, when a clever sibling, tired of waiting, would strike a theatrical pose of anticipation, and call out excitedly: *"HEY!! . . . Hey, c'mon!!"*

This would be said looking in the direction we needed to go, as though spotting a rocket ship around the corner. The toddler would stop mid-bellow, drop her angst like a shovel, and skip excitedly after her brother . . . her six-year-old brother. People skills flourish in having to figure out how to respond to challenges with ingenuity; siblings make this growth possible by providing the challenges.

The sibling dynamic certainly runs the gamut from life-long friends who'd literally give their left kidney to their be-loved sibling to detestable enemies who plot the murder of the other, full Cain-and-Abel mode. Besties or Enemies. Between those two extremes is a vast shared history that involves a lot of fighting in the basement.

Regardless of the conflicts that existed, whether born of tension or rivalry, Marcel and I tried to focus on providing what each child needed. It became abundantly clear to us, and to our children, that "what each child needed" was going to be different in very particular ways. Each child was not going to "get" the exact same thing. Keeping everything equal was never a goal, but tending to each child was. We hoped only to be equal in terms of the "tending to"—our children seemed to understand that. We tried our best; I'm sure it didn't look very good at times.

The parent of a child without siblings has their work cut out for them in particular ways too. I've watched with admiration the intensity often required in parenting a single child: there's no sharing of the parents' attention, but there is also no sharing, or deflecting, by siblings of angst, or momentum, or conflict either. Parenting a single child involves the gritty work of keeping things in balance and on track for both parties, without a sibling's mitigating interference or contribution, exhausting in a different kind of way. The same. But different.

We all work hard.

Reactions to a larger family are interesting; strangely, people tend to be either violently opposed or violently in support of. Neither reaction is necessary. I prefer the curious.

Me, pregnant, with five kids under nine years old, having lunch at a McDonald's after swimming lessons:

Older man (walks up slowly, leans over, smiling): "Is this a birthday party??"

Me: "No. This is just lunchtime."

Man: "Oh." (pause) "Well, it looks like you are having a party."

Me: "Every day is a party." (He and I smile at each other.)

That was a lovely one. I smiled for days thinking about it. That gentleman reminded me to be grateful, for everything. Grateful for the party I was living.

That "curious" line of questioning happened at home too.

We moved our children around between the shared bedrooms frequently, depending upon who was getting along best and who was needing their own space the most.

At one point, this needs matrix led to ten-year-old Adam sharing a bedroom with his two-year-old sister, Veronica. One day, during an afterschool play date, Adam and his buddy ran into the bedroom to get something. The friend screeched to a halt, taken aback not by the sports equipment, bird books, walkie-talkies, rock collection, and other stuff strewn around the room, but by the presence of a crib.

Friend: "Whose is this??" (pointing at the crib)

Adam: "It's my sister's."

Friend: "Why's it in your room?"

Adam: "Because she sleeps here."

Friend: "Oh."

Every day can be a party.

"Mu-u—u—um!" (somehow four syllables)
"Adam's being a bad example to meeee!!"
—Levi, 4, loudly, in the car, with the kids
fighting

REFLECTIONS ON PLAY

Play is the wonderland opportunity of learning for children. Play is the formula, the required work of a child.

The more free-form the better.

Duh—it's play! Toys without prescribed purposes "built in" are best. Though if children are "good players," they ignore built-in directives anyway. If a toy has batteries, take them out.

There's nothing quite like reading the paper Saturday morning and seeing your daughter sprint past you, flying Barbie horizontally above her head, which you assume is Barbie flying . . . but WRONG! You watch your clever daughter land Barbie facedown along the runway of the coffee table and witness that Barbie is actually a jet, which is corrected further, when your daughter informs you that Barbie is not a jet, she is a spaceship from the future.

Don't ask her anything about it though, a novice mistake. Your questions slow her down, break her train of thought, force her to apply limiting adult logic to her play . . . We should get into this right now:

Don't interfere.

Adults largely ruin children's play when we get involved, especially if more than one child is playing. We are joining a conversation in which we have forgotten how to speak the language.

Those of you thinking right now, *Well, that may be true for those linear-thinking, boring parents . . . but not for me! I am fun!* I hate to break it to you, but you're not that fun. Oh, you'll do in a pinch, but only if you follow precise instructions perfectly, refrain from introducing any of your own ideas, and meticulously repeat spoken lines exactly as assigned to you.

> Child: "Okay, say, 'The frilly lizard is putting you under arrest!'"
>
> Parent: "The frilly lizard is putting you under arrest!"
>
> Child (sighs): "Not like that. You have to be more mad."
>
> Parent (furious voice): "The frilly lizard is putting you under arrest!"
>
> Child: "Hmm, yeah, okay. But you need to put your arms more out to the side, like this, when you say it."

Which brings me to another point:
Kids always take turns telling each other what to say.

Even the surliest of children cooperate with this edict without question, as though adhering to an inherent, universal rule of kid-play, which is likely exactly what's happening. This is a perfect example of the kind of play that adults inevitably wreck. An adult will get all hung up on this assigned line-dictating as being limiting, pedantic, and unnecessary, even somehow lacking creativity. The adult will insist that Child X be "allowed to express himself," to "say what he wants to"—causing all the children, including Child X, to stare at the adult as if he's on crack cocaine and doesn't understand a thing.

There must be some weird developmental reason why kids do this line-dictating, because they all do.

See my point though? Ruined.

Kids use kid logic.

Children's play is free of the limitations of adult logic.

At some point our kids must have watched a National Geographic TV program, or had a library book, featuring a frilly lizard (is that a real thing?), because for an extended period, *every single time they played*, there was a frilly lizard on the scene. Domestic home event: check. Wilderness adventure: check. Robbery: check. That lizard guy got around.

"Hey, let's say the lizard worked in the mine!"

Later on, for one entire summer, our children played constantly with a large, colorful, concave segment of a torn, soft rubber ball. The segment was named "The Cap of Justice" and was worn on the head of a ruler while pronouncing irrefutable edicts, I believe. I have no idea what made them do this, but I am certain an adult would not have thought of it.

Nobody wants to be the mother.

Children often simply remove adults from within their imaginary play. It's best to just clear adults right out of the situation. Especially the mother.

A shared family memory, cherished by all of us for its delightfully savage candor, is that, for years, when the kids were playing together, or in various combinations, their imaginary game regularly began with the declaration, "Let's pretend the mother is dead."

Ah, yes. *Finally.* Limitless vistas of imagination could crack open, unfettered options suddenly piled abundantly upon the table with the ol' Mam banished from the scene. Imagine the scope now! Nobody wanted that old hag along, or worse yet, wanted to *be* her in the game. Are you kidding me?! The person "being the mom" would have to get people to wash their hands, scold them for talking back, frown if someone yelled, "Shut up, stupid!" (*"MOM! It's in the game!"*), and make the bad guys stop fighting. Ugh. No fun whatsoever. Clear that mom-cop right outta there!

I totally understood. Sometimes I didn't want to be the mother either.

NOT LIKE YOU

This might be a good time to mention that your child may be nothing like you. Nothing. At all.

No—really, think about that. We know it, but we don't *believe* it. Put another way, your child is not you. We can't help but use ourselves as a reference for our child, which is, more or less, utterly useless. We say things like:

What do you mean, you don't like "this kind of book"?! I read mysteries all the time when I was young!

I don't know why you're so upset about this. I don't see this as something to get upset about.

I wish I could have taken an art class when I was a kid!

See? Useless. But we do it all the time.

We lump siblings together in a similar misconception, in a subconscious expectation that they will be alike. I've been repeatedly bowled over, surprised over and over, by how completely different my children are from one another . . . which makes me a slow learner.

Adam was "tricky" as a toddler, a small Royalty of Resistance, of consternation and non-cooperation. So when our next child, Madeline, was a toddler, I'd brace myself, "gird my loins" as it were, when announcing something formally catastrophic, such as having to leave the house. I'd prepare myself for the inevitable meltdown. Madeline would look up, say, "Okay," put down the toy she was playing with, and walk over to wait by the door, leaving me in stunned amazement. Stupid, stunned amazement.

Fast-forward to Madeline during the teenage years, when getting her to express feelings and worries was like pushing a cart uphill, while simultaneously being carpet-bombed by thoughts and feelings being shared by Veronica, a preteen.

All of this surprised me.

I saw my own mistake demonstrated to me by another person during a high school parent-teacher conference for Madeline. The teacher had taught, and was currently teaching, Madeline's older and younger sisters and said to me, "I cannot get over how quiet Madeline is." I agreed, she is quiet. The teacher could *really* not get over this fact though, because she continued: "I mean, she's quiet, and reserved, doesn't speak up in class. She's SO different from her sisters—totally different!"

I was about one and a half decades into attending countless parent-teacher conferences at the time, thoroughly old and woolly. I was not merciful.

"Yes," I said. "It's almost like Madeline is a completely different person," which was unjustifiably savage, given my tendency toward the same error.

Message: your child is not you. And she is not her sister. She is herself.

"Mom, sing 'Rumpa Pum Pum'??"
—Madeline, 3, requesting we sing the
"Little Drummer Boy" Christmas carol
at bedtime, literally *every* day for months,
which was peaceful and weirdly calming
every time. All summer.

LEARNING TO READ

Things happen with our children that are like a mirror being held up to us, revealing something ugly in ourselves, especially when viewed next to the shimmering, fresh beauty of a sweet child. I've spent a lot of energy insisting children are not "all sweet," but honestly, mostly they are.

I was sitting with four-year-old Levi as he was "learning to read" in the kindergarten's early reading program. Which is to say, we were holding one of planet Earth's most repetitive, mind-numbingly boring books, repeating the "sounding out" of syllables, to form single words, to form brief sentences . . . over and over and over. Let me be clear: these were the same words. No, really—the exact same, every time. Levi approached each and every time as if it was entirely fresh, brand new, each and every time, on repeat. Know the kind? *The cat is fat. The cat sat. The fat cat sat on the mat.* Actually, no, that last sentence is too zany to be a legit example. Too interesting.

Levi sat propped beside me, legs fully bent, heels of both feet dug into the couch underneath him. His little face was the picture of concentration as he patiently repeated this process with every. single. word. It was a chaptered—did you get that?—a *chaptered* . . . "easy reader" about plants. What is wrong with these people?

Child: "Pl—pl—pla . . . pla-n . . . pla-n . . . pla-nn-t . . . pla-n-t . . . plan-t . . . plant . . . plant! I think it's plant!!"

Mother: "Yes. Do you recognize it? See? It's the same word from this page, and this page, and this page. Same. Plant. See?"

Child: "Yup, looks like plant for sure! Right. Okay, we got it! Plant. Alright! G, G-g, g-r, gr . . . gr . . . "

Mother (inwardly): *Help.*

Mother (outwardly): "Do you want to maybe take a break? We could read again tomorrow."

Child: "No, I want to keep going."

Mother (crestfallen): "Oh. Okay."

This process was repeated, while my mind longed to be free or, at least, not tortured. I composed grocery lists in my head, tried to think of gift ideas for upcoming birthdays, wished I could file my nails. Each page turned was "a new day," as though never seen before. We shoveled our way through this, as we had for weeks, through *plant* and *grow*, *bug* and *sun*, and *leaf.* Maybe I had low blood sugar or something, but it was all I could do to stop myself from running screaming out of the room.

At what seemed to be the peak of this process, Levi paused, looked up at me, smiled broadly, his eyes animated, and said,

"Whew!! We're getting there, Mom!"

I am a shithead. Really, what a loser, begging *him* to stop the difficult thing he was valiantly trying to do. This darling little soul, trying to learn to read, was *encouraging me* that his efforts would bear fruit, if I would just hang on. He, encouraging *me.* I almost burst into tears, at my being so terrible and he so lovely at the same time.

His upbeat encouragement worked wonders: I was shamed into a refreshed determination to "keep going," sitting or lying or propped with this small bulldozer of a boy and the most boring, repetitive books ever put to print. He'd learn to read despite me. And suddenly, one day, many weeks later, he could read. Just like that. He got it and was off.

Children's learning appears this way sometimes, sits hidden, simmering below the surface, as though being stored but not accessed, or at least not expressed, until some critical mass of understanding is reached, and then BOOM! The child can "suddenly" read, or understand division, like overnight. Or ride a bike. Or swim, or get what North-South-East-West means.

Be patient. Remember too that children cannot, and will not, be the same in how they learn things or do things. Why would they be? We adults aren't. Be honest with your kids: they quickly realize what they are good and not good at. It's weird for them when you say things they know are not true.

One time when Adam and his cousin Carson were drawing together, I saw Adam look startled as he glanced from his drawing of a dog with stick legs, heavy eyebrows, and a tail remarkably like a kitchen broom, over to his cousin's realistic sketch of a hand drawing a hand.

Later Adam made the statement, "Carson's a way better drawer than me."

"Yes, he is," I said. "Everybody's good at different things." Adam paused a sec and looked satisfied with this answer.

Apart from raw talent though, a common trajectory for learning is as follows:

learn > learn > learn > learn > learn > GOT IT

That's not how it actually works of course; that's just what it looks like. They, the children, and we, the parents, have to keep on going during the "learning below the surface" part. Sometimes all it takes is a little encouragement . . . for the parents.

"Wassat culled? Wassat culled?"
"Err lar looooo . . . ?"
"Wa do dat, Mum? Wa do dat?"
—every 2-year-old, asking questions.
All. Day.

CAPABLE

We seriously underestimate what children are capable of.

My mom, the second youngest of a very large family, was six years old when her mother died. The eldest sibling, Eva, returned home, at twenty-seven years old, to help Pop, as they called him, run the show, a Herculean undertaking of sheer will. For Aunty Eva, and my mom, and her sibs, and Pop, the years that followed required a lot of "personal grit."

My mother tells stories from her youth, of growing up on their family farm, in her signature, down-to-earth, unembellished style, as a series of facts that leave my kids "shook." This helped earn her the name they gave her—"G-ma"—because she's such a G (look it up if that term's meaningless to you).

Here's a barn burner G-ma shared one time.

G-ma: "I used to pick up my younger brother, John, after school. Schools were real crowded at that time, so we went in shifts. I was in the morning shift, until noon; the other young kids were in the afternoon shift. My sister Eva was back teaching again by then, so John—he was three or four years old—went to the neighbour's house every morning. She babysat him.

"After morning at school, I'd walk over to the neighbour's and pick John up. We'd walk home together and I'd get him lunch and, you know, chop wood and start the fire in the woodstove to warm the place. I'd heat water on the stove and peel a big pot of spuds—we had potatoes with supper every night. I'd sort of get things going before everyone started coming home, from afternoon shift of elementary school, and high school, and after work, and stuff."

Grandchild: "Wow. So G-ma, how old were you when you did all that?"

G-ma (thinking for a moment): "Mmm, I was about seven."

All grandchildren (standing up, shrieking, swearing, or mouths hanging open): "G-MA!! WHAAAT? Seriously, seven?? What a boss! Unreal! . . ."

Years later they still refer to that conversation.

I know, crazy. We all likely agree that, by today's standards certainly, my mom's seven-year-old situation was not ideal for her own care and nurturing. But in terms of building capability, it's got what we are currently doing beat all to hell. Nobody's recommending purposeful pursuit of barren, arduous, Dickensian childhoods here. Though the stacks of compelling literature featuring remarkable people emerging out of such bleakness are noteworthy, greater still are the numbers of children who likely emerged from such conditions damaged. No, we protect children now.

Maybe too much?

Perhaps we should at least teach eight-year-olds to practice critically crossing the street rather than just blindly following us. Or get them to make their own lunch, or a supper occasionally, take out the garbage, or make the phone call about the thing they want to know, or be otherwise capable in non-dangerous ways. Seriously, children can do much more than we think they can. Even small things are valuable.

I remember Adam coming home in Grade 4, thoroughly disgruntled that his teacher had "made him clean some cupboards" in the classroom. (Important note: always, *always*, find out the actual truth of what your child says "happened at school" prior to believing it, or reacting to it. Always. The story and reality are often curiously mismatched.)

Adam was frequently bored and agitated in school, and his wily, experienced teacher knew what he needed. One day he'd completed his work, and the classroom cupboards were a mess. It's safe to say that cupboard-cleaning was not a pre-scribed part of the curriculum, but this kid thrived on having something to do. Knowing this teacher, she probably provided detailed instruction, such as, "Clean up these cupboards." And that was it.

Adam removed everything, piling stuff all over the counters. He sorted out the garbage, taking it to "the garbage in the furnace room" (uh, does that sound like a good place for garbage, everyone?). He assessed the remaining stuff for purpose and meaning, sorted, and grouped it. He cleaned the cupboard itself, with cleaning spray and a cloth, then arranged everything back into various sections, in accessible sets and ordered fashion. This nine-year-old exercised a bunch of skills getting the job done, got the cupboards hella organized, and probably gave himself a sense of accomplishment. Win-win.

Anyone who'd consider this teacher lazy or unprofessional for requesting such a thing is missing the point entirely. Kids are capable if you let them be; she knew that and put that fact to work for her, and for him too.

As we were sitting together later at home, Adam described all that he had done. After we'd chatted about it a while, he hesitated, still somewhat agitated at being randomly assigned this chore. He asked, "Yeah . . . but why'd she make *me* do it?"

"Because she knew you'd be good at it," I answered.

"Oh," he said quietly, in a way that revealed he'd never considered the possibility the assignment could be viewed as a compliment, not a punishment. He walked away thinking, as one often saw him do.

"Mom, when I die, could you die with me?"
—me, 7

"No, dear. That's something everybody has to do by themselves."
—my mom

FUN & GAMES

GOING FOR CANDY

Life with children isn't all chaos and disorder and exhaustion. There is fun to be had too, lest I fail to mention it. Even some routines are fun.

During the years our children were in elementary school, which seemed to stretch on forever, we had a lovely Friday routine. The kids loved it, and so did I, because it made them all happy. This routine was like a reward for getting through a long and busy week, the kid equivalent of sitting with a beer and a friend on a patio in the sun on a Friday's late afternoon.

There was an ordinary convenience store near their school. We walked there together every Friday after pickup, hunched over wearing rain jackets in winter, or skipping there without jackets at all in the spring. I had a chunky baby perched around my shoulders, or I pushed a toddler in a stroller. We entered the store and immediately they dispersed. Much of the joy in this routine was the search for and selection of a treat.

We were there "for candy."

My adult kids are all still candy freaks. If their obsession was caused by this routine, so be it. Pure sugar, pure fun. The question was: Would you choose a prefab cup full of sour gummy worms? Or a chewy chocolate bar? Or a bag of crunchy chips? Or a sweet, freezing "swamp-water" mix of slushy drinks? Or the peak of fun: bulk mixed candy, selected with tiny plastic tweezers and placed in a small plastic bag??

Because that was the deal: you could only get one thing. My children acted as though they were choosing a car.

Their backpacks strewn all over the place, they wandered about, jackets skew-whiff. Children often look haphazard, ill-put-together, like small, absent-minded professors. After they'd chosen, they stood a few paces behind groups of teenagers, not intimidated, just waiting, well aware of the "pack rules" pecking order that dictated they wait for older kids to go first. They would have their turn later. (Kids need to know these things and are wise to observe them.)

We got to know the store manager, a kind and friendly Indian man who greeted us each week like friends. He always commented on my dark-chocolate bar, the one with coconut that he knew I always got (routine) to have with my tea when we got home (routine). He patiently helped the kids with the tedious counting out of bulk candy, since some cost a dime each, some a quarter, then helped them with the arithmetic to total the purchase. (This is sounding like a visit to the general store in a *Little House on the Prairie* book . . . No, we didn't hitch up horses outside.) I felt a fondness for our manager as he pointed out the "bargain of the week" to me, as if showcasing local fruit in-season instead of a jumbo bag of caramel popcorn. He chatted with the kids, and me, and asked us questions.

I pointed this man out to the kids as a most excellent example of the greatness some people bring to their work. They "own it" and go out of their way to engage people. They know their stuff and do a fantastic job. I mentioned how much we'd grown to *like* this man and that being good at his job seemed important to him. Our candy-store man was the original prototype of our *look how great this person is at his/her job* role model, leading us to notice the same thing in many other people, over many years to come. Barbers. The doctor's receptionist. The winter tire guy. A pharmacist. The delivery person. A compassionate airline agent. Some bus drivers—the key word here is *some*. Good ones of all these are "worth their weight in gold," Levi once said solemnly. Indeed they are, gems in our midst.

I digress.

This is all to say we loved our Friday routine. We loved our convenience-store guy. Afterward, we ambled to the car and clambered in, ready for another fabulous routine: singing along, as best we could make out the words, to a live-version CD of Peter Gabriel's melancholy-joyful "Solsbury Hill" blasting all the way home (sing the lyrics to yourself now).

We arrived home, and the kids piled on each other in the family room, and lay about, eating their candy happily, like lizards in the sun. I sat with them, having tea and my chocolate bar, relaxing with my feet up too. There was double joy because on Friday they were allowed to play DS until their brains froze.

Lots of people: "What's DS?"

Me: "DS was a little hand-held gaming thing, with tiny cartridges you pushed in, and you could play with multiple players. I have no idea how they worked, or what they were really. We got them at a toy store. The kids loved DS and played it for hours if they could, talking and yelling, and laughing, leaning up against each other, eating their candy, engaging in high-stakes 'tradesies' of that candy, loving life. I found out later they sometimes snuck their DS's into bed at night, to play multiplayer under the covers, especially if they shared a room. They'd fake sleep if I walked by or came in. I always knew they were feigning sleep by the theatric fluttering of their eyelids. But I admit to never knowing about the DS's in their beds. Or the walkie-talkies."

Same lots of people: "Oh."

Recently Emily reminded me of yet *another* part of our Friday routine that I'd forgotten. For years, after the candy store visit, we stopped by . . . the video store (!) to get a VHS movie for the evening.

EVERYBODY: "What's a VHS movie?"

Us: "Bruh."

> "Mom, I'm happy with the way you and Dad are raising me . . . The rules seem good, you get mad mostly when you have to, and I really like our school. Yeah—I think things are going pretty good."
> —Emily, 9

"Oh. Gee, uh—thanks, Em."

SPORTS

Sports have loomed large in our family life, some in passing, some going deep. I loved all of it. Loved. I have a strange addiction to watching children play sports: I sought all opportunities to get a fix.

Of course, playing sports meant practicing them—and that meant *a lot* of practices on the ol' family calendar. I would set the oven timer to remind me to go pick someone up from one sport or another, a problematic strategy if something happened to be already cooking in the oven when the timer went off.

One evening we were having people over when the mother of a friend of Madeline's phoned.

"Hi!!" she said, with a smile in her voice, followed by a dramatic pause.

"Uh . . . hi," I answered, impatient that she get on with the reason for her call.

"So . . . I'm standing here with Madeline . . . "

AAHHhhhh!! I'd forgotten to pick up Mads from soccer practice! And this lovely lady was kindly serving as my "it takes a village," bless her heart. I am the worst. Deepest apologies to all coaches since the beginning of time who were ever delayed by this type of negligence . . . or . . . maybe we were the only losers to ever do this?

The following is a choice selection of just some of the activities that fueled my kids-doing-sports addiction:

TRACK

Elementary track meets were my favourite. The sight of children running their fastest, their movement free and loose and natural, with their entire being focused upon *going* is, to me, a gorgeous thing. I love watching children run.

Seated in the stands beside an oval track, I was the weirdo tearing up at the sight of children running their little hearts out—or, conversely, delighting in those children strolling along completely nonchalant, seemingly unaware that a race was happening and that they were in it. An iconic family quote was delivered at a track meet by a daughter who was deeply unenthusiastic about having been entered in a long-distance event, one she had no intention of running in: "If I walk fast, but really pump my arms, people will think I'm running." Phenomenal.

SOCCER

Our children all played soccer when they were young, with Emily, Madeline, and especially Veronica continuing on through high school years because they loved it so much.

"Soccer" begins as a pack of small people wearing long jersey nightgowns, roaming all over a field in a tightly packed group, collectively chasing a ball. Gradually some skill and understanding of teamwork develops, becoming magic if they love it.

I remember being parked beside a soccer field one evening, waiting to pick up eleven-year-old Veronica. Driving rain, illuminated by field floodlights, pelted down so heavily I could barely make out the players sprinting, jockeying for position, trapping the ball, and sending it during the end-of-practice scrimmage. I was feeling sorry for Veronica, when she flung open the car door, her face and ponytail and clothes running water, thighs bright red from the cold. She threw herself in, exclaiming, "THAT WAS SO MUCH FUN!!" in a notedly "outside voice" as she slammed the door violently.

VOLLEYBALL

Even elementary school volleyball games, where getting a serve over the net was cause for jubilation, provided me with a cherished memory. Picture it: every member of Levi's Grade 6 boys volleyball team, *entirely* focused on the ancient, bulbous school knee pads they'd been given to wear, obsessively performing repeated diving, knee-slide maneuvers throughout the game, apropos of nothing, entirely unrelated to the volleyball game they themselves were playing in.

BADMINTON

A bit of badminton was fun to watch, because I knew my kids knew nothing about badminton.

CROSS COUNTRY

I was at a school cross-country running practice—standing in the park near the school, holding the hand of Levi, and stopping Eva from escaping, as my kids and their classmates ran around the park—when I realized I was in labour with Veronica. I'd loved doing cross-country running myself as a teenager, and, though not typically considered a spectator sport, for an addict like me, it was.

Cross-country running bestowed beauty on me in two acts, performed a few years apart.

Act I came a couple of years before Veronica's birth, as I watched the annual, district-wide elementary schools cross-country meet, a run through a park, finishing on a track inside a large, open stadium.

I was waiting for Adam's age group to weave their way around through the park when suddenly Adam came flying into the stadium at the front of a pack that flowed, spreading out behind him. He was straining, intent, but with wrists and hands hanging limp, relaxed. He came second.

This same child did not normally run at cross-country running practices. He would walk, and stop, and pick up leaves, or investigate a tree, insisting afterward, perplexingly to his Type A mother, "Mom, it's not a *race!*" Yet at this meet, without warning, Adam, seven years old, suddenly locked on and took off. It's a mystery what goes on in a child's head to make these changes happen.

There's a lot to children.

Act II took place at the same event a couple of years later, as I held month-old Veronica in a carrier and watched Madeline run. The year prior, Madeline had tripped and fallen and, by her accounting, had been almost trampled to death before coming dead last. She chose to run again this year, and I watched Madeline *once again* finish the race dead last . . . but this time, walking and chatting amicably with another little girl. I later learned that Madeline had stopped to help the other girl, a stranger who had fallen, and walked the rest of the way with her, poetry found in the most unlikely of circumstances. Sports can give us little windows into who they are: years later, Madeline is a child and youth care worker.

HOCKEY

Adam played hockey for a few years. We were terrible at it, not Adam, but Marcel and I, for obvious reasons. The ever-moving target of rink locations, and times for practices, and games, and the outrageous amount of equipment involved all required an ability to cope that was beyond us.

After a few years of this, Adam told me he'd decided he wasn't going to play hockey anymore. I steeled myself for a count of three before saying, "Okay," as quietly as I could muster. I still love watching him skate though. Good skating is beautiful, fluid, and athletic.

BASKETBALL

I grew up in gyms and playing basketball, so volunteer coaching Levi's and then Veronica's elementary school basketball teams felt like pure fun, the play adults don't get enough of.

Making the team at our children's elementary school went like this: if you want to join, you're on the team. Done. If you committed to practices and could remember your gym clothes, that was it. Experience? Not necessary. Knowledge of the game? Also not necessary. Athleticism? Ditto.

One cherished memory I have of coaching the boys basketball team involves a player, a tiny student who'd joined the school in Grade 7, who'd moved from the other side of the world. He told me he'd never played outside, never ridden a bike, or done "anything like that." Basketball was a mystery to him, naturally, with so much to learn. But he joined the team.

Fast-forward through our fairly short season, with limited practices, to playing in a real, live basketball game. The other team was ahead, but we were holding our own. The new boy, new to the country, the city, the school, and the game, was on the floor. It was our turn "trying to score." He was passed the ball at the top of the key. He stood a moment. Without bending his knees, he shot the ball, no arc whatsoever. It hit the backboard like a brick, with a thud, and fell lifeless into the hoop and through the net.

Praise the God of the Universe.

Our team stopped dead, then exploded in collective celebration, the way young boys do, like Steve Martin on speed. Our players on the floor ran around, hugged him, jumping up and down, ecstatic that he'd scored. Teammates on the bench jumped up and went wild, high-fiving each other as if they'd played a role in his achievement, which they had. The small crowd cheered, his parents smiling. The boy stood beaming. He, that brave boy, stood fixed in place where he'd shot the ball, smiling a quiet, satisfied smile, something I'd never seen him do. Our new scorer stayed there, savouring the moment, while the game continued on around him.

That is what children's sport is for.

We lost the game, but he scored, the most awesome moment of the entire season, for all of us I think. Better than a movie.

I cease this lengthy sports saga, numbing for those uninterested in sport. Sorry about that. We all like different things. Maybe that's the message for a parent. As the bookworm son of our super-athlete, cyclist friend once said to his sporty father, "Dad, I just don't like doing things that make me sweat." Fair enough—to each his own. My "own" though has been the pure joy of watching my children, and other people's children, play sports, through childhood, teenage years, and even into adulthood. My gratitude to each one of you, you adorable young athletes of every description. You are the best. I am a fan. Go you! Go team!

> "So . . . you know you're trying to kick the ball toward the other team's goal, down at the other end of the field, right?"
> —Grandpa, gently to Madeline, 5, after watching her "play a soccer game"
>
> "Duh, Grandpa!"
> —Madeline, having spent the entire game chasing the swarm of small players all over the field

CRAZY OUTDOOR PLAY

Outdoor play was the centerpiece of fun and games for our family. Much of that play strikes me as highly questionable in retrospect, but it seemed okay at the time.

We live on the kind of quiet, dead-end street rarely found now in this city, directly across from "the forest," a huge protected parkland, in a '70s house with a driveway and a carport. Who has carports anymore? I love our carport, a frickin' gem from the past: drive in and out easily, under cover, no garage door to deal with.

Our street slopes downward toward a cul-de-sac, the "turnaround spot," as the kids called it, and we still do. Once they were old enough, our kids were allowed to play together outside, on and down the street, all the way to the turnaround spot, and out as far as the path that bordered the forest and its paths. I don't remember how old "old enough" was; I imagine it varied, depending upon the child's ability to follow directions, stay with the group, and participate, even sort of, in the play.

And play they did. For hours and hours and hours.

I want to say, absolutely and without a doubt, that free, unstructured, outdoor play influenced the best of everything my children have become. It was kid-driven, pure creative madness, natural cooperation and negotiation training, great exercise, and—let's be honest—fantastic, because they were out of the house for a while.

Here are a few of the games (the ones I know of) that our kids played outside:

"SPIES"

The youngest, Eva, Levi, and Veronica, would take walkie-talkies, spread out along paths at the forest edge, and lay on their stomachs beside and under plants, hiding ineffectively, "being spies." They reported to one another, in loud stage whispers, as pedestrians walked by. My children sometimes even (cringe) trained the wrong end of a hockey stick upon the walkers, as though in the sight of a gun. (I didn't approve this; they did not ask me.) This game involved an awful lot of yelling, and "over and outs." and sprinting back and forth, and rolling on the ground in broad daylight, for a group of people meant to be spying. "Spies" could alternatively be called "Soldiers" or "Army guys" (apologies to all women in the military). I have no idea if/how those varied.

"BEING HORSES"

Long skipping ropes were tied around someone's waist, who would run ahead in a step-to gallop fashion, "being a horse." Naturally the child "being the rider" had to run as far and as fast as the horse, but nobody seemed to mind that. The horse got to neigh a lot and could neigh out words in whole sentences.

"SPORTS GAMES"

These games were an approximation of many sports combined, or a group of individuals each playing different sports, but somehow together. Think soccer, but with one kid on rollerblades, or street hockey, using a soccer ball as the puck because all the pucks are in the bushes and everyone's too lazy to get them. Or think basketball, but you're allowed to run with the ball. And be tackled. So "sports," loosely termed. Not good for children with OCD tendencies.

"ROLLERBLADES"

This was a strange development. We had a whole bunch of low-quality rollerblades I cannot for the life of me remember how we acquired. Is it possible someone gave us, like, six or seven pairs of rollerblades in a myriad of sizes? And I cannot remember this? Maybe we bought some? Though obviously at a toy store, not a real sports store, because these were crappy, made entirely of plastic. None of them fit well; maybe you were meant to put them on over shoes? Or maybe that was just us? Why is this so hazy? Apparently I did not pay any actual attention to any of this.

The "game" of rollerblading was absurd. Imagine a dystopian movie from the future, where children (wearing terrible, old clothing from the past) skate around poorly, aimlessly, without intent. Just around and back and forth, slow and a bit faster, occasionally very fast, in random, meaningless patterns. This lasts for a time, then stops. Weird, as if *they* didn't even like rollerblading much.

I recently threw out the whole pile of them, the crap rollerblades, broken and odd. Seeing them made me feel happy and sad. It's curious, all this, what it was and how it makes me feel.

"DOING CHALK"

Any combination of our children using a bucket of large, coloured chalk to do drawings on the driveway and street, of maps or directions, pictures, or printed jokes, designs—anything really.

"RIDING BIKES"

This meant simply riding bicycles up and down the street. Up and down, down and up, just because. It was a happy thing, done together but separate, without much need for arguing or rule management; just pedaling fast or slow. Riding bikes was often combined with "doing chalk" because . . . how fun is that?

As a teenager, Adam told me something I'd not been aware of: at around ten or twelve years old, he went for really long bike rides, all over the place, by himself, that were "the best thing I'd ever done." I really wasn't sure how to feel about that at the time. Now, though, I think that was really good for him.

"PLAYING TENNIS"

The kids played tennis on the street, using an assortment of old racquets, which, again, I have no idea how we came to possess (though people did give us lots of stuff, which I loved).

"Playing tennis" meant any of the following:

- a) actually trying to volley a tennis ball, or another kind of ball, back and forth
- b) hitting a ball as far as possible, or as high as possible
- c) trying to hit someone with a tennis ball as they dodged or weaved in front of you

or, the family favourite:

- d) standing around holding crappy, even quite broken, racquets, arguing about the rules of the game

"RIDING THE SKATEBOARD"

I say "riding" because it was some time before most became competent enough to ride down the hill standing on the skateboard (which would simply be called "skateboarding"). Even children eventually figure out what's dangerous. Each would "ride the skateboard," meaning sit on it, legs bent, feet flat in front of them, and glide down the hill, wobbling, using body weight as a rudder, one or both feet as brakes.

Me (incredulous): "How on earth have you worn a hole through your shoe?? There is an actual HOLE! . . . through, to the outside!"

Child (incredulous): "I don't know!!"

A fun twist? The arrangement of two people riding on the skateboard, sitting close, layered, or lying, one on top of the other. I insisted on the most bizarre parent rule ever, like the pretense of a rule created by someone who'd all but given up: riding the skateboard had to be *feetfirst only*. I'd try to stop them doing any of this altogether when visitor-children came to play, especially ones from careful families. Bad enough my own children were doing this, but not other people's children, not on my watch.

"RIDING THE CRIB MATTRESS"

All this brings me to the ultimate, most iconic outdoor-play activity, the most celebrated of all "the games they played," the one they loved most. Let me set this up for you.

When the time came for Veronica to be done sleeping in a crib, the mattress was terribly worn, a corner mashed in where an enthusiastic and weighty jumper, or a series of them, had stomped the mattress into submission. It was time for the mattress to go. We retired the crib mattress along the side walkway of our house, the designated place for items awaiting a visit to the dump. Consequently, there leaned a heavily worn crib mattress, a forlorn symbol of misspent babyhood, perhaps a lawn chair, with a spring and too many web strips missing, and pieces of a ceramic planter the kids knocked over by accident, all greeting visitors as they came and went. Fantastic property street appeal, I know.

One day, one of our kids must have eyed the crib mattress leaning up in the walkway and saw opportunity where others saw garbage. The words *Hey! Look at this!!* were probably shouted, like the cry of a triumphant scientist after decades spent peering into a microscope. The crib mattress was dragged onto the driveway, placed teetering upon the skateboard, and *TA-DA!!*

Epic New Family Game:

"Riding the Crib Mattress . . . on a Skateboard!!"

Hell yeah!

I truly thank God our family life preceded the existence

of permanent photo or video evidence like the kind archived on social media, burdening dear families these days. Dodged a bullet there.

I must say, the image, the pure irony, of my children taking turns flying down the hill, shrieking with glee, balanced precariously upon a disheveled crib mattress atop a skateboard, the now-exposed metal frame of the mattress throwing joyful bursts of celebratory sparks into the air as it dragged upon the street, is a scene I can replay in my head to make myself laugh. Appalling, yet fantastic. The glory days.

It was as though all the worries and overprotection of nights spent hovering by said crib, and its mattress, were cast to the wind, and those same babies, grown up just a few years, were now happy pirates on a sea of risk. Where the hell was the mother? I *should* have been sipping a G & T in the backyard, but alas, I was inside dealing with a stack of unopened mail, making supper, hauling laundry, or, honestly, sitting talking on the phone with a girlfriend. I despise how frightfully domestic this makes me sound, but then, raising children is domestic.

There they were, my children, risking their lives on an object that had been purposefully designed for their earlier comfort and safety. I am not saying any of this was a good idea. I'm just saying we did it.

I realize that the freedom of unsupervised outdoor play reads as wistful reflection on a distant past, of settler times, or the '50s or '60s. But it's not. This is the experience of some young adults *of today*, currently in school or having joined the workforce. This is not an unfathomable possibility—you don't have to have six kids, or a '70s house on a cul-de-sac, or be home full time to have this kind of play be part of your child's life. It's not a prescription; it's a mindset.

Leave some things unstructured, let the kids lead, try not to interfere. Close the windows and give the garden hose to your two little girls in the backyard. Keep old gadgets that your

child can take apart and do whatever she or he wants with.
Take your four-year-old only child, and his pal, to a wide-open
expanse of beach on your day off. Bring a real garden shovel,
a tarp, a bucket, a snack he chose and made, and your book.
Then sit off to the side and read.

"You're having a yard sale . . . right?"
　　—a woman, hesitatingly, bent over in our
　　front yard examining kid paraphernalia
　　spread all over the lawn

We were not having a yard sale.

TOUGH STUFF

RIDING, NO HANDS

Accidents happen when children are around. How is it that one such accident led to my feeling grateful, overwhelmingly blessed, rich, and sad, as I held my child in the back seat of a car at 3:30 a.m. in a parking lot outside of a drugstore?

The particular accident I'm referring to, which took us to an Emergency Department early on a summer evening in September, involved simple bike riding, a reassuringly normal way for a child to get hurt. Our six-year-old daughter Eva tried to go fully "no hands" while riding a bicycle, her first attempt at ever doing so.

Recently, at twenty-two years old, she was reflecting on what surprises her about this experience, looking back. She'd seen Adam ride "no hands" and thought that was somehow something anyone who could ride a bicycle could also "just do." She'd not imagined that "riding no hands" was yet *another* physical skill one had to learn, on top of mastering riding a bike.

Back on that day, while riding down the hill, Eva saw our neighbor, a lovely man, the dad of two girls she played with, outside in his driveway. She decided to give him a big ol' wave

. . . and, hey, how about riding no hands? That'd be extra fancy! She let go of both handlebars, began to wave, wobbled, and crashed, hitting the pavement hard.

The hours that followed were chaotic and are foggy to re-count years later.

Eva had split the skin on her chin open, scraped her face badly, hurt her arm, and was holding her jaw at a strange angle I knew indicated it was broken. Her little bike helmet had done its job: thank God we had that baseline safety measure in place for bicycles, if not for crib-mattress-skateboard-riding.

Another neighbour, the mom of a family, new from Australia and renting a place up the street, who must have been outside that day, appeared on the scene. She offered to stay with my family. I accepted gratefully. It was a Friday and nine-year-old Madeline had a friend over for a long-awaited first sleepover. Being practical girls, not dissuaded by trauma, the two pals still desperately wanted the sleepover to hap-pen, despite a family member heading to Emergency with the mother. Odd, but I trusted them. I knew they wouldn't be any trouble. Helpful Neighbour Woman was fine with it (what dif-ference was one extra kid in this mayhem?), as were the vis-iting girl's parents. The friend would stay. Seems like lunacy now but there it is. The two girls set happily upon the task of making crafts for the injured, as one does. Our lovely Helpful Neighbour stayed with our family that evening, which was un-believably generous of her. Looking back, I feel bad; I didn't thank the neighbor as properly as I should have, which would have involved buying her a four-hour spa visit, or making her family's dinners for a week, or the like. I really regret not doing more to properly thank her. What a kindness.

I left a message for my husband and, holding Eva, climbed into the back of the wave-to-the-dad-neighbour's wife's car. (She was, ironically, a marvelous nurse I used to work with years prior, now a good friend.) I held a clean towel to Eva's bleeding face on the way there, as she lay shocky and quiet in my arms, much scarier than if she'd been struggling and loud.

Children's Emergency was busy, but I think they're always busy. Our evening there was long.

I carried Eva in. She was admitted, seen by various medical personnel, had an IV started, and had her chin cleaned and temporarily bandaged. She was taken to X-ray. I was accustomed to Eva being feisty and brash at home, assertive, a worldly twenty-seven-year-old trapped in the body of a six-year-old. In the Emergency Department, she was little, lost in a loose hospital gown, and propped in a bed that made her look even tinier than she was.

She observed everything with a sedate, wary, scraped, bandaged, and crooked-jawed face. Her eyes had met mine with a look of extreme distress as the nurse cut off and threw away her favourite yellow Sponge Bob T-shirt, now covered in blood. I knew she wanted to cry about that but didn't. She loved that shirt, having worn Sponge Bob almost every day since discovering it in a bag of hand-me-downs and claiming him as her own, a cherished prize. Marcel arrived, a great reassurance to us both. He and I sat on either side of our daughter's bed in the little curtained cubicle space. She glanced back and forth between us, as though gauging our anxiety in order to set her own.

We knew Eva wasn't mortally wounded, but still. Her arm was sprained at the elbow, jaw fractured though not requiring surgery, the gaping cut in her chin requiring stitches. The worst, we learned, were the gravel-embedded abrasions across her face. The plastic surgeon decided to debride, or scrub, the abrasions, to remove the gravel and clean them properly. This would have to be done under anesthetic, and they'd do the stitches at the same time.

We sat waiting in our darkened, curtained cubicle. I was preparing to feel terrible about all this when something happened next to us that made me feel incredibly, desperately, and guiltily grateful instead.

A child died in the next cubicle.

The child had a condition of some sort and had come in with oxygen equipment and other medical supplies. From the moment the child arrived, there was a suppressed but tangible buzz of charged activity all around. There was too much happening on the other side of the curtain for things to be okay; it quickly became obvious something was, in fact, terribly wrong. The child was having trouble breathing, was not doing well. The family did not seem to be expecting this. Too many medical staff began arriving, too tense a request made of the family to leave, too much equipment swiftly brought, too many orders quietly given. Busy, tense, orderly activity took place in the space a world away on the other side of the curtain.

Then quiet.

A nurse stuck her head in our curtain, saying, "Stay in here, don't look out," curt in her protection of those in her charge. A social worker arrived. A meeting was being set up in a family room. The nurse was sent to get the child's family from the waiting room. Marcel and I looked at each other over our little girl's head. In between our looks, I stared at a point on the ceiling, blinking focusing all my energy on willing myself not to cry. I wanted to sob—sob for the gift of my little girl sitting right in front of me, for the pain of the parents about to be shattered in a meeting room somewhere nearby, for life and all its tenderness and frailty and beauty, its pain and fatigue. Sob for all of it. But I didn't. The three of us sat in the quiet, waiting.

Staff soon arrived to give our daughter IV sedation and start some other lines. Eva was done with being stoic and fought them like a wild animal. Marcel helped hold her down to get the job done, and they wheeled Eva out, off to the procedure room in Emergency for her facial debridement and stitches. I tried not to imagine it.

Later, in the wee hours of the morning, I sat in the back seat of our car in the parking lot of an all-night pharmacy, holding Eva, with her arm in a sling and a bandage over her stitched, fractured jaw and scrubbed face, held in place by gauze wrapped around her head and under her chin. Marcel was inside picking up the prescribed pain medications and antibiotics, the salves, bandages, and more gauze. It was cool and dark and quiet in the car, silent even, after the noise and bustle and bright lights of the Emergency Department. I sat motionless, looking at my daughter, thinking of the family of strangers somewhere in the city who, at that exact same moment, were now unable to hold their child ever again.

Why must we brush with death to really see this life? For many, many days to follow, I thought about what had happened, with an ache in my chest, every time I looked at Eva. As I changed her dressings, or pureed food for her to eat, or took her to follow-up doctor visits, I thought of the family whose routines no longer included the pressing demands of looking after their child, of caring for and loving him or her in the flesh. I imagined the gaping void they faced while I was immersed in an abundance of loving in the flesh, in the ordinary days of my beautiful life.

Each time someone said to us, "Oh my goodness! A broken jaw, stitches in her chin, scraped face! How awful!" I wanted to say quietly, "No, not really."

HOW TO AVOID RAISING AN ASSHOLE

I want to share a set of conclusions with you, ones arrived at through observation. They're opinionated and judgey, but represent hard-earned knowledge borne of other people's grief and somewhat avoidable suffering. It's best we not allow it to go to waste. Raising an asshole is largely avoidable. Let's avoid it.

Here we go:

Do not give your child everything she wants; that's really bad for her. It is difficult if you are rich, because then you have to say no on purpose when you could easily say yes.

Teach your child he is not more important than anybody else. Be certain he knows he means the world *to you*, and is truly important, but actually not more important than anybody else. The paradox: being absolutely special and, at the same time, no more special than anyone else. Wait—what? Yup, special/not special.

Make her wait sometimes. It won't kill her. Wait for you, wait for stuff, wait for others, wait for things. It is a monstrous disservice to allow her to think she should go through life expecting never to wait. Prevent that shock. Make her wait.

Do not allow your child to monopolize the conversation, especially with a group of adults. It's totally annoying to everybody. Yes, totally *and* everybody. Your child is cute but also not that cute.

Be ruthless about manners. Ruthless. Manners demonstrate our respect for one another. People without good manners seem like assholes.

Allow your child to be bored. Ignore your child when he or she is bored. Really, who cares? Why is that such a problem? It's certainly not *your* problem, nor the end of the world. Boredom is the engine of much creativity. Don't solve it. Let him solve it. He will if you don't.

Call your child out on his or her bad behaviour. Do not let it slide. Was your child being mean? Did she just lie to you? Is he blaming someone else for difficulties of his own making? Was she disrespectful to Grandma? Deal with all that exhausting shit. (But don't nag. Now *there's* a trick!) Ignoring these exhausting things rather than dealing with them results in something *infinitely more* exhausting and wearing in the long run: living with an asshole of a kid.

That's it.

See? Easy peasy lemon-squeezy (as opposed to *Difficult difficult lemon-difficult*, as I heard Adam say about something in grad school).

There's a better chance your child will have a good and happy life if he or she is not an asshole. Do your best to prevent that. Among all the things we have control of in parenting, which aren't many, this one's largely on us. Not entirely, but a big chunk of it is. We might as well wield the little influence we actually have.

To be clear, I say this out of high regard and respect for our dear children. They are not benign recipients of our care and concern, inert vessels of humanity without agency or autonomy. They have their own will—man, do they have their own will—and their own drives and cunning and reasoning. Kids are smart. They are wily. They push their will as far as they can manage, to arrange their world around their own wants, which makes total sense but not, ultimately, if they would like to get along well in that world.

Don't underestimate the abilities of children: they have the capacity to become assholes. Do your best not to allow this.

"I WANT PICKLES!"
—toddler, from her high chair

"What do you say?"
—weary parental response

"GET IT!!!"

WAITING

Nothing about having children is efficient, to be clear. Nothing.

Children are by design anti-efficiency. Parenting is a process, not a procedure.

There's a lot of waiting. Wait for baby to finish nursing. Wait for toddler to look at a beetle. Squeeze toddler's cheeks and wait for beetle to be spit out. Wait for words they are trying to say. Wait for pee to come on the potty. Wait for them to wake from naps. Wait with them at doctor's offices, for them at birthday parties and gymnastics. Wait for her to finish her supper. Wait for his cast to come off. Wait at parent-teacher conferences, at driver licensing offices, and late at night for them to come home. Wait.

People think of waiting as "doing nothing," which it is not. Waiting is a thing unto itself, an indispensable tool of parenting. To wait. This is not efficient—I don't think it's supposed to be. But it's necessary.

Please, please, though, do not tell me, *It's a good thing you're patient.*

I am not patient. I have learned to be patient, but I am not naturally so. Parents *learn* patience, because we have to. It's called survival. We would lose our freakin' minds if we "popped off," as my youngest adult child calls it, with every inconvenience, every clashing of wills, every difficulty, every task that must be done despite our not wanting to do it.

I've grown into this, as we do, and weirdly love it now, the mess of this mothering role. I relish being needed. We become more, we fathers and mothers, more than we used to be, as we grate against what we find difficult, the abrasive stuff. I'm still a shithead, but my children have made me less of one. I value that growth in myself, the growth my children have scraped out of me.

Marcel's work has been such that he wasn't home a lot. A good number of times while taking care of our children on my own, I thought, *I can't handle this.* But, looking around, there were no other adults on-site. Wailing about my distress, real as it was, was sound and fury signifying nothing; I was it. Mom or Dad, you are it. And so we "learn" patience, a Guantanamo Bay–type of "learn," but still. We do.

Finally, years into this gig, I have the hang of it, this waiting, this adapting. *Adjust. Go with the flow. Calibrate. Underreact. Wait.* I have mellowed somewhat. Go me.

Want to hear something delicious? I can feel my adult kids' annoyance as they have to wait for me these days. I am finally, *finally*, not in a hurry. And they are. They want to get going, be on it, arrive early, do the thing . . . and now I don't care. They are the very reason I have shifted all my natural tendencies in this area, and the outcome of that transition grates on them, the ones who caused it. Ha! Life. Or maybe I haven't adapted my natural impatience at all; maybe I'm just worn out.

Either way is fine.

All kids (at 9): "Can I come grocery shopping with you?"

Parent (getting old): "Sure."

All kids: "How long will you be? It could be kind of boring."

Parent: "I don't know—not long. But yeah, probably boring."

All kids (looking distressed): "There's nothing to do here. But then . . . maybe I don't want to come . . . Uh—maybe I should."

Parent (stands holding front door handle, waiting)

CHILDREN & BOOMERANGS

Let's say boomerangs became popular among adults.

Adults were keen to have boomerangs. They found boomerangs helpful and entertaining. They started relying on them. Soon teenagers wanted boomerangs too. The parents said, *Okay, sure, you can do some stuff with boomerangs. But not everything.*

Teenagers loved using boomerangs. Boomerangs were shiny and made sounds and showed you were cool and let you talk with your friends. Boomerangs were awesome. Teenagers did everything on them.

Then children wanted boomerangs as well. Parents were not sure, but said, *Okay, you can do some stuff.* Children got boomerangs and started doing lots of stuff on them, not just some stuff. Children began using boomerangs to go to a place where things aren't real. Some kids started living a lot of their childhood over in that not-real place.

Then things got weird.

Children were hucking boomerangs around in ways adults had not imagined for them. Children became obsessed with their boomerangs. They didn't run around, ride their bikes, or play together in the real world as much as before. Children did not build structures out of stir sticks on the restaurant table while waiting for the food, or chat with Grandma when she came to visit. They preferred their boomerangs. Some children had their boomerangs with them all the time, even in bed at night. By then some children and, unfortunately, some bad adults were using boomerangs to harm other children in ways that no one could see.

All of this made adults say, *Oh dear, this is bad.*

Kids' lives became different with boomerangs. Many kids became anxious, even depressed. Children worried about stuff happening on their boomerangs and in that other not-real world, where hurts and harms had become real. Boomerangs put pressures on children that adults could not see or did not understand.

Adults worried about children's boomerangs.

But adults were busy being adults and busy with their boomerangs too.

So that's all that ever happened: the adults saying, *Oh dear, this is bad.*

The End.

That's where we are.

> Anyone: "Hey, so I was thinking that boomerangs seem super-terrible for kids."
>
> Everyone else: "WE KNOW! BUT WHAT THE HELL?! Kids LOVE boomerangs, and LOTS OF KIDS have one, and they NEED boomerangs—to be safe! Boomerangs are just 'the way it is.' You can't stop boomerangs!!! Besides, your kid will be weird and never get invited to birthday parties if she doesn't have a boomerang!"
>
> Anyone: "Oh."

It's difficult for me to participate in this conversation. My ideas are too simplistic for the problem that lies in front of parents now. If I were asked, I would say useless things like:

If you have to check your kid's boomerang all the time, maybe he's not old enough to have one. (Full disclosure: this is a direct quote from twelve-year-old Levi, about parents constantly checking their kids' actual boomerangs. I cannot take credit.)

Kids would be bullied less in that not-real world if they were, maybe, in that not-real world less.

If your child wants a boomerang when she's much too young, say, "Yes, later." Then wait, and get her one later.

Or straight-up crazy stuff: *We could take their boomerangs away and make them go play.*

See? I'm no help at all.

You are all smart. You can sort this out. I'll be sitting in the stands cheering for you, calling out, *Good luck, everyone!!* Not in that nasty, dissing way that people do when they say, *Good luck with that* and mean, *I hope you fail miserably.* No!

I will mean, earnestly, with all of my heart, *I wish you the absolute best of luck—everyone!—because this matters incredibly for our children, and we love them so much . . . and being on boomerangs constantly is harming them in ways we should fear, and we have enough collective wisdom to figure this out!!* That kind of "good luck."

We are smart enough to make boomerangs. We are smart enough to decide how to use them.

> "Excuse me . . . this is too much fries for me."
> —Veronica, 6, earnestly sliding her
> overflowing basket of fries back across
> the counter at a bewildered concession
> worker

PARENTING THINGS I WAS TERRIBLE AT

Note: The following is not a comprehensive list. Not even close.

- Children's birthday parties
- Pets
- Crafts/costumes
- Allowance
- School projects
- Children's fashion
- Music lessons

CHILDREN'S BIRTHDAY PARTIES

I didn't dislike having birthday parties for my children, but, surprise, mine were done old-school. Get the kids together, let them play, give them a hot dog and cake, send them home. Done. Fun for all. For little kiddies, I'd knock myself out and plan an actual "activity" or two. You know, an actual thing.

I always tried to "win" birthday parties offered at those auction events; the best party we "won" was a party for little girls, hosted at a high school wrestling room, with birthday cake in the school cafeteria. Another was pizza-making at a hip pizza place: there'd be no hip and no pizza-making party at our house.

Honestly, it was other children's birthday parties I didn't like: the ones at Bouncy Fun Trampoline and Archery World, an hour-and-a-half drive away on a rainy Saturday between all the sports. Or parties at Ceramics Are Us, where your kid was meant to bring a white T-shirt to tie-dye—but you didn't read that, so he has to take off the shirt he happens to be wearing and tie-dye that, putting on his muddy soccer jersey for said ceramic/tie-dye party.

I ignored all gift directives. My kids will cringe at this memory: I stockpiled a bunch of the exact same thing to give away at *all* birthday parties. Right, kids?? Let's say it all together now!

- A bird feeder (bell-shaped seed feeders you hang

in a tree, wrapped in cellophane, sold in hardware
stores)
- A box of movie-themed Band-Aids (children love
putting on Band-Aids: give them a whole box to
do whatever they want with)
- Gum (children love gum)

Don't get me started on those gift bags we give to children
for *attending* a party. Because . . . why? Cannot deal. I would
like to speak to the person who invented that idea, please.

PETS

Pets are a hell of a lot of work. You will do most of it, unless
you are a sensible farm person. But if you're down for that responsibility, well, kids love pets and maybe you will too.

Adam had budgies as a child, Phlaps and PhooFoo. He bred
them once, then hand-tamed and re-homed the baby budgies.
A self-taught bird expert and, later, bird hospital volunteer, he
pleaded incessantly to foster a Moluccan cockatoo (cockatoos
live eighty years, lots need fostering). Eventually Beaker the
Moluccan came to live with us for a few years.

Our first and beloved dog was a ridiculous, dark-brindle
boxer named Cedric who could almost talk, holding your
hand with his, flattening the jowls of his expressive face into a
pancake while mooing. Dog-training classes with Cedric were
humiliating; he was not committed to the process. Cedric
lived nine years, from Veronica's kindergarten year until the
year she began high school. We loved Cedric.

I remember the afternoon a little friend of Adam's stood
gazing upon the scene, of Beaker, bobbin', talkin', screechin',
perched in the corner of our family room, with our new puppy
Cedric scampering about amidst kid-mayhem. The lad shook
his head, saying, "You guys need this like a hole in the head."

Truer words never spoken, dear fellow.

There was a hamster, two guinea pigs initially Betty and Wilma, hastily renamed Wilson and Alex.

Later we got Winifred, a beautiful, red-brown, sensitive boxer-Rottweiler mix, also deeply expressive, with comical eyebrows and a wicked side-eye. Winnie rushes over to press her weighty care of concern against any family member in need of emotional support, before that person themselves even realizes they're feeling emotional. She also, unfortunately, rushes over to press the same strength of instinctual devotion into the attacking of strangers arriving at our house. A young school-age Veronica built an agility course in the backyard that she and Winnie played over together many days after school.

Eva got a university-hamster, named Remington, and, later, her own puppy, a perpetually happy Cavalier-beagle mix, named Gilbert, as in Gilbert Blythe (look it up).

I have developed a test to help you decide whether "now" is a good time to add a dog to your family. Picture the zaniest, most out-of-control kind of day you have. Now, insert a three-hour veterinary visit into that same day, because that will happen. But there will be super-nice moments too, of a warm dog leaning against your leg as you sit, and days when you feel like going for a walk too. So it's a toss-up.

I didn't dislike our pets, and eventually even loved a few. I did not bring an over-the-top enthusiasm or single-minded devotion to it though. Our pets had good lives with us, but I hoped they weren't comparing notes with pets from other families—they might not have loved us quite so much.

CRAFTS/COSTUMES*

I helped with all costumes and crafts by saying, "Go ahead. See if you can find some stuff then, yes, go ahead."

ALLOWANCE*

Many parents have the commendable goal of wanting to help their children understand the value of money. Me too. I think children really learn the value of money if you don't give them any.

SCHOOL PROJECTS*

Tempting I know, but school projects are theirs, not yours. Years from now you will find it extremely uncomfortable sharing a single bed in a dorm with your child when it becomes necessary to go to college with him, because, well, school projects.
(*No wonder I could have so many kids, right? I hardly did anything.)

CHILDREN'S FASHION

Thinking about the clothing my children wore while growing up makes me want to laugh, and also cry. They appear in a decade-plus of family photos wearing the same items in series, including crazy-ass things people gave us in large, full garbage bags, like we were a charity. I loved that gifting, because I don't like shopping or, at least, could never go.

We'd open the bags and just start using the stuff, including, for instance, the bizarre balloon/clown (?) denim overalls with bright, multicoloured straps and buttons that Madeline is wearing in a home video, at four years old. She is singing and doing actions for a little song learned in preschool, "Going to Kentucky." Anyone who sees the video, including Madeline, enjoys how adorable she is, with her animated face and singing voice with a darling lisp, on the verge of laughter all the

way through. Her little fingers are spread out hard, hands totally flat, enthusiastically patting a rhythm on her legs through
mounds and gathers and folds of voluminous, puffed denim.
Every person, I mean each and every single, solitary person,
who ever watches the video, asks, *What is she wearing??*

MUSIC LESSONS

We went about this all wrong somehow. Piano lessons were
reduced to a battle of wills. Flashes of interest and talent were
apparent from time to time, when a child, particularly Levi,
began enjoying himself without noticing. Occasionally this led
to exhaustive repetition of a piece they liked, replete with errors but some joy, or the bashing out of bits of popular music
they tried replicating. They probably learned something about
music—notes and some counting, the idea of chords maybe.
They certainly all love music now, but who doesn't? Perhaps
some will make music using something they learned. Mostly,
though, we just fought over an egg timer used to time the
practicing. *I heard you turn that backwards . . . !*

> "Did you happen to send us an invitation to a
> birthday party for Madeline?"
> —a lovely mom from the preschool
>
> "Yes!"
> —me
>
> "I thought so. We got a birthday invite card
> that was blank inside . . . I thought it might be
> from you."

IN THE END

A RELATIONSHIP

There seems no way to capture, really, what it means to have children, what it's really like. We all sort of know, but cannot seem to say. We look to books to help us understand it all, its complexities. There is a multitude of books available, to help you learn and grow in being a parent. I offer a caution to accompany them.

I'm not revealing much when I tell you I did not read many parenting books. I don't think my parents' generation read many (in case you couldn't tell that either). Truly, they and I made mistakes, a great number of them, some serious. Our children bear the scars of the things we did wrong; that is true for every generation of parents. My generation, and many before mine, often didn't think *enough* about what we were doing—our children will work hard to avoid the errors we made. I applaud the current generation of parents for being so intentional in their efforts to do things well.

Yet there existed for me, and all the more-oldsters, a mysterious, uncalculated advantage in raising children without the books and blogs, the Instagram videos, podcasts, and apps (are there apps??). We were less hesitant, less uncertain, less anxious. We were more likely to trust ourselves, for good and also, I admit, for bad, if that trust was not carefully considered. To a great degree, however, ignorance is bliss. I am not suggesting parents bury their heads in the sand and live out parenting unthinkingly, flailing about to the detriment of their own dear children. God, no. But we oldsters had the ease of seeing parenting as simply an extension of being, not a technique lived.

Not long ago I visited a large chain bookstore to peruse the parenting section. I stood in front of the wall of books about parenting and made myself slowly read each of the titles, trying to take them in.

Something about how that wall "felt" made me want to weep, and also have a panic attack. It's so much, you poor things, parents of children today. So much. You are trying so hard and the wall looms.

Of course we are going to try our best, of course. But be "scientific"? "Best" (what?)? "Data-driven"? *"Peaceful"*?? "Smart"?! Instillers of "lifelong success," now? *Today?* With my two-year-old . . . who just took off all her clothes and diaper for the third time this morning, and is fighting me in dressing her, though we have to leave *immediately* because we're already late getting her brother from preschool? *Today* is aimed at lifelong success?? Because of what I do with her today??

You're scaring me, brother!

Somehow combined, amassed, this wall of books weighs heavily upon parents. In their summation, the books tell us we are not good enough, that we're doing it all wrong. They convey to us, on an emotional level, if not a content level, that parenting is a skill, like windsurfing, or a strategic process, like systems analysis at work, or instruction, like teaching origami. But it's none of that. It's not. Yes, parenting is comprised of one thousand and one activities, involves a hundred skills, calls for endless instruction. But that's not what it *is*.

Parenting is a relationship.

You already know that, dear parents everywhere. And you know what to do with a relationship. You, with all your gifts and particular foibles, and your precious child, with all his or her gifts (you know those best) and foibles (you know those best), and the question of how you live your relationship with one another. You already know what to do.

You listen, you cuddle, you holler, kiss, laugh, scold, chat, and wait, be furious, cry, forgive, mess up, apologize, love, and do the hard thing, colour a picture, make a quesadilla, and take her to practice. And listen after practice. And worry, and talk through what you heard after practice, with your spouse/partner or friend. Or your mother.

You turn to people, *to other relationships*, to help you with the parenting relationship. Turn to friends who are deep in the trenches of parenting alongside you. Turn to your grandmother . . . unless your grandmother is insane, then don't turn to her; go find someone else. Turn to the parent group at the community centre. I was an idiot and didn't do that enough, too proud somehow to need a bunch of people to push strollers around with and talk about how hard it was, having a baby. I abhorred the thought of that for some reason, which was stupid of me; I was lonely and I needed support and I didn't get it.

But I would not have gotten it from a book. We need people. And *you* are one of the "people" someone else needs: it's like that. My "people" were my husband, my parents, and my sister, a wise preschool teacher, and some marvelous friends, who provided me with repeated reassurance, good ideas, and support. And listening, heartfelt listening. They saved me and kept me going. We need to be encouraged, need to be told we are doing a good job.

All I have to offer you, by way of affirmation, is that, regardless of whether you have one child or ten, if you manage only half of the failures, commit only half of the errors and omissions that I have, then, in my estimation, you're killing it at parenting. For what that's worth.

Get the book if you want to. But this is important: if you are feeling anxious about parenting, do not get the book titled *How to Reduce Anxiety in Your Anxious Child in an Anxious World*. Pretty sure that won't help. (Note to self: check that this is not the actual title of a real book.)

Trust yourself. Look inside yourself. Challenge yourself. You know what you are doing SO much more than you realize . . . or admit. You love your child like life itself, and *that love*, that relationship, is what makes you a good parent. You already know what to do. Doing it? That's the hard part, for all of us.

WHAT REALLY MATTERS

I have failed to share, in any specific way, what's most import-ant in having children, what matters. Parents easily make that mistake, mired in details of everyday life, such that we over-look mentioning the important stuff.

It's difficult to capture what really matters, but it's some-thing like this:

You're sitting with your child in the kitchen, having a bowl of soup together. It's quiet and there's no one else around.

Your child is happy, lost in his or her thoughts. He or she hums along with the clinking and the slurping, a leg swinging back and forth, loose and free.

Your child looks up at you and smiles. And you smile back, with your eyes and all your heart.

That's it. That face, those eyes, that smile, and the love that surges from within you, enveloping your child and the space that lies between you. There's not much else to say.

SUFFERING

You should sit down for this, if you happen to be reading standing up.

There is a lot of suffering.

Suffering appears as a separate chapter here, but that's not really the case. In parenting, suffering can be found in any chapter, in various paragraphs. Suffering happens between the lines sometimes, behind the stories, or, tragically, *is* the story. There's no way of getting around this.

There is good reason for this suffering, this sorrow though. Love.

It's love that makes suffering cut deep, and ache when it does. It's different from sadness; suffering is sadness for which you pay a price. What's worth a lot costs a lot—there's no suffering over something that doesn't matter. And in the final analysis, nothing seems to matter as much as your child. Love is the reason it hurts. Maybe this truth could be helpful to you sometime? A comfort maybe? Only a little, I know.

There is suffering in the everyday uncertainty and anxiety that comes with parenting, because you love. Love makes waiting in Emergency excruciating, makes hovering, pacing by a phone for some calls an agony. Love makes the struggles and sorrow felt by another, your child, become your very own sorrow too. We don't just feel our child's suffering. We enter into it, we take it on, as though it is our own . . . "and a sword will pierce your own soul too."

Notice the theme of "waiting" and the passive voice of *felt* in that. We can't stand the waiting, the powerlessness, the strain of not knowing. We are doers when it comes to family.

"What can I do?" we ask. The worst answer is "nothing."

It's just as well nobody understands any of this before embarking upon parenthood, or the human race would have died out millennia ago. We are a hopeful bunch, which is good.

I locate this non-chapter before an actual chapter about teenagers for good reason. Moving through parenting life, past your daughter's or son's childhood, things become messy. Some challenges become bigger, the stakes higher. A lot is asked of us parents, and some of it will involve suffering. Let's be honest, there's suffering too in the constant giving of ourselves, the endless giving and giving. Because that is what we're talking about here: giving 'til it hurts.

Prospective First-Time Parent: *I really want to have a child! . . . to fulfill myself!!*

Everyone Who's Ever Had a Child: *Uh, . . . so, no. That's not—it.*

Yet even this default position of one-way giving is compelling. It's good for us parents, as people. We give ourselves away and become more in the process.

"Love is the weight that drags me along."[1]

Good grief—what *am* I trying to say? Who knows. Forge ahead blindly. Like parenting.

The love of a parent for his or her child is an unwieldy mix of all sorts of human love, physical and earthy, embodied but mystical, somewhat instinctive but unreliably so, generous and

---

1. Quote attributed to St. Augustine, *Confessions*, 13.9.10.

magnanimous with an undeniable edge, an undercurrent of demand. The purest, fullest kind of love is demanding.

Love can require being a hard-ass. It takes a ton of resolve, a determination of iron, to love toward the good, when pushing against the worst kind of bad, the exhausting, terrifying thing parents are sometimes called to. Think of the true story behind the heart-shattering movie *Beautiful Boy*. How can that desperate father get at the good for his lovely, drug-addicted son? What does love look like in these situations?

It looks a lot like suffering. Sorry, team.

A non-romanticized interpretation of this? You know love is real when it costs you something, when it involves sacrifice. As in parenting.

Yet "everything hard is made bearable through love . . . What can love not do?"[2] This viewpoint could be mistakenly dismissed as an inspirational quote scripted upon fake-vintage plaques and cheap pillows these days. But truly, it is as freakin' real as it gets. *What can love not do?* I have felt everything from inspired all the way to gutted over the years, witnessing the lengths some parents go to in order to love their child, against all odds. Against everything. These parents are the best of us, their unyielding efforts for their children one of the truest examples of living the pure love "to will the good of the other" we ever come across.[3] You know it when you see it.

I end with a somber reflection, found woven in the background or savagely across the front sometimes of your story and mine, through all the actual, real chapters of this book.

Bad news: parenting involves a lot of suffering. It'll break your heart sometimes.

Good news: because of love.

---

2.   Quote attributed to St. Augustine, *Sermons*, 96,1.
3.   Quote attributed to St. Thomas Aquinas, *Summa Theologica*, Question 20, Article 1.

TEENAGERS

LOVE, DISTANCED

Bangs in through the door
Cold air, sweat. Backpack dropped,
     runners strewn,
And jacket. Ponytail swings, bag flung,
     loud
Strides, fridge open, talking
Words fly, bowl and cereal and milk,
Words spill everywhere, noise and ideas
Energy crackling, happy

Quiet
Lifts head from book,
Hair greasy, longer, flipping back. New
     voice recounts
A history, indignant
Lays facts, righteous, alive to it all
Eyes flash, his same eyes
Lecture delivered, stands, lopes
Out of room, near tall as doorway

Sits slumped, lip gloss glinting
Hovering nearby, a she-wolf with reading
    glasses
And vague instinct
To come near, and stay. Place hand on
    hers
Stay still, silent, unmoving
A moment allowed, shared
Snatches hand away, rushes out, eyes
    filling
With tears that
Spill down she-wolf's cheeks

Crammed in car, windows down. Huge
    feet
Pressing under seats. Hoodies,
Arms and knees, elbows and legs piled
Pound seats to music, loud. Teeth flash in
    dark,
Laughing, sing. Heads bob, smashing beat
Smiles at driver, mother,
In rearview mirror

KNOW THY TEEN

NOT DONE YET

I have a lot to say about teenagers, primarily, that they are not done yet.

They are not done yet. I cannot overstate how important this is, to feel this, be reassured by this. Teenagers are not finished. You need to hang on for the ride, but he is not done.

When he's distracted, and monosyllabic in "conversation," and inattentive, or kind (randomly breathtakingly so; watch for it), you must bear in mind he is not done yet. You will vigorously employ the second half of The Secret of Parenting formula (take no shit) and remain ruthless in requiring semi-decent behaviour, as endurance and willpower permit. But all the while, know this: he is not finished yet. Hold on. He has a long way to go.

When she's sullen and dismissive, forgetful and selfish, or generous (occasionally stunningly generous; watch for it), you must steel yourself to remember she is not done yet. Do not accept bad treatment from her, but realize she's not finished becoming herself. Hold on. This is not "it" for her. She's still going. Stay the course. Be tough, yes, but hold on.

Parents mope around, gloomy and disappointed, observing

their fifteen-year-old son, thinking, *Damn, he's going to be such a rude, disorganized thirty-five-year-old.* No! Fifteen does not thirty-five predict. (Well, maybe a teensy bit, but not definitively.) Keep the ultramarathon push for good character going, and be patient. Try to remember what a shithead you were at fifteen.

Be as loving as you can manage, every day. It's a grind, I know. Love sometimes doesn't flow as freely as back in the Young Children time, but remember, lots of days were terrible then too. We have to love our way through this.

> "Okay, Mom—so there was a bit of a fire in the workshop—but it's out now. Hardly anything got burned. So you don't need to worry."
> —Adam, 14, opening words of a phone call to me out at a noisy gala event

AGAIN, CHAOS

The chaos of teenagers is different from that of young children. With young children, chaos is intense and physical. It's local, in the room with you, in your face, literally right on you. With teenagers, chaos is more removed, broader, and involves more people, more movement of coming and going, more objects and events.

Teen chaos is *much* less under your control than toddler chaos; this fact might scare the hell out of parents of young children, who see their lives as entirely out of control (not worse, just different).

The chaos of teenagers has many stages, indistinct ones, that merge, stall, suddenly speed forward, then lurch backward, over the years from thirteen to nineteen years old. Our

use of the same word, *teenager*, when referring to youth at opposite ends of that age range is terribly misleading. The difference between them is stratospheric, though oddly easy to
overlook while living through it with them. The inching, stall-
ing, and lurching leads somewhere though: they grow up. They
become wiser—quite a bit actually. They begin figuring out
who they are a little (they are not you).

A thirteen- or fourteen-year-old is still childlike—and I
mean that as a compliment. At times they are an open book.
They let go, when feeling confident enough, and allow themselves to act like a child, delightfully unfettered, until insecurities and demands of teenhood beset them once again, and the
child retreats. Fast-forward, through about six years of those
demands and insecurities, surging and retreating, along with,
hopefully, bouts of buoyant fun and a couple small victories,
and he or she is changed. Of course.

Being a party to this journey is objectively extremely interesting, though occasionally it makes you feel as though you
are living in a mental hospital, or are in need of one. It's a bit
rich, my waxing eloquent about teenagers while no longer surrounded by them, the sullen and silent, the eruptively emotional. It's easy to be philosophical while not busy drowning.

A big part of teen chaos comes because of their stuff, all
the goings-on, the scheduling . . .

I must say: there was a lot of scheduling.

For years we kept a large, paper monthly desk calendar
taped to the wall at the top of the basement stairs, by the
kitchen. The rule, roughly, was, if it wasn't written *in pencil*
(small, so everything could fit) on the calendar, it probably
wasn't going to happen. As our kids got older, less of their stuff
was written there. They started making their own things happen, by themselves. Hey, but later, when they needed to borrow a car to make it happen? It better be back on the calendar
again. Just sayin'.

And *many* times, things happened that were never on anyone's calendar, never scheduled at all, yet superseded the scheduled. The weekend Emily moved out to begin university (scheduled), Adam was in the hospital, in the ICU, after rupturing his spleen and lacerating a kidney (unscheduled). The axle of his dirt-jumper bicycle broke, causing the next landing to occur without a front wheel. This "more than one thing at once" phenomenon occurs more frequently than you'd guess, somehow even with only one teenager in your life. Teens are gifted in this way.

I have none of their stuff scheduled on my calendar anymore. Well, that's not entirely true—there's a long-awaited doctor's appointment for one, a flight home for another, a driver's road test (scheduled by her, not me) to earn removal of the New Driver designation for another. Stuff like that. But mostly, I don't schedule their things. They do.

Getting there involves *a lot*—of everything. I was about to begin describing it . . . but stopped. There's too much to recount, and the details are boring to read. Besides, those details would suck us into that odd, unhelpful pull of competing for "busiest parent," itself a ruthless, competitive sport, one that nobody wins. Funny, I don't think that's the goal of all these child/teen activities anyway. Admittedly, the goal of all the kid/teen happenings becomes obscure from time to time, but I'm pretty sure busyness of the parent is not it.

Mercifully, one day the bedlam of scheduling transforms into:

> Me (7:20 Saturday morning, walk out of bedroom, see Madeline, 15, heading out the door.
>> Learn she: a) has registered for a first-aid course she needs, b) knows its location across the city, and c) is leaving for the bus.)

Madeline: "See ya!"

Me: "Okay!"

The real teen chaos, however, comes from inside, not out. The chaos of their internal angst far outweighs any external schedule. Remember being a young teenager, new to your high school, unsure of everything? Remember how it felt? That awful, insecure time, trying to fit in and find friends, then trying to figure out if they really were friends? Yeah, well, witnessing your young teenager do that feels exactly the same, again.

"HEY, SO NOBODY USE THE WHITE FACECLOTH! That's my WART CLOTH! . . . for soaking my foot!"
   —Veronica, about 9, while Adam, 17, was
   in the bathroom . . . washing his face

TEENAGER WORLD

BAD MOVIE NIGHT

Our sweet, thirteen-year-old, new Grade 8'er had arranged to go to a movie with "some new girls" she'd met. New friends are usually borne of locker proximity, or desk placement, or even seating in the caf, the stuff of every coming-of-age sit-com or drama. Plans were made, timing and meet-up location arranged, and outfit selected, aimed at looking as normal as possible. I dropped her off; she wore an ordinary hoodie, unre-markable jeans, and an anxious look.

She returned home hours later, saying she had a good time. She was quiet though, not triumphant as she would have been if it was a grand success. She reported on the movie, what the other girls wore, who they saw walking around the mall after-ward. I could see something was off.

I waited.

She mentioned later that she missed the beginning of the movie because she "got the popcorn and stuff for everyone." I asked about that, and she described being asked, just as the movie was starting, to go get popcorn, candy, and pop requests for the group. They gave her their money.

"I didn't mind though, that was okay," she said, putting on a brave face.

Oh.

Later still, my daughter mentioned casually, not casually at all, that the other girls talked throughout the movie, leaning together, without including her sitting beside them. "They know each other already though . . . They don't really know me much yet." I put on a brave face, and listened. "Katelyn sent me to get another drink near the end," she added quietly.

Later that weekend, out of the blue, my daughter said, "Katelyn and them didn't talk to me while we walked around the mall."

"Oh," I said, dying inside.

Quiet a while.

"I think they're not really my friends." Tears in her eyes.

"Yeah. I think you're right," I said. "That's okay, you can find different friends." I felt sick for her. "It takes time." She nodded.

I might as well have been thirteen again too, for how this made me feel. That's how it often feels having young teenagers: not good. Their turmoil becomes yours.

Damn. It was hard enough the first time.

SHOES AT THE DOOR, AGAIN

You need some comfort for the hard times ahead. Here's a sneak peek ahead that may offer some reassurance.

Older teenagers continue to bring chaos, often (not always) in a less heart-wrenching form. They're more confident now. They're figuring out who suits them and have established some friend groups, still shifting but more stable. They're potentially more settled behind their chaos, making things easier to take, even fun.

Once during a university reading break, while Eva was living at home and Levi was home from away, both went out with friends for the Friday evening. No longer did I ask what they'd be doing exactly, or when they'd get home, or how. No longer did I wait up for them, as I still did for Veronica, in high school. None of that for them anymore. *Okay, have fun!* was the extent of it.

I got up the next morning and found a note on the floor immediately outside our bedroom door, with the words "There's a lot of ppl here, FYI" scrawled upon it. A couple of steps further, I froze at the sight of the front door. A landscape of shoes littered the space, as though a counsellor at a Camp for Very Large Children had shouted, *OKAY, EVERYONE. TAKE YOUR SHOES OFF AND THROW THEM HERE!* before they all ran for the lake. It was unreal. I had difficulty matching them visually, to count them. (Eleven pairs, two belonging to my kids . . . though I didn't know what their shoes looked like anymore, as I was no longer part of that either.)

What had happened? More importantly, how had I not heard any of it?? How had I gone, in a few short (long) years, from waking multiple times per night, Spidey senses tingling, predicting and responding to nighttime events almost before they happened, to sleeping through a home invasion by a group of young strangers? What had I slept through?

Marcel poked his head out of our room. "Whoa . . . lots of shoes."

I walked into the kitchen in my pajamas and robe to find a young man sitting on a stool at our kitchen counter. He had a friendly face and a forward manner.

Him: "Hi! I'm Joshua. I'm a visitor."

Me: "Hi, Joshua. I'm Sue. I live here." He laughed.

Another young man skittered into the kitchen, making a beeline for the table, with bare feet, narrow sweatpants and the most disheveled hair ever, carrying a laptop.

Him: "Oh, hi, Sue. How are you?"

Me: "Hi, Tyler. I'm good, how about you?"

Tyler: "Good. I have an assignment due in a couple of hours." He sat down at the table and opened his computer, glancing at Joshua with a nod. "Hey."

Joshua: "Hey."

Eva and friends had come across Levi and his group late in the evening, and they'd all bused and walked together to our house. Eva's crew were in upstairs rooms, and both basement bedrooms, including Madeline-away-at-*non*-reading-break-university's bed. Three or four of Levi's friends were sprawled on the big ol' sectional couch in the basement, some still asleep. The rest were lying on the carpeted area around the couch, on the floor or on couch-back cushions, a coat or kids' play-blanket pulled over them. When you're young and probably drunk, you can sleep anywhere.

I made them all pancakes. Our kids' friends of colour, many in number and colour, say that white moms always make pancakes when kids stay over. They are right. In defense of my predictable white-momness, what else am I going to make for you kids? I had tons of cereal on hand, but not necessarily four jugs of milk to go with it. I might have had bacon and eggs for eleven, plus us, but that's too much work—it was my weekend too. One time I made a big pot of porridge with raisins and apples, a standard for our family but a mystery to some. I heard one young guy whisper, "Is this camping food? I've never been camping."

What's my point in all this? I hardly remember. I think it was to say that the early teen years are really hard, often more emotionally taxing on everyone than later years are. It gets easier somewhat, even fun, for parents over time. You earn it.

In between is a lot of mess. Hang in there, it gets better.

FRIENDS

Your teenager's friends matter more than you do.

You are correct, yes, this is ridiculous. Completely. Because, really? After . . . everything? A morose chick with too many piercings, or some cocky dude with BO they met some two weeks ago? *These people* matter more to your child than you do?

Yes and no.

Yes, friends matter more *to your teen* than you do right now. And no, of course these friends do not actually matter more than you do. You are infinitely more important in the course of your child's life history. But that is not the point.

These friends are necessary. Our teenagers need this carousel of new people and personalities, to learn and grow and figure stuff out. Young people are hardwired to look away from you, and look around. You are the given—or you're meant to be, if things have been going well on your end. For a child to be uncertain about you, dear parent, is the biggest of problems he or she can have. Or, put positively, to have certainty about you is a lottery prize in the life of a teenager. You're meant to be the given, the sure thing, the taken-for-granted. Not that we accept doormat treatment, but we understand, if all is right in the world, we parents are the insurance policy, not the risk. Don't be offended if you're taken for granted . . . okay, maybe a bit. You're reportedly human too.

Your children will meet fabulous kids over years of new friendships, and terrible ones, and they need all that. These relationships have nothing to do with you—again, the point entirely. Some friends will remain, most will fall away. And you will stay.

Your teenagers need to be with the new people in their lives. Indeed, "being with" is ideal, hanging out, in person. Doing human, old-school, like *Little House on the Prairie* days (there I go again). Our fundamental human needs haven't evolved since the Ingallses' days.

One time, in Grade 11, at sixteen years old, Veronica went out to the driveway to talk with a couple of friends who'd stopped by. She re-entered the house four and a half hours later. Talking. There's an almost unquenchable need for this peer interaction.

Teenagers need the group too. The group can be brutal, inattentive, and cruel, but it can also be the most fun your child has ever had in her life. Fabulous opportunity lurks amid the risk. Teenage friend groups are ever-changing, amoeba life-forms, melding and splitting over the teenage years, as though expressing a mysterious migration pattern inherent to the adolescent human, as narrated by David Attenborough, which is likely exactly what's happening.

Teenage boys and girls, on average, approach "the group" quite differently (don't get ragey on me—I said "on average").

Teenage girls are more discerning and individualistic in their approach to pursuing and finding the group. It's less a package-deal endeavour; girls more readily see variation and nuance *within* the group: those who don't suit each other, others who are naturally aligned. I don't deny the power of the group for teen girls, yet they often choose smaller packs, of two or three. Be crystal clear on this though: the dynamics of girl packs, regardless of their size, are exceedingly complex. If you're lucky enough to have a daughter who talks to you about the dynamics of that complexity, be grateful, despite how utterly exhausting it is. All that talking, like the tide rushing in, is your window to her world, a gift in parenting world.

Boys do a lot less thinking at the same age. (Not always! I KNOW! I get it—some boys are big thinkers!) Most/many/some boys are drawn to the large group, especially around Grades 8, 9, and 10. Young teen boys are pack animals; "en masse" is how they roll. (No, not all!! Some roll with one or two friends max—I'm talking averages, people. Sheesh.) I love a pack of teenage boys. I've never had a bad experience with one. Still, it's understandable that a group of teenage boys approaching them on the street might make people uncomfortable; it all depends on what the group is up to, what bonds them. The power of the leader, the thoroughly maligned alpha male, truly sets the tone in this dynamic, for bad—but then logically also for good. The pack follows; that's just what happens, but a leader can be good. Funny, parents all want their kid "to be a leader" these days, but much of being socially aware involves cooperation . . . which looks a heck of a lot like "going along with the crowd." It's tricky.

The physicality of boys in their early teens is surprising and endearing. They lean, shove, sprawl, and drape on one another like large puppies while in conversation or on the move. It's lovely.

While away one weekend as a driver for a boys' junior high school basketball tournament, I waited in the hotel lobby with the team before heading to the gym. One boy sat overtop three others squeezed together on a short couch, his legs stretched out over them, big feet hanging askew. Another stood behind the couch, patting a sitting teammate's curly hair, the "pattee" trash-talking a teammate across the lobby, the "patter" quietly focused on his task. Two others sat close in one chair, bobbing, listening to music together, sharing a headphone. They all passed around a deodorant, for quick pit-stick application, there in the lobby. At an age when being overly self-conscious tends to kill the freedom that allows for a lot of joy, their relaxed unselfconsciousness together was charming.

Unfortunately, boy groups *think* "en masse" too, collectively, in a pack-dynamic mentality not aimed at what might be called "seeking collective wisdom." Uh, no. Boy packs are masters of moving directly toward the lowest common denominator of any wisdom. Accompanying their physical prowess and zest for life is not yet an abundance of "group critical-thinking skills." Straight up: young teenage boys in large groups do dumb-ass things when they're together. Ugh—now *there* lies legit parental worry. Girls do asinine things too, but not as much.

The soundtrack you wish you could play, like a mantra, in your teen daughter's or son's head over these years is *Is this a good idea?*

Is this a good idea, jumping off the roof to land on a stack of chairs? Getting in a car with seven other kids? Trying a drug some kid gave you? Leaving a party with a guy you don't know? Ack. You've had many conversations with your child, delivered numerous speeches, in years leading up to these outings. Odds they will think of you and your speeches, when danger presents itself as fun? Who knows?

Suddenly much of this has nothing to do with you, which feels foreign, scary.

It helps to think of yourself in this way:

> You are a train station, grounded, set in place,
> providing food, shelter, and reliable security.
> You are fixed, you can be found on the map,
> we know where you are.
> You are always open.
> You are the ticket agent in the booth in the
> station, ready to be helpful.
> Our teenage children's lives are a convoluted,
> evolving, and uncertain series of train trips:
> simple rides, brief outings, and long voyages.
> Their trips require multiple tickets, many trains
> and tracks and exchanges, with numerous travel
> companions and plentiful reasons for travel.
> Teenagers are travelers who visit the train

station in order to keep going. The ticket agent
provides the tickets, making direct eye contact
and squeezing the traveler's hand as the ticket is
handed over.
But the agent does not go on the trip.

You help make travelling possible and arrival at a desirable destination more likely.

You are where your teenager gets tickets to keep going on voyages he or she must make without you.

Your teenagers really, *really* need you right now. It just doesn't feel like it, when they walk right past you without even a glance. For a while, their need is largely a selfish one.

> "M-UH-uuum!! Emily's corrupting my child-hooood!"
> —Veronica, 8, listening to her
> eighteen-year-old sister talk about
> who-knows-what

LEARNING TOGETHER

HOW ARE THEY DOING?

If you ask a parent how their teenager is doing, you usually get the answer to a different question. You're given a description of *what* she is doing: what she's involved in, what she's up to, often what her achievements are. Those responses are interesting but do not answer the original question.

How are they doing?

No, really, like, how are they doing? This is *the* vital question for our teenagers. How are things going? How do they feel—inside, about things, about life? Adolescence is always hard, but is it getting too difficult? This is what we parents need to wonder about, and listen for. Most of the time we're listening for what they don't say.

It's a heartachingly difficult time, with so many pressures, so much self-critique. The dance of social belonging is complex and negotiated over many issues. Much of that costs them dearly, on a personal level. It's always been so, but seems somehow supercharged for "kids these days." Because social media. Because identity development. Sometimes, because parents. Which is worse: abject neglect or toxic levels of pressure? Hard to say.

We resist our teens' rebellion, yet some rebellion is necessary for them. They need to push away, which, weirdly, can be
as hard on them as it is on us. Hair, its colour and/or style, is a
fantastic form of rebellion for parents to pretend to resist. Hair
grows back. Piercings hold the possibility of being temporary.
Tattoos are more permanent than most people realize.

Nevertheless. You help them, try to talk, listen, worry. You
get them the stuff they need, or want, trying to hit that sweet
spot with the crap you buy, where it's good enough to avoid
them being *that kid*, the one with weird shoes and uncool jackets (we were pretty close sometimes; sorry, kids, my bad), but
not so good that the teen gets everything he or she wants—
which stunts them. And you'll never be done.

But still, there's a sadness in teenagers, a loss in the changes
of moving out of childhood—that has always been true. One
wants to say to a teenage son or daughter, *Yes, darling, you are
suffering, and most of that is* normal. *It is hard, and that's normal.* There's so much that is heartachey . . . even while he or
she is being a total pain in the ass.

Back when one of our daughters was in high school, maybe
Grade 10, she hadn't been sleeping well, a barometer of "How
are they doing?" usually indicating "not good." (Pay attention
to their sleep.) One night, something woke me, a sound, not
a bad one, but odd. It was the repeated, distinct "clink" of a
spoon against the side of a bowl downstairs, as when someone
is eating cereal. Who was eating cereal at 3:18 a.m. and why?

I went down to the kitchen and found our Grade 10
daughter fully dressed for school, backpack out, lunch bag
on the counter. She sat hunched over her bowl, mechanically
spooning cereal into her mouth, looking desolate, tired. It was
dark out. The wall clock, oven clock, and microwave clock all
said 3:21.

Me: "Sweetheart, why are you up? It's the middle of the
night."

Teenage Daughter:

She turned to me, a blank expression on her face. Her eyes moved slowly from the dark windows, to each of the clocks, then randomly around the room of our quiet house. She put her head down on the counter and began to cry. I hugged her, held her and rubbed her back, took her back upstairs, and got her to undress and climb back into bed without setting an alarm. Tomorrow she could sleep in.

The next day she told me how strange the whole thing was, being in some obsessed, autopilot mode, resistant in the face of all logic. She said she looked outside and thought, *Wow, weird how dark it is this morning.* Then, *Why is my clock wrong, saying three-something, when it's morning?* Which it wasn't. Later, she thought, *Gee,* all *the clocks are wrong.*

So yes, bizarre. All this was a function of her fatigue and anxiety, her perceived pressure around social stuff, and routines, and expectations, not even because of schoolwork, because schoolwork was easy for her. Teenagerhood is fundamentally just hard: seeking to fit in, hormones, body changes, the newness and challenges of high school, complexities and pressures of their social world and shifting friendships— the whole thing. The young girl who has no breasts, or huge breasts. The skinny fifteen-year-old boy who appears to be about ten years old, or the one who looks about forty. Any of these with bad skin.

One of our sons had a young substitute teacher stop mid-sentence, as she was giving him hell about something (that he probably deserved), to demand, "Why are you wearing such ridiculous shoes?" They were ordinary shoes actually, only ridiculously large, size 12 then, attached to skinny legs on a body that was not yet tall. He was a human approximation of a right angle. He told me, with a complicated look on his face, "She thought they were joke shoes—like clown shoes or something. She wouldn't believe me that they're just my normal shoes."

Why am I even mentioning these things? These are *nothing*. They do not even register on the trauma-meter of shit some teenagers have to deal with. But they reveal a teensy sense of the day-to-day, wearing heartache for our teenagers. These things made my heart ache, at any rate. Friend groups, being included in them, or not. Growth of bodies, all the changes, or not. Academic demands, revealing aptitude, or not. Good-looking faces and clear skin, or not. Confidence and coping, or not. Finding their way, or not.

"Mom, want to tuck me in?"
    —a most-cherished bedtime request from
    all my teenagers every now and then

Yes. Yes, I want to.

COMMUNICATING

STYLE A

Daughter: "Trina said she wants to go with Loren, but she doesn't mean it. She just doesn't want people to know she doesn't like Loren, because Loren's locker is close to the cafeteria, and she gets the table we sit at for lunch every day."

Me (trying to memorize that Trina is the new friend and Loren is difficult): "Oh."

Me (thinking a moment, something my daughter never asked me to do): "Couldn't some of you go sit at your own table?"

Daughter: "No."

Me: "Oh. Okay."

STYLE B

Me: "How was your day?"

Daughter (walking past, out of room): "Fine."

I've experienced both styles and can tell you, for a parent, Style A wins hands down, no contest. It's full open-book disclosure; a lot to take in, yes, but saves you from sickening worry about what's left unsaid, because nothing is left unsaid. Style A Communicators make it abundantly clear, constantly, exactly how things are going, and how they are doing . . . *at all times, whenever they are present.* Emotion tsunamis, as it were.

Before recoiling at the sheer intensity of that, especially if it's happening to you, pause. Consider the plight of the parent whose teenager makes nothing abundantly clear, who shares not, who does not express his or her feelings. True, the teen may simply be an introvert, or quiet, or prefer being alone. The quiet child is more easily overlooked though, dangerously less demanding of a parent's attention. You must seek him out, on his terms, and sit back interiorly, and wait for a response, inviting one with your silence.

I was schooled in this needing to not talk so much by Madeline, not when she was a teenager, actually, but when she was only about nine or ten years old. We were driving somewhere together, and Madeline was quiet. She looked out the window, appearing relaxed, content. I was chitchatting, spouting my ideas, asking her about recent goings-on in her life, trying to pull her out and get her to talk—probably driving her crazy. She'd give a brief, few-word answer, without much elaboration, and fall into a comfortable silence once again.

During a pause in my interrogation, she turned to me and said mildly:

"I think I'm a kind of person who doesn't need to talk much."

"Oh," I said, pausing. "Okay." (quiet)

So there is that.

But none of this is easy when you are worried or frustrated, as a parent naturally is when he can't tell what the hell's going on with his teenager. The key seems to be seeking routine moments of connection rather than crisis intervention. That, and mentally applying duct tape to one's own mouth during those moments. Our talking only impedes his talking. (Our yelling also impedes his talking, in case you wondered about that.)

Connections with teens are made easiest over food, like back in the toddler days when you'd sit with them while they ate, or while watching a show they like, these days in the evenings when you throw yourself beside them onto the couch and rub their back while you sit together. You need to pat your teen lovingly as you walk by, kiss him on the cheek when nobody is around, throw your arm around her after a good laugh over a funny TikTok that she saved to show you . . . because you asked her to. Your teenager will not be able to tell you this, but she or he desperately, desperately needs your physical affection. Never for show though, only for real.

One teen will blast his emotions at you with a fire hose; another teen plays poker, emotions as cards held tipped right up against her chest. While your poker-player kid is a teenager, you need to keep an eye on all *the other* messages that come with the not talking. A dad or mom feels the yawing chasm between a child's contented quiet and his or her stressed-out quiet, a silent difference that becomes deafening, the loudest thing in your life.

If the quiet one walks straight to her room with tears in her eyes, follow her. And shut up.

"Mom, I'm pretty tired. I don't really feel like talking about preschool today."
—Adam, 3, responding to my questions from his car seat on the way home

WHAT ARE THEY DOING?

Teenagers are frequently loud. A din can surround them, a backdrop of noise and movement, of high-voltage silences, and the mess of all their stuff. The mayhem and dispersal of their things can distract you, becoming a curtain of busyness obscuring that which needs to be seen. We all know teenagers can get up to no good, but it can sneak up on us parents.

We know our child; we have an impression of him or her. Naturally we keep going with that impression, with the familiarity of the child we know. It's easy, during the comings and goings, away time, school time, friend time, and phone time to miss a change, a shift, to miss what is actually going on. We need to ask ourselves, *What are they doing?*

Again, no, really—what are they doing?

In the messy middle years, around fourteen, fifteen, or seventeen, it's terrifyingly easy to miss that she or he is up to no good, or experiencing something fearfully no good. This realization can come to you all of a sudden, like an emergency flare going off, eerily similar to the way a child "suddenly" learns something. Without being aware of it, you've been noting and archiving unusual happenings, discrepancies, peculiar observations. The leaving of a room too quickly. A strange comment. The nervous attachment to a phone. An inconsistent story. A look that says something is wrong. In the middle of the night, you bolt awake, suddenly seeing it, thinking, "Oh God, something is wrong."

Which means it is.

I remember a moment of this, a flash of abrupt realization about my teen, my teen's friend group, and what they were up to. It snuck up on me, that they were up to no good. I'd known it, but somehow, not really. The next day, at a pickup, I did not start the car as that teen got in. I turned, put out my hand, and said quietly, "Give me your phone." A wary face, holding a look that knew what was coming, stared back at me. "We need to talk," I said. And thus it began: Love Fiercely and Take No Shit.

You are no longer coasting. All else is pushed aside, as if nothing else matters, because, also suddenly, it doesn't. In some cases, parents pull back that curtain of concealment, look around, suddenly seeing clearly piles of shit hiding all over the place, or, frighteningly worse, evidence of a sickness all over the place. Let's gather still a moment, in care and love, around shattered parents among us who discover something truly terrible, signs of darkness or sickness, stashed all around. Life becomes shadowed, heavy for parents of a child mired in such problems.

But parents begin, as parents do, huddling as a team when two are together, leaning on each other for differing wisdom. Clean up sickness and shit, wade through lies, and truth, try to pull darkness into the light. Phone the school guidance counsellor. Cry with your mother. Pray. Hope not to call the police, but do if you must. Talk to your doctor, or your work benefits counselling program. Meet with the principal. Who knows?

About this "parents huddling as a team." I need to say more. Throughout parenting, spouses/partners talk about their children. And talk. And talk. You gift each other with that differing wisdom. You disagree about that difference and argue, compare, throw around ideas, think together. Single parents have to do this too, find trustworthy gems in their lives who will do this with them. It's too much alone. Then together, you arrive at a path, the path you will all step onto, together, without knowing where it will go. And along the way, you keep talking. You do this with ordinary things, but during times of crises especially.

You go to call your kid's best friend's mom and realize you don't know who that is anymore—not the mom, the friend.

If you're lucky, your teenager, though possibly furious with you, is momentarily safe and, deep down, relieved you are blowing apart her world. Pulling her from a horrible group of people. Laying out the sickening anxiety and depression he's been feeling inside. Saving her from an addiction, as much as we are able to save another person, which usually isn't much. A parent's love goes far, far, far though—only, this kind of love doesn't look or feel like we expect love to. This love is a pressured, exhausting, determined act of the will. It takes all the time you can give it, is infuriating and scary, makes the person you are trying to love temporarily hate you, and makes you feel sick: that kind of love. A barren, terrifying place.

Yet. Love "bears all things, believes all things, hopes all things, endures all things." We hear that reading at weddings, but it speaks perfectly to times of duress with our teenagers. There is reason for hope. Your child is young; there is help; things change.

You are not alone; you have more company than aloneness in this. Everyone has problems. Everyone. Some people hide their problems better than others, that's all. We should be more like elephants, who encircle the hurting ones, gathering, leaning close, swinging their trunks over the shoulders of the vulnerable. We could take turns being the vulnerable.

Get help and sleep. Watch for the tiniest crack of access to real, honest moments with your teenage child. Sit right beside him when he'll let you. Look for the beat of time where *I love you* won't sound sanctimonious, a moment where your quiet company is welcome. You think that will never happen, but it will. Keep going. Love like this is hard, but you can do it—you've got it in you.

> "It gives me bad minds."
> —Veronica, as a young child, tearfully explaining how anything scary made her feel

LEARNING TO DRIVE

Some of my favourite memories of being with my teenagers are of when they were learning to drive. No, really. I loved that time spent doing something completely novel to them, something all at once exhilarating, serious, frightening, and permissible, a scarce combination in adolescence. And I had a front seat.

You're not fooling around learning to drive. You're focused, together, on the same thing, something high stakes, important, and, mercifully, not the teen herself or himself. You are not "checking in," not asking them stuff. You're just driving . . . okay, and maybe yelling. It's a strange sort of relief, comfort found within a fundamentally terrifying activity.

I remember my sister saying, about one of her sons, "I really wonder about him learning to drive a car. Some days he can't even pour orange juice."

The oddity and intensity of these driving outings, randomly inserted into ordinary life, on weekends, late afternoons, or evenings after supper, were refreshing. It was fun, being out in a car with that "adorable little toddler" now about to make a left-hand turn too late on a yellow.

My kids were keen to learn to drive. Not all teenagers are, which is fair enough; it's a gong show out there. Still, if you have a car available, and live in a reasonable place for driving, there seems something important embedded in learning this, an engagement in their own independence. Apparently teens aren't as interested in learning to drive these days; we should wonder about that.

A few of our teenagers had never driven *a thing* prior to that first outing—as in, nothing, ever. Those inaugural lessons were doozies, the teen amped with apprehension/excitement, me with apprehension/amusement. Each time the car rolled forward, one gal screamed and jammed on the brakes, laughing. Roll, scream, brake, laugh. Soon we were both laughing, legitimately in hysterics, especially after high-speed lurches when she "forgot which one was the gas." In the dark of a weekday evening, we'd do a few lengths of our street, that street she'd played on for hours. This involved turn-arounds in various driveways, lengthy, traumatic ordeals. It took days to recover.

I feel compelled to mention that first outings are no indication of final competency. One of those screaming lurchers recently drove all over Ireland, in a stick-shift rental, on her own, on the "wrong side." This is true of many things with your teenager: the beginning is no indication of the end. You have to hang on in between.

My learner soon progressed to parking lots, again late in the evening, after supper and homework, soccer and laundry, after the recounting of a friend drama and an argument with a sibling over dishes. Mall parking lots are empty and quiet then. We'd pretend certain stalls were the lanes of a make-believe road, like the chalk roads they drew upon our street, with imagined intersections outlined by thick yellow stopping borders found throughout the lot. My driver would repeat imaginary left-hand turns, practice backing up a long distance, which is terribly difficult at first. They'd choose a particular point to be a car to parallel-park behind. He or she would practice reverse-stall parking, unnecessarily quickly once they'd improved at it. It was all so much fun.

We'd foray to quiet streets behind the malls, later weaving through familiar neighbourhoods. The leap to daytime driving would eventually arrive, driving for an actual purpose. The learner was the driver, me the copilot, with other family member(s) stashed in the back—going to a gym or a field or stopping for something at a grocery store.

My sons would beg to do "threshold braking," a procedure I'd never even heard of, but one they tried desperately to convince me was mandatory practice. This essentially means slamming on the brakes while going full speed, reserved for emergency situations.

I was well aware their interest in this maneuver had nothing to do with learning a safety skill, and everything to do with being peak fun for a teenage boy. I was thinking three-car pile-ups, metal on metal, airbags slamming against bodies. They were thinking, *Jam on the brakes? Going full speed? Hell yeah!!* This led to the routine weirdness of a son driving along, with me riding shotgun, on the quiet, curving road to our house, or even a main city street, and his sudden pleading, "Mom!... *threshold braking*?!?" with the same look on his face as when asking for candy. Unlike candy, to this I said no.

Hot Tips for Teaching Drivers
Happening too fast for words?
Use Hand Signals!

- *Direction:* Shoot arm out straight, aimed right, left, or directly ahead. Hold arm in position, silently providing a strong visual cue to your young driver as to what's immediately required. No pesky spoken language, no shrieking, swearing, flailing about, grabbing the wheel. Only strong visual signals: clean, unambiguous.

- *Stop:* Shoot both hands forward, palms flat, facing the windshield. A naturally occurring signal. Perfect.
- *Exit:* Closed fingers, straightened hand, directed at an angle aligned with the identical trajectory of the desired exit. Painless, stress free. Refer to hockey referee signal for a goal: the goal, in this case, is the correct bridge or freeway exit.
- *Slow Down:* Options: heels of both hands pressing forward in a digging gesture; two hands, flat, in a *down-down-down* motion, rapidly, in driver's visual field; a piercing *eeEahhHH* sound. It's personal really. Use your discretion.

Eventually this progress led to a summit of learning: the teenagers driving themselves to school one day instead of busing, student as driver, me as passenger. They loved driving to school, pulling up in the hurly-burly of morning arrival, the extreme uncoolness of mother being present offset by the teen driving the car, his or her music blaring.

We'd pull up in the drop-off lineup and spring out, at the same time, like game show participants. She'd grab her huge backpack and sports bag from the back seat as I ran around, taking the large magnetic L for *Learner* off the back of the vehicle as I went. My kid would call out a happy "see ya!" and hurry off, melding into the swarm of students. I'd hop in, more often than not having to pull the driver's seat way forward. I'd continue on my day, and she on hers. I felt happy driving off. This little thing, their driving to school sometimes, felt like a game, a fun one, that we played together. God knows, parents need fun with their teenagers.

"Real driving" advanced rapidly, becoming scarier for us both. We'd go downtown if necessary, over bridges, taking exit overpasses and one-way streets, parallel-parking with some idiot pulled up too close behind, honking. Highway driving felt the weirdest. I'd lean back and, honestly, enjoy the view while my kid sped along, concentrating and changing lanes, quietly holding the wheel tight, or tapping their fingers on it to the music playing from their phone connected by an aux cord, even changing gears in the old standard car we had.

Driving became a literal interpretation of what was going on between us on a larger scale or, at least, the direction we were heading in: teenage child takes over, parent sits back, providing guidance, encouragement, and correction when necessary. I remember asking one of my sons, driving on the highway with friends along in the car, to slow down, a number of times, yet his speed kept creeping back up. I remember saying then, "If you drive too fast when I'm *sitting right here*, why would I ever let you take the car out on your own?"

The long-awaited road test day is fraught with tension and stress. Off they'd go, to do their thing, huge dejection if a fail, overflowing joy if a pass. If a pass, they'd be vibrating with excitement or quietly pleased, sharing details. Soon afterward all of them suddenly stopped, and in a moment of realization, each would make a new request for the very first time.

"Can I borrow the car??"

I would say yes. I had to; that's why we'd done all this. After confirming the where/when, she or he would run around the house, gathering their stuff, then walk out the door without looking back. I'd watch them drive off on their own for the very first time. In that moment, everything shifted, a high-speed lurch this time.

"Have you seen a bag of clothes?"
    —teenage boy, rushing around during
    early morning bustle for before-school
    practice

"A plastic bag of laundry? Yeah, I threw it
downstairs to be washed."
    —me, having seen a rumpled shirt with a
    shoeprint on the front

"I just got that ready! It's my stuff for the day!"

"Oh. Sorry."

NOT COOL

I need to bring up something awkward with you, like telling
you there's spinach between your teeth or something. This is
what friends do: say the difficult thing, out of care and concern. This is to help you.

So here goes.

Do not try to be cool with teenagers. Do not. It's a deadly
mistake, the veritable kiss of death.

Not trying is preferable to trying, by far. Unexpected advantage (get ready for it): not trying increases the odds by about
90 percent that you will, as a side effect, be ever so slightly
cool. Slightly, possibly. But that is never a goal.

Fact: teenagers have the wonderful, highly valuable super-
skill of being genius-level readers of authenticity. That is what
they evaluate and judge us on, our authenticity. That and our
taste in comfortable shoes. Teenagers are heat-seeking mis-
siles for the truth, for realness. I'm not saying they always want

the truth, or will follow the truth, or do not storm out of the room slamming a door when you tell them the truth, but they are looking for it. And they are definitely looking for it in you.

Teenagers are critiquing you. They see, really see, better than adults do, whether or not you actually *do value* the things you say you value, do *care about* the things you say you care about, aka whether you put your money where your mouth is.

What does this have to do with anything?

Authenticity is cool. Honestly, with teens, it's the only currency we've got.

Let's lay it out here. You are not able to participate, or God forbid, compete, in any arena of "being young," regardless of how much potential you think you have in that regard. These are teenagers! Adolescents! You are not going to be successful in a show, a weird power struggle (which is how they'll see it), of attempting to demonstrate *any* aspect of "being young" with the very embodiment of youth itself, that's for damn sure. Sorry, team—that horse has already left the barn. They cannot see you as young.

You may have a keen sense of fashion, regularly dressing in styles from the current decade/century, but by definition, a teenager's generation is compelled to think your fashion contrived (while theirs is totally contrived), dictated (while theirs is totally dictated), and kind of boring (credit where due, theirs is often not boring). So we're not going to impress them with style either.

Finally, for God's sake, do not, I repeat, do not attempt to engage in their teen world *along with them*, trying to be cool. Egad. THAT is a huge chunk of kale stuck right between your two front teeth! Do not comment all over their Instagram, try to impress them with your taste in current music, Snapchat with their friends, get a tattoo "the kids will like," etc., etc.

That is a Hard No.

Case in point: when YOU were fifteen, would you have

wanted your mother to dance in the kitchen, to show your friends that she's a good dancer? That she is "cool"? Horrors, shudder at the thought, I know. Definitely not. The image evokes *Seinfeld's* famous Elaine *Want me to get it started?* dance scene. Of course, *now*, a decade or two later, as an adult, you would LOVE to see your mom dancing in the kitchen! It would be awesome! You would cheer!!

That is different. We are not there yet.

So *now*, real time, if YOU, Mom or Dad, were to start busting a move in front of your teenage child's friends, to show them you are cool, that you've still got it, your teen will stare, break into a cold sweat, and turn inwardly, in desperation, to a Higher Power:

Dear God of the Universe and all Created Things, if you exist, sorry if I doubted you 'til now. At this moment, I need you, badly. I beg you—please—please, make my mother stop dancing. I'll do whatever you want, just make it stop. Do whatever it takes—make her fall and break a hip if you have to. Have mercy on me, God of Everything. End this, now. Amen.

This will happen *even if* you think you actually *are* a good dancer! Sorry. (Besides, insisting, *I'm a good dancer!* is rather like exclaiming, *I'm a good driver!* Suddenly, all is in question.)

To sum up, for all the teenagers in your life, you cannot be dope, rad, sick, or fire. (If you don't understand those expressions, I am proving my point. And yes, I realize this will read as dated in about fifteen minutes.)

Okay—stay with me now . . . This is where it gets complicated. I am NOT saying to never dance in your kitchen, or play your own music in the car, or wear whatever the hell you want, whether a kilt, embroidered acid-wash denim, or all leather. You do you, for sure. But never, never, *never* do it to try to be cool. Because then you won't be, by definition.

Follow?

When you be yourself, freely, your real, authentic self, and *do not care one tiny bit whether the teenagers like you or not,* then, maybe then . . . maybe . . . you might be slightly cool. Not a goal though. Too lofty.

I would like to give you an example.

The mother of a high school classmate of one of my sons embodied this principle, naturally of course, like she wrote it. She had a strong build, wore mom jeans, actual mom jeans I mean, not fake ones purposefully designed to be a style (confusing, I realize; some women will understand, otherwise, never mind). She wore her curly, reddish-grey hair in a plain ponytail every day and carried a heavy-looking purse in such a way that it seemed light. She knew sports well, *extremely* well, meaning the inside-outs of a game and its current leading pro players. She had strong opinions and lots of interesting life experience, none of which she was shy about sharing.

More often than not, she had a group of teenage boys gathered around her like fruit flies on bananas, chatting, arguing, laughing. She would ask them questions, challenge their answers, laugh, listen well, smile, be sarcastic if they were lame. She exuded not the tiniest whiff of the impression that she cared an iota what they thought of her, because she so obviously did not. This mom attracted teenagers like bees to flowers, so authentic it oozed out of her.

So damn cool.

There it is.

The summary? Don't try to be cool. Be yourself around teenagers, and everyone else too if you really get good at it. Let's keep spinach out of everyone's teeth.

"I was like, what the beef? How are you even an adult?"
—Veronica, 17, about a grown man's immature behaviour in public

CARING

THEY CAN HEAR US

I need to get something off my chest. I'm going to "pop off," as my youngest teenager called it. The Hard-Ass Mother appears.

We're doing a shit job of something with our teenagers.

It's what we say about them, right in front of them—it's appalling.

We need to examine this strange phenomenon together, one that happens much too often somehow.

Let's go back, beginning with the coworker who bores you to tears with endless, proud stories about her toddler. Kind of tedious, but also sort of cute. You give your coworker a pass because, well, who doesn't feel this way about their precious young child?

Fast-forward about twelve years. You bump into this person, and are taken aback as he or she expresses a tirade of negative, critical disdain about that same child. *Their* child.

Quite the dramatic shift—and they go on and on.

How is it that the same parent who fretted, deeply invested emotionally in the most minute details of their child's early development, such as sleep scheduling, autonomy in food choices, and safe expression of "big feelings," a whisper of time later seems to toss such considerations in the dumpster, and begins hammering those same children with the worst? I have heard breathtakingly unkind things said about, *or to*, teenagers, by their parents, while the teenager is standing. Right. There.

To clarify, I get it, that a parent must offer "correction" (i.e., animated feedback regarding behaviour and/or choices) to his or her teenager from time to time. That is necessary. True too, we occasionally go overboard in that process, myself especially. We apologize and try to do better, just like back in toddler days. What I'm talking about is something different: it's a harsh negativity, a meanness. It's unkind. How and why is it that this change to negativity takes place?

Parents of young children often fear they will damage their child if issues aren't dealt with "properly," *even when the child in question will not explicitly remember any of it.* Yet, at fourteen or seventeen years old, that same child *can* remember things, explicitly, and does. He hears what is said and remembers it, even when he appears not to be listening—especially then. And what does he too often hear?

That teenager hears adults, sometimes his own parents, talk shit about him, right in front of him. Even *to* him.

They are listening! They will remember! *This*, now!! Not toilet training days, but mean-spirited put-downs and dismissive disdain—coming now from the same parent who patiently read the "correct" number of bedtime stories each night when they were little. *Now* they remember! Now it has influence! The negativity some parents heap upon their kids at thirteen and fifteen and seventeen is soul crushing. Our teenagers *hear* us when we say that they're lazy or useless, that they're lousy students, that we can't wait to have them out of the house. They are listening.

Teenager's mother: *She doesn't want to come on the holiday, and trust me, I don't want her to come either.* To Grandma, on speaker phone. In the car. Teenage daughter right beside her.

Teenager's father: *I have no idea what he's going to do for a living—not sponge off me, that's for sure.* Said in the living room. Teen in the kitchen, listening.

Teenager's mother: *God, teenagers are the worst! I can't wait for "been there, done that" with these teen years.* This was said to me, with the teenage daughter, wearing a rude T-shirt, standing beside her mother.

They notice us walk past them without smiling at them the way we do to total strangers. They notice us looking at our phones instead of looking at them—so they do the same. They notice us dismiss their opinions with an eye roll or a scoff, while we lose our crap when they do that to us. How are they supposed to feel about this?!

One thing is clear though: our teenagers will never forget how we made them feel . . . especially when it was like shit. Where did the tenderness go? A teenager needs tenderness as much as a three-year-old does, maybe more.

Adding insult to injury, piled on top of this broad, cultural attitude of negativity (which teeters upon age-old, normal angst and pain of coming of age), these teenagers are saddled with another burden of blame laid upon them: the injustice of constantly being told they are entitled.

Young people today expect something for nothing—they have no idea how to work hard.

These teenagers are so entitled!

Kids these days are too indulged.

Uh, *DUH?!* If that is true, whose fucking fault would that be??! Being overindulged and entitled and lazy is a ridiculous thing to blame *them* for! That would be *our fault*, not theirs. Man up, parents!! Stop giving your kids every freakin' thing they want and doing every single thing they demand of you, and they wouldn't *be* entitled! Have the balls to say no when you must. We are the grown-ups here.

Note: I like the use of *man up*. I use it intentionally. My teenagers used it, even our daughters. Similar to the expression *having the balls* to do something, these are not gendered aggressions. They present the idea of certain behaviours, courageous ones in fact. Gender stereotyped, yes, but let's not go there. Besides, it's useful and powerful for a young woman to tell someone to "man up" or to tell a female peer she needs to "have the balls" to break up with her horrid boyfriend. Leave it. I will not be sidetracked. I know that trick—I've had six teenagers.

Teenagers are our children. Without breaking into song, they *are* our future. I know they say and do things that make you want to put your fist through the wall or drive over them with your car a little bit, I get it. But imagine ever saying to the tiny, adorable version of that same person, at two years old, that she's an idiot. You would not.

If you do that now, when she's fifteen, she will remember. Worse yet, she might believe you.

Alright.

My apologies to anyone I have unjustly accused.

But if the shoe fits, wear it.

> "Mom—that wasn't a snuggle."
> —Adam, 5, being tucked in at night, asking for a snuggle and receiving a hug
>
> "Do you know what's the difference between a hug and a snuggle? A snuggle takes a while."

NO ONE CAN MAKE YOU FEEL INFERIOR

When my siblings and I were children, my dad taught PE at a junior high school. We were at the school a lot.

I remember, in wintertime, throwing off our coats and boots to run around the empty gym like wild animals. We enrolled in a drama club for children, held one evening a week at the school. I remember, on those evenings, the scandalous, almost unparalleled kid-fun of sprinting and sliding in our socks through long, shiny-floored hallways lined with lockers on both sides, on our way to drama. A hazy memory, like a happy dream.

Over those years we often waited for Dad in the gym, sitting in noisy, crowded stands watching a game, or in its quiet emptiness beside the gym office door. Occasionally we'd cram in the back seat of our family car with a student or two as Dad drove them home after track or volleyball practice, back to their farm to do chores, or because they didn't have a ride.

I was a weird little kid with thin, dark-blond braids, watching everything closely. The students were beyond cool, about thirty-two years old for how they seemed to me. I studied them carefully and watched my dad with them. Dad would chat with these teenagers, and laugh, or reprimand them in a firm, demanding way if a kid made that necessary. He'd go stand and chat with them, or walk along with them going places. It was obvious to me that my dad cared about these young people; I imagine it was obvious to them as well. I could tell they really liked him back. Some adored him.

I loved seeing all that; it made me feel good.

I'd walk around the school, looking at displays in the entrance area, halls, gym office, equipment room. I would see things hanging about: schedules, warning notices, awards in cases, announcements, banners, sign-up sheets. Dad had many inspirational posters in the gym. He's a Jonathan Livingston Seagull kind of guy (a character and book worth looking up).

One poster stood out to me. It was plain, written in Dad's neat, script-like printing, on medium-sized poster paper, done in simple, black felt pen. It said:

No one can make you feel inferior without
your consent.

I thought about that, as hard as my child-brain could think. It pulled at me; I spent a lot of time trying to figure it out. Maybe the junior high students did too. I came to love that saying. I admired the personal power it offered the teenager who read it taped there, with *you* and *your* in the statement.

Looking back, these experiences with Dad, these memories, that poster and my thoughts about it, all rolled up to become what I believe about teenagers and how they should be treated, formed back when I was a school child myself. This is the kind of care, the kind of respect and attention, effort, and love our teenagers need and deserve. I am convinced we are difference-makers for great good in the world when we work hard to provide this to them.

> Dad, at church, everyone singing the classic "Amazing Grace" (drops his voice, leans close, pretending to be nonchalant but suppressing a smile, sings):
> "... that saved a wretch like youuuu ..."

LETTING GO

MY GRANDFATHER

In 1912, my grandfather, my father's father, a man I never met, left his family home in the north of India and travelled to Australia, by ship of course, to begin a new life there. He, William Winter Home Purves, was eighteen years old at the time. He never returned home to India again. Ever.

Eighteen.

I'd always considered this from the point of view of that young man, my grandfather. What was it like, arriving in Australia? How did he make his way, go about building his new life? Did he feel he might die of homesickness? Did he ever regret his absolute uprooting?

More recently, I've thought about his story from the viewpoint of his mother, my great-grandmother. How on earth did my grandfather's mom say goodbye to him, those oh-so-many moons ago? How did they say a goodbye like *that*?

Semi-adult Child: *Well, mother, I'm away now. Thank you for bearing me and raising me. I shall think of you fondly.*

Mother: *Alright, dearest flesh of my flesh. It's been a delight. I shall cling to memories of you as long as I live. Have a good life.*

Mother (calls out as he walks away): *Hey, honey, careful with the drinking water in the bowels of the ship—it'll give you nasty dysentery! I tucked Vitamin C tabs in your rucksack to prevent scurvy! Write me! Love you!!*

Mother (begs inside her head): *Don't go.*

I cannot.

Yet I wonder if there could be a powerful case of "the past whispering to the future" woven in there for us now.

We need to let go a bit.

Our generation of parents cannot bear our eighteen-year-olds traveling two hours away without texting "to see if they got there okay." That's in a heated car, wearing a seatbelt, armed with a cell phone, a bottle of clean water, maybe even road-side assistance, zero risk of scurvy, dysentery, or piracy. Why do we do this? That's not a rhetorical question: I do it too, and I wonder why we started that. Really, is our text making him "more safe"? Is it truly helping in some way? I don't think so. Maybe we should stop. How did *we* get so fragile? So worried?

Text me when you get there.

Why?? Why does she need to text you when she gets there? What scenario is going to be made different/better/safer/somehow improved by her texting you?

Back to my grandfather again, on the other side of planet Earth from his parents when World War I broke out. Imagine them learning their son had joined the Australian Infantry Forces, in the Light Horse Brigade, and been sent overseas a few days shy of his twenty-first birthday. William took part in the godforsaken campaign at Gallipoli, went on to Egypt, Palestine and the Sinai region, Beersheba, Jordan, and Damascus. I have a photo of him, Grandfather William, a swarthy, deadly-handsome young man in uniform, wearing tall boots with riding spurs and holding a broad-brimmed hat. The photo was taken Christmas Day 1917, while he was on leave in Cairo, Egypt. He was twenty-three years old.

William was away at war for four years. His parents would have waited desperately for news, a handwritten letter arriving months after it was sent, opened with trembling hands.

There were no reassuring texts. *hey mom warfares hell. BTW going out in Cairo rn. talk later.* We are blessed with the reassurance of instant communication these days. Still, maybe some of this checking-in we do is too much. Maybe it robs our teenagers and young adults of experiencing accomplishment without our involvement, without the need to constantly re-assure us.

I was chatting about this with some girlfriends, sharing that my parents didn't seem to worry about me making de-cisions, going places, and coping while I was growing up and as a young adult. One friend said, "Maybe they did worry, but covered it up, to hide their worry from you." That had never dawned on me.

I asked Mom about it. She looked perplexed, then pro-claimed indignantly, "No! Why on earth would we worry about you? We knew you could do all those things." Classic Mom.

And there it is. Our current constant checking-in with our older teenagers and young adults does little to convey the empowering conviction that we know they can do all those things. Let's get brave. We have to start letting them go, now, in little bits, so they learn, as we do too. We can love them hard in between all the letting go. Start saying he doesn't need to text you.

No, don't text me—just go have fun. Tell me about it later sometime, when you get back. Back to the train station.

> "No . . . I'll send the email."
> —Levi, 15, feverish, sick in bed with the
> flu, about to miss morning basketball
> practice

LAUNCH

Now, after insisting we have to get tough in letting our teenagers go, I will do an about-face and admit right here that the Big Letting Go, "the launch" as it were, is terribly hard. I'm referring to that decisive moment when your child does actually go, and that is that. Not permanently of course, but still, a decisive "gone for now."

During a most recent university housing move-in, my daughter and I were pushing a cart overloaded with her things across a courtyard from storage toward her new building. We approached three people gathered next to a car. A petite teenager with a huge ponytail and an oversized sweatshirt was standing, head inclined, wiping her eyes. I noticed because the mother with the exact same big hair wiped her eyes at the same time. Their simultaneous movements and identical hair caught my eye. Then the dad wiped his eyes too. The mother and daughter clung to each other intensely a moment, then broke apart, the girl walking away quickly, head down, and the mom moving toward the car.

As my daughter and I heaved our crabbing-cart alongside them, the dad forced a smile at us, calling out, "Busy day!," nodding at our cart.

"Heartachey day," I replied, inclining my head toward their daughter. Both parents immediately turned toward me, faces pained, all pretense of nonchalance or bravery dropped. "Yes," they responded in unison.

I talk tough but I am not. This step of letting go is a birthing of another kind, equally painful as the original sort, only in a different way. Your heart aches; you feel homesick and slightly ill. You know him or her inside out. You know that look of nervous excitement or suppressed apprehension on her face. You have seen the same look many times before, when she was six, and eleven, and fifteen. She will figure it all out, or not, as the case may be. But she will be seriously absent from you for the first time, after these years of being physically present to each other. You've been with her in your thoughts too, night and day, for years, in that "thinking twice" that parents do, once for yourself and again for your child. Now you will be neither present nor required to think twice.

This feels sudden, gut wrenching, wrong.

Parents seem to feel curiously obliged to be upbeat! Positive! Light about dropping their kid off at college, or at the airport, or waving goodbye as she drives away in an old car to start her something new.

Parent (out loud, at work or a social gathering): *Oh yes, he's on his way! Launched. Very exciting. All good.*

Same Parent (inside his own head): *Yes, and I'm not prepared. I feel sick leaving him—more than melancholy, like physically sick. The house is empty without him. It's weird walking past his room. I hope he makes good choices. I sure didn't at the same age. I wonder if I gave him enough of me? But it's too late now. Did I get enough of him? I feel pressured to say his leaving is fine. It isn't.*

So yeah. We're painfully individualistic and independent in our culture, so strangely bent on not being or, at least, appearing sentimental. But the launching is hard. And, like back in toddler days, what were you thinking of saving "sentimental" for?

I felt mildly emotional at the pomp and ceremony of my teenagers' high school graduation events: the pretty dress or handsome suit, the walk across the stage, the gaggle of fresh-faced friends smiling together. That was sweet and happy and a bit wistful—but not a gut punch. For me the sucker punch of raw emotion came a few months later, at the moment my teen child walked away from me, or I away from her.

I admit how deeply difficult, how raw and complex, I found that moment. Nothing was "wrong." My situation wasn't sad in any objective way; *I* was just sad. Those goodbyes were nothing, meaningless compared to truly unbearable things some parents have to cope with. Refugee camp separations. Vicious, drawn-out custody battles. Terminal illnesses. Next to those, I should be ashamed of my weeping about, only saying goodbye to my teenager I'd see again in some four months. Mine was a pampered dream, my children being able to attend and afford university. No hardship whatsoever.

I just found their leaving hard, that's all. I'm overly sentimental compared to . . . I don't know. Other people, I suppose? But there it is. I have always been.

I remember, as a nine-year-old, being at the end of my family's month-long visit with Nana in Australia. Before we left for the airport, I went from room to room, quietly by myself, throughout her house, touching the walls, and studying everything. I cried because I might never be at her house again. I saw my nana a few more times in my life, but I never did see her house again. Why did that matter to me? I don't know. It just did.

Early in my marriage, when I was away with my brand-new husband for a year of his study fellowship, my colleagues at the rehabilitation hospital where I began working came to mean the world to me. These new coworkers were my lifeline, my social world in a city of strangers, my everyday fun and new place of belonging. I saw these people at work only. They weren't even close friends; I would not travel to see them. We did not intertwine our lives in the way friends do. But they were a world to me at the time and I liked a good many of them, some very much. Ten months later, when my husband and I were leaving that city, my coworkers hosted a lovely little farewell gathering at someone's house. I could barely suppress my desire to bawl like a baby because, again, I thought, *I'll probably never see these people again.* And I haven't.

I confess to you here that I am painfully sentimental about partings and such things. These moments, these people and transitions, are the stuff of life, a measure of time, a weaving of acquaintances and places and friendships that make up our life story. These things feel intense to me and matter *so* much more than many dry, heartless issues we give our attention to.

Now imagine me a mother. Yeah, it's that bad.

> **Walk-away moments**
> **that had me heartachingly sad and happy, mel-**
> **ancholy and proud,**
> **yearning, content and restless,**
> **all at the same time, needing to be in the quiet**
> **and think for a long time**

Son in a parking garage. We finish unloading his stuff and setting up the university residence room. He walks me back to the car. Smiling, his face some nine inches above mine, he says, "Well, Mom, I guess my childhood's officially over." We both laugh, and hug just a moment. He walks away through the garage, literally into the sunset, the ubiquitous residence-lanyard thing attached to new keys swinging from his pocket as he goes. I steer our big old car out of the garage and see his figure striding away, his familiar walk. I drive away, thinking of my son.

Daughter in a single room, all cozily set up. She is tearful. We hug one more goodbye. I squeeze her tight and say I know she can do it. One step at time. "You'll get to know people. It just takes time." Looking distraught, she closes her door with her eyes trained upon me. I walk away down the long hallway of doors, of kids and parents milling about, carrying stuff. I have a lump in my throat. I drive around past her building.

slowing down to look across a courtyard, to the second floor, third window in from the corner, and picture my daughter in there. I drive away from that city thinking of her.

Daughter, early morning on a busy sidewalk in Paris. A third-year university term of student exchange. We'd found the rooming house, a dark, depressing place. We'd Metro'd around to find buildings of the "campus" spread over the city. We'd communicated, sort of, in the most painful butchering of the French language ever to be heard in the City of Lights, trying to set up a cell phone. We'd obtained some crucially necessary piece of paper at a bank that, *"Mais, non,"* could not simply be handed to my daughter over the counter but, rather, had to be mailed to her rooming house, because France. She'd stayed overnight with me in the tiny hotel room, a third-floor walk-up atop crooked spiral stairs.

Early in the morning, we walk out onto the street, for me to go to the airport. It's sleeting snow and is cold. She carries the bag of random groceries we found the day before. We don't talk about this goodbye. It is too much, but our eyes hold the words. After our parting, I can't help myself: I stand and look back along the sidewalk of pedestrians to watch her easily trackable, crazy-curly blond hair gradually disappear into the sea of bobbing heads above black jackets and coats, moving along the sidewalk. I fly away, the city shrinking away from me, thinking of my daughter down below.

Another son in a different parking garage. We carry empty bins and bags back to the car. A bright, sunny day. Much fun setting up. He wears a look of anticipation, exudes excitement. I say Mom things of encouragement, and he replies, "Thanks, Maaam," with a kindly, soft look on his face. I drive out of the garage, watching him walk across the grass and disappear be-tween buildings. I drive out of that city thinking of my son.

Daughter, on the side of a quiet roadway near the edge of campus, by our parked car. This competent, independent seventeen-year-old kid is suddenly overwhelmed by the both of us, her parents, driving off, and her continuing on her own there without her hurly-burly family. She's crying, set to go for a run. After our hugs and kisses with tears falling, my husband and I drive away. I watch in the side-view mirror as she stands, arranging her earphones, and begins to run along the road we are driving away on. I know she will be fine, love it in fact, but my heart hurts and feels heavy. We drive out of that city in silence, and I think of my daughter.

Daughter in another dorm room of another residence. Efficient and orderly getting the room set up. A minimalist. Carefully selected, sparse personal items, books and supplies all set. Ready. She knows from sibs to leave her door open as a sign to hallmates to stop by and say hello. We say our goodbyes and smile at each other. I walk out of her building wistful and smiling, thinking of my daughter, sitting in her room with her door purposefully ajar.

It gets easier as each year passes. Eventually it really is "all good," to varying degrees. They come to know what they are doing, more or less, and I become accustomed to them being away, more or less.

Eventually their moving away, after a summer of work at home, becomes easier, as the sharing of something fun even— thank God.

Daughter, fourth year, moving into a residence tower . . . after "move-in" is over. We're hurrying, the cart-thing stacked improbably high, poorly packed and wobbling. As we wheel across the large, open reception area en route to the elevators, the stockpile of personal possessions falls, spilling across the open floor space. We are hysterical with laughter;

I'm not sure whether it was really that funny or whether we were both tired at the time. We huck her crap up into her new room, close the door on the mess, and leave together. We hug and she rushes off. The early evening sun is shining.

Son at the international departures gate at the airport. Third-year student "co-op" work placement in Germany. Never been to Europe. No confirmed accommodation. Does not speak German. One big suitcase and a backpack. A phone number. He is smiling. We both laugh at our incredulity of it all and the good luck and excitement of an opportunity of a lifetime. I watch him walk through the security gates, and I walk in the other direction, smiling and shaking my head.

Daughter who was teary in the dorm room back in first year, third year. She'd found herself a place with a hot plate and a mini fridge, in an old, converted downtown hotel, away from campus. She feels at ease there, coming and going in the bustle of the city core. She finds the longer bus ride to and from campus a leisure time. I feel content as she waves good-bye to me, smiling, from her window above a street-food vendor and a liquor store. She is happy there. So I am happy too.

The Best Move-In: "Drop-Off for Two," a second time for the youngest, at the same university as her fourth-year brother. This is when I witness the curly-haired mother and daughter clinging together, weeping by their car. I understand their pain entirely, in my gut, grateful to be in an easier place now, after eleven years of doing it. I am painfully aware of how blessed our family is in all this—who gets this? I'm grateful and reflect on what these blessings demand of us.

For me, this particular drop-off scenario offers the deeply satisfying contentment of seeing my youngest two children away relaxed, confident, happy. I listen to my daughter natter on excitedly, stashing away the mess of stuff strewn all over the room, a Frisbee and organic chemistry set, soccer cleats and a frying pan, a printer and a fake plant. Her brother arrives from his setup, that I was not involved in, to be supportive— meaning, he stretches out on her newly made bed amid the mayhem and falls asleep.

I see them finding their way.

It is *now* that I feel the emotional "graduation moment." My graduation. They need me less, these young people of mine, which, sadly, was the goal all along.

I have a best memory of driving away after that double-kid drop-off. I was driving west into the intensely bright, setting sun of a clear early evening in September, toward the truly majestic range of mountains rising above the stretch of highway in front of me. (Most of these emotional drop-offs were accompanied by bright sunshine. I do not embellish: it was common for the time of day and of year, I guess.)

As I drove, thoughts of my children's childhoods floated through my mind, like dreams that were real, their richness matched satisfyingly by the scenery around me. It felt fitting of an opera, a soaring aria. But instead I played their music, music we'd listened to together many times over the years just passed, my teenagers and me. "Sunset Lover" by Petit Biscuit felt right, oddly melancholy yet happy for electronic music. I know nothing about this artist, but his music felt good, perfect even, with tears of sad plus happy. The best of human experience, heartache and love and yearning mixed all together.

Again, that adage from when they were young children: Observe it, feel what is happening. Don't let it pass you by. My sister said it well, in some texts to me, after this trip:

Oh yes, I understand. Both those emotions of happy & sad and letting go but not really . . . as well as the NEED to FEEL it!!

Exactly, dear sis—"the need to feel it." The bittersweet moment of my children leaving that I wanted to sit with. Not hurry to get over. Not talk about. Vulnerable and conflicted, and wanting to stay right there, immersed, and hold it awhile. Even when "everything is fine," it's hard, in a very particular way. The sixth time was no easier than the first. Familiar, yes, but no easier. My kid is away and I am sad. For now. And I want to feel it.

THE MOST

LIFE, LIVED LARGE

For parents, their child's teenage years might be some of "the most." The most of parenting. Most emotion, most change, most intensity.

For me, teenagers are the most sentimental. How can they not be? A glance at her face is a snapshot in time, signaling both past and future. You still see her toddler face, that animated, little chub-cheeked wonder, yabbering on about something. Now here she is, the curve of cheek somewhat lessened, her face now guarded and more wary, yet sometimes shockingly and wonderfully the exact same. And you have a window to her adult face now too, the woman she will be at thirty-eight, with the arch of her brow in questioning, and her deliberate way of speech when she is angry. It almost makes me cry with how beautiful it is, but then, I'm a weirdo.

Yes, I know she can be *such* an asshole sometimes. I know.

I have the advantage of looking at this from the easy place of having survived it. I have space to wax eloquent, to reflect on what it all means. I'm old and woolly now (Marcel and I always use *woolly*—captures it better somehow). Please allow me to counsel you, if such a thing ever works.

Try, try, try to slow time down. Notice him changing. Make note of how adorable he really is, while he still lives with you.

Again, the line of argument of your hopeful, healthy life expectancy of eighty-seven years still stands; the period of your child's life from thirteen years old to twenty years old is seven years. That's 8 percent, my friends. During this 8 percent of your life, moms and dads, you get to feel more than you'll ever usually feel, except, of course, when *you* were the teenager. You get to experience "more."

It's funny—inspirational messages on cloth bags urge us, *Do What Scares You!* and *Live to the Full!* Teenagers make you do that on the daily. Truthfully, we desperately prefer our lives to be predictable, with even-keel emotions and manageable routines. Not with a teenager in your life—no way, José. You get *Push Boundaries!, Argue!, Send It!, Eat a Lot!* every day of the week.

Remember though: 8 percent. A tiny window of time, during which he might grow thirteen inches, go from loving dodgeball to English Lit or mechanics, sound like his grandfather sometimes, and take care of you when you have the flu. She might move from brown hair to blue and back, ditch all her mean friends, find great new ones, and become an artist, all on her own, painting you a small, touching painting of your parents' house "for no reason." He may leave dirty dishes in his bedroom, smoke weed and try to hide it, and argue with you about the stupidest things. She might use way too much eyeliner, use the word *like*, like, constantly, and fly off the handle without warning. He is not done yet. She is not done yet.

Neither are you. Dig deep, live "the most" of it all, as much as you can manage. Love crashing.

ADULTS

HERS

Her coffee mugs
Her apartment
Her nimble fingers on a phone
Her shortcut
Her breakfast place

Her lead

My visit
My daughter

HOW THINGS CHANGE

THE HOCKEY GAME

It's not cold inside the ice rink at a professional hockey game, though it feels as if it should be. The indoor stadium, or sports arena, or entertainment bowl, or whatever it's called is open and cavernous, with an enormous sheet of ice at its centre.

Once the players are out there, suited up and skating around during the pregame warm-up, the ice appears much smaller.

My daughter in her early twenties and I are going to a game, a fun evening out together. We arrive to a show. It begins as we walk into the noise and high energy of crowds pouring into the arena through the packed concourse. We weave and push a route toward the gate to our seats, past or through line-ups for food and drink, swimming through sounds of programs being hawked, antsy voices of pregame announcers, and loud music that fills the space.

My daughter is a hockey fan. I am happy to have a night out with her.

We settle into our good seats in the lower arena and get ready for the game, as if we somehow need to be ready. A few men step carefully through in front of us, each carrying a tower of beers in plastic cups with snap-on lids, stopping at their seats next to ours. They're boisterous, polite, animated, and friendly.

The lighting lowers as the pregame show begins. The crowd goes wild. Spotlights swing in the darkness. Massive screens lower to display gorgeous still shots of the city and of players, some gorgeous too, moving to rapid-fire video sequences of previous game highlights flashing over the screens, choreographed to a soundtrack of pumping music laced with the audio of frantic play-by-play broadcasts. "He drives hard to the net . . . He shoots . . . He SCooooRES!!"

Centre face-off. The puck is dropped, the game underway. My daughter and I yell and scream along with the crowd, soon clapping, later booing. We join in "the wave" when it rolls by, laughing, needing to holler at each other to be heard. Pure fun. The game is good too, with players flying end to end on the ice, cutting fast, skates carving, across and into the corners. The passing is impossibly sharp, as though the puck is pulled by a powerful magnet between hockey sticks, on the fly.

Along with his friends, the man seated next to me is caught up in the game too, but he seems to be watching us as well, as though taking in something curious. During breaks in the play, he asks us questions, inquiring loudly for our opinions on the last shift, or about certain players' defense, or for power-play predictions. My daughter answers knowledgeably.

Later he leans over and calls out to my daughter, "Are you her daughter?" and points to me. We both laugh and say yes. He doesn't seem to be trying to pick her up; he's too old for her. He's definitely not trying to pick me up; I am too old for him.

But I can tell he is watching us. He is listening to us, my daughter and me.

He drinks his many beers through the game but does not appear drunk. He and his friends step carefully over us for both period breaks, returning each time to repeat the same awkward stepping-over routine. We shell peanuts and chat with him, our seat-buddy, on and off, loudly as one must, about the game and little bits about life.

Partway through the third period, during a break in the play, amid pumping, break-in-game music, our beer-drinking seat mate sits plainly watching us another moment. A look, impossible to define, flashes across his face, a blend of envy, curiosity, and a surprising amount of wistfulness.

He leans close to me with an earnest, almost melancholy look on his face, and yells at me, "I wish I could pop out my own best friend."

I smile at him the way a mother does. The puck is dropped at face-off, and the game plays on.

NOT QUITE

Your adult child is not a best friend.

Close, but not quite. If all goes well, and you're blessed, your adult daughter or son is a friend, a confidante even, a supporter, a pal. But you are not your child's peer, not a best friend—you cannot be. You are something else. The parent/adult child relationship is unique in all the world of friendships, one in which a distance remains intact, a remnant of a hierarchy. We'd be naïve to think otherwise.

Before you go all protest-mode, ponder this, or better yet, try this: speak your mind with your adult child, about something you prefer, or think, or want, during the tiniest moment of tension between the two of you, and observe oh so carefully. Observe her face. Watch his body language. If you are honest, you will see it there, that archived original distance.

We have a past founded in raising them, for good and for bad. We know, and must admit, we are nails on a blackboard to them sometimes. Our history, it's all there, in our tone of voice, the way we raise our eyebrows, lift our chins. These serve to remind our child of what was before, and maybe still is. This drives our adult child crazy.

And to that I say, "Whatever." You are not going to stop being who you are or saying what you want, because it might occasionally piss off your adult child. But there it is. You are not peers: there is baggage. Hopefully mountains of love, but definitely baggage. C'est la vie.

Reflecting onward, or more accurately, backward, that same distance is preserved in our relationship with our own parents too, as they age. They are not peers, but rather our elders, not beholden to us, not under any obligation to temper their opinions either. Given a standoff, the respect differential is arguably meant to tip in their favour.

Still. My wistful, beer-drinking hockey-buddy had it damn near right, with his "popping out your own best friend" idea. It's astounding really. Company and close friendship, shared experience with and support from this person who arrived to form your family, even literally by emerging from one's own body, whom you carried around and led by the hand?? Now, here, you find yourself sharing a laugh and a beer with that same person at a game, or hurrying together between trains in another country, or resting after an exhausting day of moving house (maybe yours this time)? Bizarre. Wonderful.

You do become equals. This adult belongs to you and also doesn't at all. You can't help but worry over them, but their life's their own gig now. You can relax a bit, loosen the grip. This person is making his or her own way, and that's not your job nor your business anymore. The transition is gradual, similar to their going places on a bicycle as a child, or learning to drive as a teen. The gradualness, apparently aimed at having the child take on more responsibility, seems equally aimed at allowing *us* time to let go of seeing their responsibilities as our own.

MISSING

DEATH OF A CHILD

Sometimes the unthinkable happens and a child dies.

There is a large, hurting club on this planet made up of people who never wanted to join and cannot ever leave: those whose child has died. It seems heartless to use the word *club* for such a shattering grouping, but its members all know it to be true. The reason I know this is that one of the people most dear to me on this lovely planet, my only sister, Joanne, is a member of that terrifying club. My sister's son, the third of her four children, died in a car accident when he was twenty-three years of age.

Time stops. No words suffice. It is a nightmare you cannot wake up from.

The days that follow blur and make no sense. If you are blessed, there are too many flowers, too much food, too many people—that's if you are blessed. The opposite of all those things is worse, and many suffer that too. There is no game plan for the coming days and months, no road map, no "way to do it," and certainly no *right* way to do it, to survive and keep going. Grieving is a unique, acutely personal experience. Grief and mourning look very, very different on each person, with that difference becoming yet another intensely painful thing for those grieving to deal with.

In the days immediately following her son's death, my sister took in and absorbed somehow, *somehow*, a wall of grief that surged at her, especially from all the young people who loved her son. A group of her son's friends—musicians, farmers, students, artists—descended upon their small-town family home and sought her out, his mother, for comfort and solace.

That she would comfort them.

Such is mothering somehow. Young folks gathered, cried, hung around, even slept at their home in the days following her son's death. Joanne hugged them, held them, listened to their stories, and had someone feed them, and she and her husband and her children and all of them wept together. But every single person who entered their house went to find her. I never once heard her say, *Leave me alone, I cannot do this for you.* Staggering under her own cross, she helped them to bear theirs.

I hovered at the edge of all this, unable to really enter in. Grief is ultimately a solitary pursuit, each person stumbling about, trying to cope. I don't have much to offer to anyone suffering this, though I did notice that it's helpful to go outside as often as you can. There's something about the sky, particularly at night—its enormity is somehow reassuring, the only thing large enough to encompass how you feel. The sky helps you breathe against that dense weight in your chest.

We've all had the experience of not knowing what to say to someone who has had a child die. A dear childhood friend of mine, whose son died at four years old, even after an organ transplant from her was very clear on this point.

"I cannot be made 'more sad' by anything you say. Just don't ignore that this has happened—that is what hurts me."

My sister would add that it's normal, healthy, expected to cry a river, cry innumerable, endless numbers of times, for years, many years. Other people sometimes find this display of grief distressing, in its initial wracked expression and its later quieter forms. But that's the observer's problem, not the mourner's.

One day, not even many months after her son's death, Joanne was talking with a woman in a grocery store. My sister cried as she spoke, and the woman asked, "Do you think maybe you should be on antidepressants?"

My sister answered, "No. I think I'm just sad because my son died."

There's a weirdly practical thing I should mention, something many of us do wrong, though with the best of intentions. It is this: I have witnessed, through my sister, that having eighty-three individual people separately say to a bereaved person, *If you ever need anything, just call me, anytime* is, unfortunately, absolutely not helpful in any way whatsoever. I cringe admitting I've done that myself, many times. I share with you now my observation that these broad offerings are useless. Utterly. Sorry.

No devastated person is going to think, one afternoon two and a half months from now, when she or he is having difficulty rising from the couch, *I think I'll call Brenda and ask her to bring homemade soup,* or *You know, I'm going to ask Ryan if he's available to go for a trail bike ride, right now—on a Wednesday afternoon, like, in ten minutes.* You, the offerer, *literally do hope that they will do that,* call you and ask. But that's never going to happen.

No, you have to make a specific offer, for a specific day and a specific time, and you have to specifically do it. Get out your calendar and schedule yourself time to make a phone call, or take a meal, or drop off a small token of care, or mail a card, or go for a walk, smattering these throughout *your* calendar over the coming year. Concentrate your offerings a few months from now, when the bereaved person feels the world moving on without them, leaving them behind, weighted down by grief that settles heavily upon them with a singular loneliness.

Given the unfathomable pain of this loss, there's a stunning truth that speaks to the ferocity and enormity of parental love. If you ask members of that terrifying, unthinkable club whether, given all the raw pain, all the searing loss and soul-searching of their child's death, they wish they'd never joined that more enormous club of people who are parents in the first place, the answer would almost always be No.

No, most often, they do not wish they'd never become a parent to the child gone from them now, after too short a life. Their love for their child is so great that, even given the chance, many would knowingly inflict the pain of suffering and loss on themselves again if it meant they could have their child with them once more, if only briefly.

There it is, in its most savage form: the ever-present mingling of suffering with love, never so mingled as when a child, your own child, regardless of his or her age, dies. Suffering and love.

Focus on the love. At the end of the day, love is all we've got. My sister and my dear nephew, Carson, gone now from this life, taught me that. Bless you both, always.

Rest in peace, dear Carson William Ruhland
May 6, 1992–August 1, 2015

A POEM AWAY

My father wrote me a poem after I left home.

Is that not the most fabulous thing you've ever heard of?

I was lonely and painfully homesick at the time, away in a big city at university. The first piece of mail I ever received in my mailbox, my own tiny box within the banks of small, metal mailboxes at the university residence commons building, was an envelope containing a letter written in familiar, script-like handwriting, bearing this poem:

September 5, 1984

Hello sweet Sue—how do you do?
How comes it I'm so far from you?
Just yesterday—a babe in arms.
Today—a young lady with endless
    charms.
The days, the months like rivers flow,
Oh those years—where do they go?

So many times we've said aloud,
That of your deeds we're very proud.
But above those many things you do,
We love you just because you're YOU.

No doubt for long you have been yearning,
To attend that place of higher learning.
As different challenges you will try,
Like J. L. Seagull you will fly.
That you'll do well—we all know—
You'll make a terrific physio.

****

Today a thing of note I saw,
As I walked by your bedroom door,
The bed, the chair, the floor were clear,
I knew at once that you weren't here—

Since you've been gone things aren't the
    same,

Poor John has had an itchy mane.
Around the house this cry has hatched—
"Millie, you want a scratch for scratch?"

Your notes we're finding by the hour,
Tonight Mum found one in the flour.
Of no surprise it'd be for me,
To find one floating in my tea.

****

May God smile kindly on you, dear,
His love for you—our constant prayer

Forgive the rhyme and clumsy meter
Remember my name's not Willie but Peter
I know my style is often bad . . .
But greater love hath no Dad.

"Love ya, Sue
& miss you too"
x

As long as I have memory, I will remember how that poem
made me feel. I was accompanied and comforted in those
first few weeks, repeating those first two lines to myself, while
walking around the enormous campus, finding buildings, eating alone, going to the library, sitting in my small dorm room
at night. My dad hugged me close and pushed me on with that
poem.

Decades later, looking back, I think of that poem and what
it did for me as a model of what we try to do for our adult kids.
My dad did not take away any of my hardship, as it felt to me

back then, or any of my heartache. He loved me in my distress, made it easier to bear. That's what we parents try to do.

The kids gotta do their thing. We gotta get out of their way and love them as best we can without taking anything away from them. It has to be hard.

Viewing one's own pursuit of university education as hardship is ridiculous, I realize now, but what did I know? It felt hard to me, with homesickness burning like a visceral illness in my gut and bowels, being on a campus with three times the population of the town I grew up in. I felt alone. I worried with every payment and purchase that my carefully saved money might barely be enough.

The point in helping someone who is worried or struggling isn't to fix how they feel; it's to respond to how they feel. Dad knew that.

. . . Do I help my adult kids in the same way? I hope so.

MY HORCRUXES

This awful missing of each other goes the other way too.

I've recounted my experience as a young adult missing my parents, my family home. A similar thing happens again many years later, in reverse, when, as older adults—and the parents this time—we miss our children who are gone. This sentiment is illustrated by a conversation I had with one of my older teenagers.

Backstory: my kids loved the *Harry Potter* books. Loved. Still love. It's accurate to say those books played an influential role in their growing up, their immersion in story, their imaginations, their bonding over discussion of plot and detail and meaning, in excitement when a new book was coming out, in that very first reading of books they'd read again and again over years to come. As the movies rolled out, they watched . . . and watched them. It is impossible to even hazard a guess at how many times my children, collectively, have watched each *Harry Potter* movie. Boggles the mind really.

I witnessed them "playing" Harry Potter when they were little, complete with costume pieces received as a celebrated group birthday present given to Levi. I overheard countless discussions about the books over the years, arguments and explanations, thrill and upset. I beheld scene after scene of the movies passing by the TV while my children watched, in groups, or alone, or all together, at Christmas or in summer or anytime. Hell, our eldest daughter threw herself headfirst into a law school literary moot (fake trial) theatre production, simply because it was based on *Harry Potter* and she knew the material—by heart.

Many years prior, back in Grade 5, one of our daughters was silent-reading in class when she read of the death of Dumbledore. She sat distraught, tearful, feeling, as she said, "fully shattered." Thank God her teacher had read the books and understood the significance of what just happened. The teacher allowed my daughter to go to the library alone, to gather herself. One of those stellar adults again! The many difference-makers who care more and give more than is strictly required of them. Bless up that teacher.

In the pleasant, small library of a sweet little elementary school sat my young daughter, taking in the dark fact that Dumbledore had died, had been killed at the betraying hand of another, and all that his death meant. She told me of feeling, "on Harry's behalf," the loneliness of the moment, the weight of facing Voldemort alone, infinitely more daunting now without the guide of Dumbledore. "It was a lot to handle," she said.

You get the idea. In our family, *Harry Potter*'s been big.

Fast-forward ten years or so. One day, I was discussing some detail around the concept of horcruxes with one of my aficionados, or rather, she was discussing it with me, in relation to an English paper she was writing. As you may or may not know, in the world of *Harry Potter*, a wizard could ensure his immortality by committing an evil act while using dark magic to shatter his soul into fragments, called horcruxes, which become embodied in other people or things, a dark way of living on through the splintering of self.

"I feel like all you kids are horcruxes of me," I said to her.

She froze, silent a moment. "Oh—yeah, no. No, Mom," she said. "That's not . . . that's terrible."

I tried to explain: I didn't mean horcruxes in the sense of any evil being involved, or my children existing as shards of my shattered soul! Nothing like that. My children and I are each distinct souls. They are not me. I know that.

But in a way weirdly similar to the horcrux idea, my children are, *to me*, horcruxes of my love. I have a vague sense of displacement, of being fragmented, splintered, as my children, embodiments of my love, leave and are away from me, off here and there, and all over the place.

Literally, yes, like a piece of me is missing. *Exactly* like that.

This sensation would become amplified when a few of them were away at once, especially if for the first time—new to them and thus to me. My children were away from me, me at home. I was away with them though, in the back of my mind, all the time, as I went about my normal days, during my waking hours, even in my dreams. My thoughts were displaced there, like a soundtrack playing in my head behind the scenes of a different movie from the one I was living, away there with these children who once lay in my arms, slept in my bed, filled my car, and took over my life. Now gone. Or just away.

A young adult daughter, having saved her money, travelling alone through Europe and beyond. Me, constantly translating the time difference, following her in thought.

A teenage son away, rowing in a national regatta, on the

other side of the country, without us there. He away, me with him there in my thoughts.

A young adult daughter moved to another town, to begin a job and try something new. Brave, alone, away.

A teen daughter away with us on a trip, but then staying on to visit a dear friend, travelling home alone. Not with me.

A teenage son, invited to join a basketball team he didn't know, playing away at a tournament in a big American city. Away.

My "baby" daughter on a high school trip, taking the subway to visit community programs all over the boroughs of New York City. Not with me.

I was away with them, there in those places too, fragmented in my thoughts. They are pieces of me scattered all over the place, at least for now. I sometimes have the eerie sense I've transferred some of my abilities to them as well . . . without, you know, the murderous, evil, dark-magic bits, or an attempt to become immortal through them and all.

Perhaps that feeling of displacement, of fragmentation, will wane as they make their way, and I become accustomed to their absence. Maybe then the massive spotlight of my life that's been trained on them will be turned down a few notches and begin straying on to other things. There's likely some complex psychoanalysis to be applied to my feeling this, but I don't care. We feel what we feel.

I miss them, these horcruxes of my love.

GIVE & TAKE

TWO-WAY STREET

The discomfort of letting go during the teenage years fades as children become adults. Your adult "kids" don't need you as much. In the day-to-day, normal problem-solving of their life, you're off duty. On call maybe, but off duty. It's nice, this new state of freedom.

The new friendship-type relationship that evolves has a unique, built-in advantage for the adult child over all their other friendships: a parent is willing to listen to, and is genuinely, oddly interested in, excruciating detail no other friend would tolerate. Parents take on the boring, the inane, the self-absorbed, the vulnerably personal, and the boasting celebratory. "All is welcome" with a parent, no detail too tedious, too small. The full gamut of life experience is on the table for sharing and asking.

THINGS PARENTS HEAR ABOUT, WITH
INTEREST, FROM THEIR ADULT CHILD

- The weighted blanket he's addicted to, though can barely roll over under

- A fun drinking night out with a new Scottish gal on her rec soccer team, made extra-fun by being unable to understand half of what she said
- A new tailpipe he installed on his motorcycle that sounds sick (meaning good)
- The lack of women's sizing in outdoor-supply stores, and how's a woman supposed to find a good pair of steel-toed chest waders??
- That his car blew up in the night, probably while being hot-wired to be stolen, the subsequent three-alarm fire, and the detective who asked, before opening the trunk of the charred wreckage, if there'd be a body inside (this call began with, "I'm okay . . .")
- A big toenail that keeps becoming ingrown and hurts so much it's dumb
- A research building that was built for . . . research, being taken over by university administration
- Her dog's fur that's horribly dry even though she puts coconut oil on it
- A girlfriend's cheeks so nice and squishy he almost can't stand it
- Riding a bicycle to work these days because she could never quite get used to someone eating loaded hot dogs right beside her on transit at 6:40 a.m.

And on and on. A parent is interested in these conversations, not because the content is important to us, but because the other person is, this impossibly young and beautiful adult you know so well, and love so much.

We parents also reciprocate more readily now, sharing our stuff back to our adult child. They seem to hear us less like the adult voice in old Charlie Brown shows (still worth looking up) and more as an actual person.

THINGS ADULT CHILDREN HEAR ABOUT, WITH LIMITED INTEREST, FROM A PARENT

- The dog having diarrhea, despite the special dog food, but needing to avoid the vet because the dog tries to kill the vet
- Would love to play a sport as exercise, but never do the exercises that would be required to get fit enough to play a sport
- Older parents having a hard time grocery shopping, but refusing online ordering for delivery, because G-ma wants to go "choose the stuff herself"
- Failing to make—yet again—an appointment to get the winter tires put on, and why is that?

This ordinary "life-reporting" is repeated again with the even older generation too, with us in the role of adult child, exchanging tales of life with our elderly parents.

This is the circle of life: listening to crap, with love. Woes are made lighter, joys happier. It's the gift we give each other within a family.

Some dynamics aren't two-way, but rather "pass it on."

One summer I helped Madeline move to a new town, to a new beginning, in the midst of a global crisis. We forgot "Hello Dolly" (as Marcel *always* calls a dolly; Veronica legitimately thought they were actually called that—we had to play the Liza Minelli song to explain), so the move was a highly inefficient affair, like a live demo of "what not to do."

The day wore on to mania that evening, both of us crouched in a bedroom, too hot and too tired to be assembling an Ikea bed, as we were not succeeding in doing. We went and sat on her living room floor, on a rolled up sleeping bag and unnecessary comforter, leaning against the wall beside the open balcony door, with warm night air barely moving, drinking cold beer out of cans. From our resting place we could see the hills just outside of town, dark against the very last of the sky's light.

Only a few years later Madeline took that same sleeping bag and the folded comforter to go sleep on the floor of my parents' place for a few days, "passing on" help to her grandparents during a particularly rough patch. Madeline's experience of helping wasn't fun though, as her move-in had been for me; it was distressing and heartbreaking. Sometimes help expands in the dynamic of being passed on. Same as love.

RANTING

Sometimes the best kind of give-and-take with our adult children involves one party actively talking and the other actively listening.

I remember one time when our youngest daughter phoned home from away in her second year at university. Mostly she texted us little notes of love and such; she said phoning made her feel more homesick. I remember feeling that too, after hanging up the pay phone in the hallway of a residence so many years ago.

Veronica didn't phone often, but when she did, she had something to say. In this case, she recounted events around a recent chemistry lab.

Now, this chem course was brutal, and the failure rate for the lab portion, infamous. She'd studied for the lab, to understand the steps, the when and how to do what. She had rarely used some of the equipment, so she'd reviewed how-to videos. (She'd even presented a burn on her hand over FaceTime as recently acquired evidence of this lack of practical experience.) Such was the situation before the class in question. And then the day of the lab came.

She reported in her call that, at first, things had been going well; she was carrying out tasks, ticking off the steps.

Coming down the home stretch, with plenty of time to go, the lab teaching assistant called out, "Five minutes! Only five more minutes, people!"

Five minutes??! Really? *How could I have lost track of time so badly?* she asked herself. When the time is up, students must stop immediately . . . and not finishing almost certainly results in a zero out of five, substantially increasing the chance one fails the course, I was told.

My daughter reported feeling panicked, glancing again at the clock, confused. She tried to calm herself, to envision ways she might combine the final steps, knowing full well that wouldn't work. She quickly added drops of something, or heated it, or put it in a spinner thing, or did whatever it was. Just as she could see her action not working, the TA called out again.

"Oops, sorry, guys! Actually, you're good! You've still got twenty minutes left!"

The following is a limited selection of what my nineteen-year-old daughter shared with me next:

- I was like, *WHAAAT? What did you just do??* Really? Why? Are we also supposed to be double-checking the time for you too, you shit-for-brains?
- Does the TA chick know she just wrecked a lot of labs? Does she care? *She* will be the very reason a lot of people fail this course.
- The prof will not care, Mom. Seriously, they just go, *Yeah, well, you did it wrong. Too bad.*
- There's nobody in the faculty to talk to about stuff like this. It sucks, nobody will care.
- Why should we do this insane prep when the TA can destroy it all by reading the freakin' time wrong, then go, *Whoops, my bad.*
- Arrrgh! This pisses me off *SO MUCH!*

After a solid amount of this, she slowed down and paused.

Then she said quietly: "Thanks, Mom—I just needed to rant. How do people survive who don't have someone to rant to?? Some kids here have nobody—I don't know how they do it."

I don't know how they do it either, my sweet, survive life without someone to rant to.

This is one of the most important things a parent does for their young adult daughter or son: listen to them rant. As it turns out, listening is more helpful than trying to help. Listening to ranting *is* helping; trying to help is not.

> "Let's do chatting."
> —Adam, as an adult, mimicking a favour-
> ite expression of his young childhood

WHATEVER

I had a sense of disquiet the other day, realizing I'd advised my adult child to say something to herself that, when my children were young, I'd rage at them for saying. Let me explain.

Back when they were sweet young children arriving at an age when they needed to begin resisting, be less cooperative, more edgy, and "attitudinal," the expression my kids frequently threw out as a rebellion of sorts was the word *whatever*. It irritated me no end having my kids respond to a question, or an option, or a piece of information, with *whatever*. I knew they were only trying to push back, but *whatever* was a common response among kids at the time, one I detested. *Whatever* was completely dismissive in its passive-aggressive disregard, which was, of course, entirely the point.

It is possible that a *whatever* could be an expression of

lovely, easygoing cooperation, such as a singsongy *Oh, whatever,* pleasantly delivered in response to, say, *Do you want to go in our car, or with Grandma?* That kind of *whatever* demonstrates a willingness to be flexible and nice.

But a diss of *whatever* in response to any of the following was annoying as hell:

I've asked you twice to take out the garbage.

No, Toronto isn't the capital city of Canada.

Hey—that's your sister's shirt you're wearing.

As usual, I could only repress my irritation for so many of these offhand *whatevers* before I'd lose it. Randomly—or, truthfully, predicably—I'd explode.

"NO! Not *whatever. Whatever* is for lazy people and dull minds. *Whatever* is a cop-out. *It's rude!* And crap. NOT *whatever."*

Intense, I know. Some kids can tell their parents to fuck off without pushback, and mine got a verbal beating for tossing out *whatever,* poor things.

A peculiar thing began happening when those same kids were young adults. They'd be telling me about their struggles, about persevering, apparently in vain, to overcome a challenge. Courses in which the professor's vague or moving criteria were impossible to meet. A relationship breakup not resolved well. First jobs where complicated procedures were assigned without mentoring or guidance. Coworkers who remained angry about a misunderstanding.

I could hear the persistent futility they felt in these situations as they tried to figure out how to frame their reactions and deal with their challenges. Each time, the perfect imagined response crept out of hiding and stood alone in the spotlight, a word I'd heard years ago, from those very same children.

"Whatever," I said, with a sense of déjà vu.

The adult version of the twelve-year-old child stared at me in disbelief. *"Seriously . . . ?* WHAT THE HELL, MOM!!"

"No, sweetheart, not 'whatever' *from me*! I'm suggesting it to *you*—as the most helpful response *you* could have, internally, to this problem."

I explained to my indignant adult child that their situation appeared in desperate need of a *whatever*. I meant it. After years of my cursing *whatever*, here now it shone.

If you, my dears, are doing your best, being diligent and conscientious, trying hard—and that's not good enough? Not working, despite your best efforts? Well, "whatever."

Inside your head, in the voice of your twelve-year-old self, respond to these dispiriting problems with a serene *whatever*, and carry on. Just try to pass the course. Accept that past loves aren't always resolved well. Learn what you can about the new procedures. Be okay with a coworker remaining mad at you. The relief in that letting go is great medicine, though hypocritical advice coming from me.

Hell, I've even gone a few steps further, possibly a step too far but I don't think so, holding out the option of a polished *Who cares?* to my adult kids at times. I'd literally never say *Who cares?* dismissively to a child, but here, with adults, as an internal response to coping with demands they seem unable to resolve, it's the perfect thing to think. Imagine that. *Who cares?*

My message to my hardworking adult children: A situation is chock full of problems that seem almost unsolvable? Who cares? Do your best. Someone doesn't like you? Whatever. The world will not stop turning. There are people you cannot seem to please? That will happen sometimes. Maybe it's more the other person's problem than yours. Who cares?

Who knew a carefully chosen *whatever* or *who cares* could be so damn helpful?

Actually, you did, years ago.

Shout-out to my children as preteens: you were right. *Whatever* really does hit right sometimes. Use it wisely and sparingly.

FAMILY LOVE

NOT MY STORY

You may sense I am not telling you everything. You're right. I
am not.

Many of the hard stories in our family, some that affect
me, are not mine to tell, a critical consideration when one is
parent to an adult. Indeed, this concept is important at every
stage of parenting. Just as you would not post a photo of your
nine-year-old that might embarrass her when she is twelve,
or tell your friends about an intensely private heartache your
teenage son is suffering, you don't blab about personal events
in your adult children's lives.

There exists overlap between what happens to them and
how those things happen *to you*, but a parent always errs on
the side of favouring their child's privacy over their own need
to share, lest a parent become a source of gossip about their
own child, a vile thing.

There are hard things though. I just want to mention that.
There always are, for all of us. Delightful, fabulous things too
of course, but lots of hard.

"LEAB IT 'LONE, BABY! . . . Leab it 'lone!!"
—Eva, 2, warning her grabby baby
brother, Levi, off of her things

BECOMING MORE

I should mention that they change, your children. Really change. A common problem with big families, and perhaps smaller ones too, is that its members get pegged, slotted into a spot too easily, too early, unfairly. Young adulthood reveals ongoing change, showing you even more deeply who they are, as they continue becoming who they are.

These days, easygoing Levi is training for Ironman Triathlons. For his twenty-first birthday he asked for a selection of books, to begin a library of books that mattered to him, one being Viktor Frankl's *Man's Search for Meaning*. He was young when he began a full-time professional career. So . . . also, not easygoing at all.

Madeline is still quiet, but brave, and oh so resilient. She has a determination of iron, that girl, combined with gentleness. Such a powerful combination. Madeline is artistic in the way she does things, like printing.

Emily, a caring, serious professional, ever an eldest-child "most responsible adult," increasingly guides her life by placing huge value on fun—just fun, like play. She recently went kayak-camping with a friend, plays beach volleyball in the winter wearing funny rubber booties, and enjoys wearing a blouse with somewhat puffed sleeves to work. For fun.

Eva went into English Lit at university, something she says she fell into, a path of least resistance, "because it was easy and [she] was good at it." But it wasn't grabbing her. Eva faltered, a humble move, and hesitatingly embraced the risk of disappointment in considering veterinary school, the path she'd always really wanted to take. She began taking science courses, action taken without knowing where it would go. The sure thing had proven easy, and the uncertain thing was not. But she would try, and the action has made her brave.

Veronica has grown from a serious, sometimes apprehensive child into a bundle of energetic extroversion. She is also one of the kindest people you'll ever find. Her vibrancy and all the noise happening when she's around could distract a person from noticing how consistently Veronica's abundant energy is used to fuel her compassionate thoughtfulness toward others.

Adam is still analytical, ruthlessly so, just as he's always been. Now, though, his broad musings more readily make use of messy, human, emotional interests to drive his decision-making as often as the analytical. He's a quant with a heart—but he's always been so.

That's what Marcel and I are most proud of in all our children: their ability to understand people well, a most important form of intelligence and always the beginning of something good. They are all becoming more, our kids, and we love all the ways they "are," as people.

Don't decide who your young adult is because of what he or she was like at six years old, or twelve, or twenty. It doesn't work like that. Deciding who they are based on one age would be no more fair to them than it would to you. None of us are "just one thing." And we change. All the time.

GATHER

Sometimes something magical takes place within a family, as recently occurred before my very eyes.

All of "the kids," our young adults, were home, from hither and yon. They were sitting about in the kitchen late at night after an evening of drinking special beers and watching movies together. I was still up, enjoying their presence. The group chitchat and banter meandered to a place where it paused and hovered. Someone in the group, shining eyes and lips trembling, quietly revealed a painful struggle, a suffering.

The usual bravado and pecking order and dynamics ceased, fell away, disappeared.

What happened next was one of the most beautiful interactions that can happen between the children of one family.

The others gathered around that sibling, these same people who used to punch each other to get the seat they wanted in the car, two who fought like a cat and dog for one entire exhausting summer, those who were once light-years apart in development, as a two-year-old in toilet training and an eleven-year-old dealing with preteen challenges, those who teased others mercilessly, cruelly homing in on the exact thing they knew to be a vulnerability.

Those same people now gathered, listening attentively. They sat leaning forward on kitchen chairs, or perched on the side of an armchair, or up straight very still, on the couch, in a "locked-on" posture.

One by one, in turn, and in no particular order, they offered reflection on their own similar experiences, passed on helpful advice they'd received from others, shared strategies they developed through their own trials by fire as well as general commiseration of understanding . . . plus a couple of hugs of comfort for the difficulty their sibling was expressing. They provided this young adult, whom they had grown up with, their attention, care, and collective wisdom. Most of all, they listened. They sat and listened to the emotional sharing of that which was burdensome.

I was present for this magic but not needed. I said a couple of things, but it was clear that, of those present, I had the least to offer. The particularities of how life is difficult for a young person are best understood by young people. This group of young people knew how to help and did just that.

They were amazing, all of them, the person sharing and each one offering back. I was the invested bystander in a movie, in a scene of a heartfelt drama about young people, one with sharp, well-written dialogue, the kind that transports you back to how you felt at the same age. It was the scene in which the young characters reveal themselves in a way all at once vulnerable, direct, and compassionate.

Witnessing this natural outpouring of love and support between my young adult children was, for me, the engraved-gold-watch-and-applause-presentation-at-the-firm moment of my parenting career. I rolled into bed in the wee hours of the morning, my heart full, and lay contemplating my blessings, these people, pondering all I had heard.

OLDER ADULTS

THE TREE

Yesterday I bought a house.
Today I sold a home.

Yesterday my children planted a small
    discarded shrub
found at the local dump.
Today, they are able to gaze at a majestic
    fir tree
towering over our home.
That tree, in spite of being attacked by a
    lawn mower
and often visited by passing dogs, like our
    family,
took root and flourished.

My wife and I watched as each of our
    children set out
on his or her first day of school.
From kindergarten to Grade 12, they
    journeyed through

the school system being daily welcomed
    home
by mother and the large green sentinel
    pointing the way.
Like the tree, the children grew, spread
    their limbs, and
moved on to start their lives away from
    home.

In their absence Mr. Green quietly aged.
He even produced speed bumps, slowing
    down the pace
of life for all who entered.
My wife and I willingly obliged.

The children have regularly returned to
    celebrate special
occasions—birthdays, Christmas—or just
    to visit.
They are always welcomed by their tall
    green friend.

As my wife and I sadly say goodbye to our
    good
and trusty friend
we do so very thankful for the wonderful
    memories
we take with us.

Very clever men build houses for all to see
but ONLY God can build a tree
as well as other neat things, like:
friendship, love, joy, happiness, security,
    mercy,

and all the other things that form a family.

And in doing so change a House into a
    Home.
Olive Oil, good and trusty friend.

Peter E. Purves
May 6, 2017

CHANGING GEARS

PARENTS

I am changing gears here, big time, but I think you can handle it.

This chapter is not about *being* a parent; it's about *having* one.

It makes sense to do this now. It's usually what happens next, around the time your kids are grown: a refocusing on your own parents. You've been hacking away at "being a parent" yourself for a couple of decades, and the jungle is beginning to thin out. You are emerging from the wilds. The ground starts shifting under you though, and you stumble. You turn to look backward, like, *way* backward, while trying to move forward. Life has you look back at your parents again, anew, while peering ahead at your own children, young adults now, and, in strange new ways, at yourself.

Ah, and it's complicated. Through your own weary, parenting eyeballs, all that you were sure of you're not quite so sure about anymore. And about other things, you are more sure than ever—certain, in fact.

I hit the jackpot when it comes to parents. Lucky me. Amazing people and good parents. There isn't much bigger a blessing in life than being born to great parents, an advantage that surpasses all others. I am unspeakably grateful.

They are the best, those two lovebirds, my mom and dad. Married sixty years, engaged a week after they met. You read that right—one week. I KNOW!! Cray-cray. Ain't love grand? She, from a huge French-Canadian family, and he, a travelling Australian working temporarily in Canada, "on his way to Europe." At their wedding, in 1961, he reportedly said, *I came to Canada not knowing anyone, and now I'm related to half the country.*

They are getting old now. None of us want to get old, not really. The alternative to growing old is being dead though, so there is that.

My father wrote the poem "The Tree" that begins this chapter, the day before he and Mom moved out of their home of forty-nine years, the modest house I grew up in. Classic Dad: sit down and write a poem, reflecting thoughtfully on something as simple as the joy a single tree brought over many years, capturing within that a sense of what home is. A tree is easily overlooked but remarkable, in much the same way that those who build a life together over many years can be overlooked yet are remarkable.

My parents, in their early eighties, had just completed weeks of paring down, distributing, recycling, gifting, selling, and throwing away the stuff accumulated over decades of family life together, an epic amount of work. They tackled it as they did all things: as a team, head on, focused, and effective, accompanied by a lot of direction and aggressive cleaning courtesy of Mom. Their house was always neat as a pin, and small as houses go. Everything in its place, simple items, held for a lifetime. Their generation has little need for recycling— they straight-up keep the same stuff forever. Less replacement. Less accumulation. Less crap.

ABOUT MY MOM

My mom would tell you what they took to the thrift store yesterday while mashing eggs for curried egg sandwiches with the force of a jackhammer, all 5'0" and 103 French-Canadian pounds of her. That's how Mom does everything: full on.

If my mom offers to vacuum your living room, she will vacuum under every single piece of furniture, meaning she'll move all the furniture out of position, vacuum, and move it back again, *and* do inside the cushions of your couch, which you might have forgotten was even a thing. This kind of makes you feel bad, as does her saying she doesn't like your new couch very much.

I love her with all my heart.

Mom will take your newborn baby from you and tell you to go lie down. She'll set up and bathe him thoroughly and lovingly, doing his ears and folds carefully, talking to him the whole while. She'll dry him and put Vaseline on his bum, dress and wrap him expertly in an old flannel receiving blanket, and rock him in a chair, patting him firmly but gently on the back. She will lay him asleep in the bassinet, then do your dishes. She will start supper and go read a book until the baby wakes up. Then Mom will bring the baby to you for nursing, along with a glass of water that she will hand to you first, saying, "Drink this." She will wait for you to finish drinking before she hands you your baby.

Firm but soft—very soft actually, in the real way of truly helping someone. This is goddess material, the stuff that holds tribes, families, and communities together, the kind we would have run our governments if we were wise. Mom would say she's run the most important organization that exists, and that is a family. I can hear her say it.

Me, 15: "I wish I had longer legs!"

Mom: "Well, at least you *have* legs."

Me (eyeroll)

Me, 24 (working with a patient who for the past month has had no legs)

ABOUT MY DAD

My dad is a measured individual, the King of Moderation, though not in the way moderation is sometimes mistakenly viewed, as being timid or retiring. No, his is the moderation of being grounded in what is, no matter the situation, similar to being humble—another word with a bad rap of misunderstanding. He's humble in the way of being deeply assured about what is, confident enough to be there, in what is grounded and real.

After being a high school physical education teacher, coach of many sports, elementary school teacher, special education program teacher, a high school vice principal, and elementary school principal over many years, Dad declined a move further up. He returned to a classroom in a small, rural elementary school just out of town, next to old farms and open fields. He delighted in that simple setting, teaching his very own students once again. This is a moderation based in knowing yourself and what you want, without concern for what others think of your choices, yet without any self-righteousness or disdain for dissimilar choices. There's peace.

Another example? Dad had always wanted to do an Ironman Triathlon. So in his retirement, he decided he would.

For those unfamiliar with this madness, an Ironman involves a 3.8-km swim, a 180-km bike ride, and a 42-km marathon run . . . all on the same day. He followed a studied, mapped training schedule for more than a year, and, at age sixty-seven, Dad completed the 2002 Ironman Triathlon in August in Penticton, BC, Canada. I was exhausted only spectating, following to points around the route to revel and cheer over that long day, while eight months pregnant with my sixth child, my own odd little endurance event.

Okay, so you think: none of that is moderate; it's crazy. Here's the moderation part: Dad knew he'd take a long time to complete the event, and did, finishing within ten minutes of the time he predicted for himself. *Within ten minutes*, over that distance. Dad got up early the next morning, in the tiny, old, motel room where he and Mom stayed, and felt fine. His feet didn't even hurt. They went for a walk together.

I want to be like both of them when I grow up.

I watch with admiration as they move on, literally in this case, from their family home of many years to an independent retirement place, because the lawn-mowing, snow-shoveling, firewood-carrying, grocery-shopping, tree-pruning, and furnace-maintenance-ing was all getting too much.

On move-out day, Mom said they looked together around their house, immaculately clean and empty. Then they left, locking their front door for one very last time. Mom said, "I didn't even look back, it was okay." My practical mother. A moving on, taking the next thing in stride, together.

As my kids say when they see my parents walking hand in hand: *Life goals.*

> "Olive oil!"
> —Dad, over my entire lifetime, grandly

calling out his standard farewell, in joking
lieu of *au revoir*, a playful stand-in for an
elegant departure

GRANDPARENT WISDOM

My dad retired early, and my parents had a ball, were "a goin'
concern," as Mom would say.

They enjoyed a lot of travel. Some was unusual, such as
their wacky, converted-school-bus camping tour of Mexico
with a fledgling company and a random array of people. They
travelled to exotic places, like Egypt, Turkey, and Jordan,
went on a couple of cruises, dancing to the live music every
night, going ashore in every port. They travelled locally too,
around the province we live in, up north and along the coast,
to wild beautiful places, in their old van, in the glorious days
of September when highways and towns, motels and family
restaurants are shed of summer vacationers.

Their most common travel destination though was their
adult children's homes, to visit or look after grandchildren,
when new babies were born or when the younger parents were
lucky enough to go on a vacation for two. My mom and dad
were the ultimate babysitting team, blessing their beleaguered
children-as-parents, like Marcel and me, with the chance to
escape, recover, recharge. I'd have weirdo lists posted everywhere, of meal ingredients I'd bought, of instructions for routines, for school and preschool times, lists of sports scheduling
and lessons plastered about. They'd arrive and take over.

I have a funny memory, of Marcel and me arriving back
home, exhilarated to be home embracing our children once
again. I asked breathlessly how the activities and scheduling
went while we were away.

"Oh, we didn't do any of that," Mom responded offhand-
edly. "None of it's necessary."

I remember being vaguely miffed. Like, really? None? You
did none of it? (Apparently they did school.)

Looking back, I laugh at myself, my intense, misled, scheduled, uptight-young-mom self. *Really, self?* They should drag a
toddler in and out of a car and a preschool, or a kindergartener
in and out of kindergarten, instead of bringing them with their
grandfather, a master teacher, on a slow-motion stroll through
the nearby forest, looking at trees and stumps, moss and
mushrooms, talking about insects and rays of sunlight, about
wily coyotes and how plants grow? Really? They'd go to preschool instead of staying home with their grandmother, who'd
get them to help prepare and serve a healthy lunch and sit
chatting with them, toddler in high chair included, and later
sing songs with them while the kids did playdough, then set up
the miniature china tea set for a tea party? My young children
would miss this, *this*, to go to preschool or gymnastics class??
What was I thinking?

It's easy to get locked on to routines we create as parents
to help us survive, or to fulfill some perceived expectation of
what we "should be doing." It's important to remember that a
day can roll out about twenty different ways and still be really
good . . . or way better.

AGING

Watching your parents age often lines up, more or less, with
the time of life when you begin to notice your own children
watching you age. We might overlook changes in ourselves,
but our own aging is made apparent to us as our *children* notice it—*that* we see. Early inklings of this aging business start
appearing in us, as we observe our own parents living out
"where we are going." Oy vey.

Much seems a matter of good genes and good luck, but not entirely of course. Though a bit depressing, our own beginnings of aging serve to prevent us from being smug. Watching your father need "a few tries" to get out of a chair is tempered by becoming aware that you must actively suppress old-guy sounds when dropping onto the couch at the end of the day. Your mother repeats details of an entire event to you on the same day your daughter stares at you flatly and says, "You already told me about this." Oh.

You go to stand on one leg at the front door while pulling on those small exercise socks and begin to lose your balance, but in slow motion, such that you fail to abandon the putting-on-sock activity. This leads to wild hopping all over the place, a deranged, one-legged kangaroo struggling with a human sock. Just as you slam against the closet door, you notice your adult child stopped still on the stairs, watching the whole scene, a look of discomfort on his face.

And there it is, the moving on. Getting old. The dilemma: resist like hell, or gracefully accept. I assume we all plan on resisting like hell for as long as humanly possible. Yay, us! Damn right. Go for it, and keep on going.

One of the grandest, most spirited, inspirational older gentlemen I have ever had the pleasure of getting to know, Don, in his nineties, states plainly the choice faced every single day by a person in old age:

Growth or Decay, that's it. I choose growth.

Don regularly wishes people "health and miracles!"

My father wields his sense of humour as a weapon against aging. He fell for the first time a few years ago, a terrible thing on so many levels, least of which is the ego-blow indignity of falling. Hard. In public.

My mom said about it, in her practical way, "Your father

is athletic, having done gymnastics and all that, so he knows how to fall *properly*. Some people fall like a ton of bricks—but not your father. He rolls into it . . . you know, gracefully," an untarnished sheen of pride in her husband still spilling out around the edges.

Dad, overhearing this, dry humour all times loaded, at the ready, called out, "FALL?! I didn't fall! I thought I was on fire! I was doing Stop, Drop & Roll!"

Grace under pressure, baby.

There's a critical balance to be found in fighting aging tooth and nail (whatever that means) and having the grace, wisdom, and strength of spirit to adapt to what cannot be helped. Age gracefully or go down in a ball of flames? Hard to say which is better, but it's quite the trick to do both at the same time.

Ack—never mind, all too much. I'm off to put socks on while standing on one leg, in defiance of decay.

"He's zero."
—Adam, 6, holding his new, one-week-old baby brother, Levi, introducing him to his Grade 1 class, answering the question, "How old is he?"

CHANGE

LOSS

Loss begins to unfold for your parents. It's subtle at first but, soon, not subtle at all. Losses begin that go deep. Their seventies have been pretty damn good, with lots going on, interests and engagement, routines and abilities. Same for the early eighties, but maybe a bit slower. Nice routines, good days.

That "okay status" begins to change, not always, but often. You watch these changes and help out, and soon it starts to hit different. It hits hard. You begin seeing up close how perplexing and demanding these changes are, witness the loss those changes bring, and the letting go, both figurative and literal. Loss of balance. Inability to get hearing aids working properly, causing frustration and silence. Not driving at night. Not driving at all. *Should* not be driving at all. Falling out of bed. Not reading for pleasure.

If none of these things are happening for your parents, and they keep a-rollin' along all good, count your blessings, or theirs I should say.

My father became unable to carry a bag laden with groceries. Seeing this, I was hit by a childhood memory of him carrying a massive stack of firewood down the snowy back stairs to the basement door. It felt impossible to reconcile these two images. The starkness between them flooded me with a nameless emotion. I'd never felt it before, couldn't even begin to say what it was, but it was complicated, and it felt terrible—mostly terrible anyway, with a fragment that was only wistful. Time passing.

Dad was diagnosed with dementia just before his eighty-fifth birthday. Even as I wrote that, I had to push it away. Changes came fast and broke my heart in slow motion. This loss is a whittling away, losing oneself slowly, such that the more of yourself that's lost, the less you know it. Painful, painful to watch. Unfathomably worse to experience, I can only imagine.

I felt the need to fall apart but could not allow myself to begin. It was too much, I wasn't ready, I needed to keep going. I put it off for later, as women do: stowed my meltdown on a shelf for a more suitable time. Nobody would ever advise you to push feelings away like this; I simply had the need. We women do this all the time. It's how we get shit done sometimes, women all over the world. Just hold on and keep going. Men too of course, but men are less aware of their need to have a meltdown. Women know it; we just put it off.

This loss was not Dad's story. I was not going in for a closer look, would not allow myself to think about it too much, this terrifying thing. Not yet, not then. Keep going, like Mom had to.

DRIVING

Dad had always been a good driver. He arrived in Vancouver in his early twenties and somehow got a job driving a wealthy family to Mexico. Details on this have always been murky, as in . . . *how??* Who? And why?! Nevertheless, this is what happened. For weeks he drove them, using paper road maps of course, navigating on "the wrong side of the road" through enormous cities he'd never seen before, like Los Angeles and Mexico City.

This story makes me laugh for so many reasons. I mean, really, Dad? You, twenty-three years old or so thought confidently, *Yo, sure! I can be a professional driver . . . across a brand-new continent of cities I don't know . . . all on the right-hand side of the road, which will continuously feel entirely unnatural to me. Sure—why not?*

Dad taught us all to drive, Mom included, since she got her driver's license late, at forty-two years old. He's a good teacher and good driver, so we were lucky. He taught me some critical techniques, ones I taught to my kids.

> *Drive through the curves on a windy road, especially on highways. Don't float, or drift, or coast around big, swerving bends; you don't control what the car is doing that way. You drive, using the engine. Set the turn of the steering wheel, locking in the curve you are entering. And drive, using the gas, curving around the big bends. Drive the curve one way: it straightens out, foot comes off the accelerator. Then drive the curve the other way: "lock" on, accelerate, and drive. Don't use the brakes. Drive.*

I loved this. It made driving a winding highway a pleasure for the rest of my life.

Recently, after years of a remarkable amount of driving really, at eighty-four years old, Dad had a mix-up at an intersection in their town. He turned into the left of a highway meridian, onto the left-hand side of the road, which, some seventy years earlier, was the correct side. I don't think he realized it was wrong, but Mom did immediately. They got out of that precarious situation okay, thank God, but it was devastating, as was confirmation from a lovely doctor, respectfully put, that, *It's time to retire from driving, Peter.*

Retire from driving.

See? All so loss-y. I'm trying desperately to "not be sad" about all this. Their lives, Mom's and Dad's, have been, and are, something beautiful, extraordinarily excellent in what matters. I admire them in so many ways, such outstanding humans, so good at being themselves. I'm determined to cling to this and resist sadness.

Dad continues to be able to laugh sometimes at the crazy things he does or, at least, persist despite them, when glasses he fetched turn out to be a watch, and a mask becomes a toque, and words for what he wants to say won't come, and a light won't turn off because it is a thermostat, and a cane forgotten is meant to be a walker, and keys are gathered for a car that should not be driven. Between the quiet, fearful looks he rarely allows us "kids"—my siblings and me—to see, there is humour and grace. Dear God, so much grace.

At the close of one such day, replete with staggering losses on full display, Dad was hugging us goodnight, Mom and me. As he turned to walk to the bedroom, he called out, "Dear friends, once more unto the fray!"

I know this to be Dad's variation of a quote from his old pal "Willie" Shakespeare's *Henry V*, "Once more unto the breach, dear friends, once more."

How mysterious is the human person, how achingly lovely, this gift of being. We keep driving around the bends as best we can, for as long as possible. Don't float or drift or coast. Drive.

Mom expressed a similar persistent intent during the same visit, when, in a quiet moment, she said, in an uncharacteristically tentative way, "I hope I can take care of your Dad. I really want to." And a moment later, "I hope I can do it."

So brave. Aging is demanding and foreign, strikingly similar in its foreignness to the way a newborn baby is foreign in its newness. My parents' generation is tough though. Are we that tough? I suppose we don't know yet. Their generation possesses a stoicism, a resolve, that is remarkable. Just deal.

"That'll be fine, dear."

Ignorantly, I used to interpret a placid response of *That'll be fine, dear* as passivity or complacency, but it's neither. No, often times it's generosity: broad, steadfast, fucking tough generosity.

They are tough in the deepest way possible: with themselves. Or at least, my parents are.

> Emily, a young girl, watching my mom get ready for a dinner out, doing her hair, putting on jewelry and lipstick: "I don't know why old people do all that—they never look very good anyway."
>
> Mom laughed 'til she cried.

HELPING

Gradually, or maybe suddenly, comes a fairly universal turn of events in a lengthy relationship of having a parent: needing to help them. The nature of this help shifts things between you, dramatically. You become caregiver for the ones who cared for you.

I'm struck by how unfamiliar this is to me, my parents needing my help. They never needed me. I don't mind at all of course, except it feels so . . . melancholy. Their needing help is normal, or okay—fine even. Why does it feel so bad?

Memories drift by of times they did it all, did all it was that made me feel safe and cared for.

LOST AT THE FALL FAIR

I am the young daughter my mother searched for and found, years later now, helping her as she feels lost.

I remember becoming lost at my hometown Fall Fair when I was very young, maybe four or five years old. I became separated from my family. Many details are hazy—except the terror. That I remember exactly. I distinctly remember thinking, *I will never see my mom and dad again.* I had no image of how this would play out, but the parents? They were gone. I was an orphan now (according to my somewhat flawed understanding of the concept). I wandered the displays of sewing and home goods, the barns and club animal pens, past stands of popcorn and cotton candy, game booths to win prizes, tables of candied apples. I remember trying to push away the panic of being on my own. People moved about in waves, lineups blocked openings to get through. I couldn't get clear of all the people to see.

Of course they found me soon after, or I them, and I cried and cried, relief flooding over me. I had parents again, so much better than whatever I thought had come to pass. On the drive home, Mom sat in the back seat with me, which she never did, and held me all the way home.

Seeing now that same woman, my mom, looking so terribly lost, even panicked, sitting wringing her hands, feels disjointing. I do not write "wringing her hands" as a cliché in describing her state; she is literally wringing her hands with worry. She has become unwell, which can happen to any of us at times, her mental health and sense of well-being shot all to hell. Seeing her like this knocks me off kilter, reminds me how much I have relied upon her steadfastness, now that it's missing.

One could say I'm being ridiculous. My mother is old, worn out, and feeling anxious. She's been helping other people since she was a little girl, and now she needs help. True, all that. It just feels so . . . What is it? Something close to sad, yet with a sharp edge of brutal reality, the harshness of our collective frailty. But there it is.

"I need my Mama," Mom said to me, out of the blue, something she must have felt innumerable times as a child, but rarely said. Things buried in us find their way back to the surface again late in life, needs laid bare once again.

You and I take our aging parents to doctor's appointments, argue about medicines, write things on their calendars. We fight about the lamp they've plugged in beside the kitchen sink, "to see better." We badger them to get the home assessment they need, the help they don't want. We make the call anyway, overriding their wishes in a way we'd normally never dream of doing. We repeat things as many times as they repeated things to us as we were growing up, as many times as we similarly repeat things to our own children. We attempt to rearrange their possessions, as they asked us to do with the wasteland of our bedrooms back when we were teenagers.

I am the agitated mother now, doing the nagging, and my mom is the teenager, resisting like hell.

I suppose it's all okay. We just have to get over this hump and things will smooth out. It is a very large hump.

TRAVELLING

I am the young daughter my father towed through multiple airports to traverse the globe, the middle-aged daughter he supported to complete a slow but important run not long ago, assisting him now to traverse a room.

Memories of our family trip to Australia when I was a child loom large probably because the whole thing was so epic. That trip, two months of our summer in Australia back in 1974, was remarkable by the standards of most people we knew at the time. We had saved for two years, a group exercise in shared, rigid frugality in order to make it happen: we children understood its value.

When the voyage finally came to pass, I remember being flabbergasted at my parents' knowledge of how to do everything, of how it all worked, at each airport along the way. Each step was a mystery to me, making my parents even more invincible in my eyes.

> *Look!! MY mom and dad know what to do!*
> *Here—in this huge, scary airport—know all*
> *the stuff a person has to do to get on an air-*
> *plane! How do they know this?!*

Once in Australia, Dad drove our family everywhere in a friend's car. I was astounded that Dad knew his way around (not having properly processed that this was "home" for him . . . but nevertheless).

Some three decades later, in 2003, when Veronica was eight months old, I ran a special half-marathon together with Dad—not special because we clocked any blistering times, but because we did it. I had asked Dad to help me train for a road race, one we could enter together. I needed a goal provided by an event, a thing to aim at, something just for me within my life of demanding "otherness."

So Dad coached me, meaning he sent me lovely letters in his neat, distinctive, script-like handwriting, combining news from home along with the outline of a *moderate* training schedule. The PE teacher in him. I knew that if I just followed the neatly written schedule, it would work. And it did.

I hope for the memory of running the course together with Dad, under cloudy skies next to a still lake one morning in May of 2003, to stay in my head, even as other memories fall out.

All of this is to say that my dad literally took me around the world and helped me run a slow race when I needed help to do it, and now he was having trouble walking across a room. This felt wrong, shoved me, again, already unsteadied by Mom's all-encompassing anxiety. I have viewed my parents in a shiny, protected bubble of invincibleness for a much greater quota of time than normally afforded to children, with that child-like confidence borne of naïveté and trust, a blessed problem to have really.

It's like my parents are tired of standing on the pedestals I've put them on, and have climbed down to sit slumped on the edges, weary. They're close to me there though. I can lean in and hug them easily, my cheek against the tops of their heads, as when I'd sit my too-tall teenagers to hug them properly. I'm relieved to be leaning against something myself. We're together there, all resting against those pedestals.

There is more "needing help" looming, which begs me to spring into action, and start planning for needs likely to come. I'm learning slowly though there's little point spending mega-watts of energy on events that may or may not come to pass. Inspirational messaging on cloth bags and such tells us, *Live in the moment!*, but very few people actually want to do that. No, we wish we could predict the future, and we want to plan the hell out of everything. Yet the biggies, we cannot plan. As my little niece Freya says in her kindergarten weather forecast report, "We will see what today will be . . . like."

Mom hasn't been hungry lately, with her new anxieties. Her weight is going down and down, under ninety pounds now. We have peculiar conversations, she and I, me encouraging (badgering) her to consider various foods and times to eat more, and she explaining (arguing) why she cannot.

"I'm telling you, I cannot eat a whole sandwich! That's *way* too much—I only want half!"

Mom hollers this over the phone, our conversation taking place as I watch Levi stand at the counter eating an entire pizza he'd baked from frozen. He then pulls a massive tub of leftover loaded fried rice (i.e., a whole family meal) from the fridge. I gesture at Levi madly.

Me, to Mom: "Okay, well, try to eat all that."

Me, to Levi (covering phone, whispering): "Don't eat all that!"

Mom, to me: "The other night I had toast before bed."

Me, to Mom: "Oh, that's good! Put peanut butter on it too."

Levi, to Me (whispering): "Do we have a bag of pierogies?" Then, "Or can I eat these?" (holds up a carton of eggs).

This transition from strengths to frailties in my parents has made me more aware of the gift lavished upon me all these years, of having parents who are generous, competent, reasonable, kind. They handed me an assurance and encouragement not routinely distributed as a universal participation medal for being a member of the human race. How did I get so lucky? Affection without smothering. Encouragement without handholding. Education without expectation. Freedom to make my way. Given this, my desperation to help them now isn't virtuous at all, only natural, simply an extension of how good they've been to me.

The experience of many, many people is a stratosphere away from the care I have received; some parents are a source of pain to their children. It is beyond impressive, a wonder of being, really, to witness people who have experienced hurt and suffering at the hands of their parents yet manage to make their way, somehow becoming generous even, in their own lives. If you are one of those people, making your way without much parent-love, you are a wonder, a miracle of greatness. I am in awe of you. I am so sorry you have suffered, but your strength of spirit astounds us all. We applaud you. Keep going; you are an amazement, a gift of sum-total good in the world.

SIMPLE PLEASURES

In the midst of all the helping, you will begin to notice birds tweeting. Seriously. In the early morning, awake and lying in bed with the window open, or later, outside, or in the evenings, out walking the dog, . . . the birds!! Have they always been doing this? Chirping and tweeting and calling out in earnest, in complex patterns on repeat, with outrageous levels of intensity and commitment? I'm not sure what's going on, but there's something with the birds.

I remember some twenty years ago Mom phoning me in autumn and going off, something about the trees—the colours of various trees around their town. She described each tree's location, so I'd know which ones she meant (that works in a small town). She seemed beside herself with amazement at the beauty of the trees that fall, even walking around town to take photographs of them with her old Instamatic camera. She kept saying, "It's unbelievable!" And I thought, *Hmm.*

Now I am doing the exact same thing, badgering my adult children about the birds tweeting and receiving pretty much the same response. What is this? I'm doing it with other things too. Intricate shapes and shades of flower petals, rays of sunlight slicing through trees, obsessing about the smell of rain on dirt in the garden and of cut grass, long shadows in the early evening, the feel of the wind. Weirdo material.

It seems that in aging, as I am, the simple and beautiful begin to take on greater significance, bringing more pleasure. It's as though age cuts through the din of debris gathered around you over the years, pointing you toward what is most worthy of notice, presenting that to you. The aged notice what the young are too busy or too impetuous to take in. Finally.

A simple slice of delicious bread, toasted and buttered while still hot, crispy to bite into but soft inside. No wonder that's all your mom wants for supper when she's not hungry.

What tastes better? My Filipina friend tells me that if you're Filipino or Chinese, the ideal food is a bowl of perfect rice: plain, simple, delicious.

A glass of cold beer. The sight of a child running back and forth in a room. That same, familiar, favourite piece of music. A tree in autumn, leaves brilliant orange and red, shimmering with light and colour, dancing against a clear blue sky. The quiet company of an old friend. And, it turns out, the layered sound of many birds chirping and tweeting, calling out and singing early in the morning.

Eventually much of everything else becomes background noise, unimportant.

This discovery has helped me be more useful to my parents as they get on in years, in their mideighties. Make the dish they like, get the cardigan they've worn for sixty-five years, turn on the same TV show, press play on favourite music tapes. Serve hot buttered toast and a strong cup of tea with a bit of milk. Fair enough. A lot of that is starting to sound pretty good to me too.

> "Cuppa tea, dear?"
> —Mom or Dad, calling to the other, on any given afternoon throughout their retirement years

LIFE

IN THEIR OWN WORDS

"We have no idea what's next. No idea," said Mom.

Mom said this to me as we were chatting on the phone, she on the wall phone they had installed in their little retirement-living apartment, with the same phone number they've had for more than fifty years.

We soon agreed that we "had no idea what was next" back when we were younger either. We were just more oblivious to the fact. Nobody ever knows what's coming next, not really. It's a comforting delusion to think we do—one we all indulge in.

A PREDICAMENT

I had a stunning conversation with my father on Friday, March 11, 2022, many months into his life with dementia. I was keeping him company while Mom attended her new weekly care-giver support group, a breakthrough undertaking for her. I'd planned to take Dad out for an outing, a change of pace.

He was intent otherwise; he led me to sit and have a conversation, despite that having become an arduous thing to do.

We knew Dad's memory problem impaired his ability to

store language long enough to say what he wanted to say. He began a sentence but soon arrived at a word or phrase that caused him to stop and shake his head. The word was not available, or not correct. He paused, frowning, and inclined his head, leaning forward, trying to grab at the word he wanted from his whirring memory system. Those words often whirred right past him, out of reach.

If he was far enough along through a sentence, I could sense and guess at words for the idea he seemed to be expressing. My offered words were met with a clear, relieved *yes*, or an emphatic *no*, which came with a head shake and, again, the head incline of leaning in, trying to access the correct words.

Dad knew what he wanted to say.

We persisted for two hours, and he expressed terrifying revelations about what he was experiencing.

We knew that Dad's perception of spatial relations between physical things was impaired. That's what led to the curious sitting crooked off the edges of chairs, or on the arm of one, or trying to eat from a plate placed too far away, or setting a full cup of coffee barely onto a table edge, things Mom originally began noticing as unusual. One time he tried to buckle his seatbelt all the way across the console of the van into her buckle; she thought he was being funny, the teaser he's always been. He may have laughed at the oddness of it all, but he had not been joking.

During that morning he and I spent together, Dad was determined to express the profound and frightening realities of the world as he was now experiencing it.

He succeeded.

His problem with the relating of physical spaces had escalated, taken over his world entirely, such that wherever he currently physically was, other places "did not exist" to him; those were his exact words. They were unknown to him, could not be understood nor imagined. The bathroom or the bedroom door some few steps away? Might as well have been in another country. Or on another planet.

"Places away do not exist," he explained, clearly wanting to convey this sense of things.

He waved around himself, around the small, one-bedroom apartment they'd lived in for four years by then.

"I don't know any of this. None of this makes sense to me. There are so many rooms, and I don't know where we are, or why we are here." He told me this haltingly, the two of us piecing together the words he wanted to say.

Dad could no longer remember him and Mom making their shared decision to move to the retirement home. Their apartment felt continually unfamiliar to him now, despite being filled with the same old furniture and things they'd had for years, *like another room in their house,* as Adam aptly put it.

The location of the dining room they walked to for meals, on the main floor of the retirement home, was now a perpetual mystery.

"The place where we eat? It doesn't exist; I don't know it. It's over in another building somewhere, with so many hallways to get there. Your mom explains where it is over and over, but it makes no sense."

A pause.

I find myself in a predicament I cannot understand.

I wrote that down as soon as I could. Such grace it makes my throat and chest ache.

We were planning to go to the church later that afternoon, for a little visit and some prayer time, as they liked to do. I asked Dad if he knew the church, if it existed for him, a place he'd gone hundreds of times, to commune with God and neighbour.

"No. I don't know it," he said.

I had a question, one I desperately hoped he'd understand. I asked whether going to this now-unknown place of nonexistence, the church, felt *entirely* unfamiliar, strange and terrible, or whether, upon arrival, he had *some sense* of being comforted by something familiar, any inkling of knowing and belonging once he got there?

His answer was immediate and emphatic: "Both."

My mind grappled at this mystery, pulling at its edges, unable to get any hold.

He and I discussed the possibility that he try to let go and just trust Mom, try to simply accept her explanations of where they are and where they're going, as true.

He looked uncertain but said he would try.

"Your mother is helping me a lot. Without her I'd be lost."

There it is—the give and take of a long marriage, the 100/100 giving, because 50/50 doesn't work.

I thought back to a time around Mom's menopause when she had her first severe, long bout of depression, completely disappearing from herself, and from us. Dad made Mom get dressed every day—made her—and took her walking with him, an hour-plus-long walk every day. Every day, until, with the right medications, and care, and time, she got better.

And now she walks him through every day, every day.

It's all so heavy, but clearly what love looks like.

When Mom returned from her support group, I was elated to share with her, purposefully in Dad's presence, how well he had communicated his thoughts to me, to help me understand.

Dad looked satisfied, this courageous man trying to think his way through a predicament using an instrument that wasn't working properly, in which the instrument causing the problem must itself be used to solve the problem. A foreign land.

Mom expressed a similar experience of foreign unfamiliarity in an email to me a year earlier, that she would have

tapped out on their iPad with one straightened finger, much
more firmly than is necessary:

> *This getting old does present some anxious mo-*
> *ments. Our bodies do not function as we ex-*
> *pect them to. We haven't been this old before,*
> *so we do not know what to expect, to ignore, or*
> *to bother about. Your dad feels we should just*
> *leave it for now. One day at a time.*

> *With love,*

That email was back when neither of them wanted to investigate any of the difficulties Dad was experiencing, because,
What good would it do? They weren't wrong.

Mom recounted recently that, over the past months, in
the evenings, Dad gathers the clothes he is going to wear the
next day, folded carefully and stacked into a pile, and carries
them out of the bedroom, a practice she thinks perhaps was
extracted from long-ago days of his youth living at an agricul-
tural boarding school back home in Australia.

He emerges into their little living room with his neat stack
of clothing and asks, "Where will I sleep tonight?"

She told me she walks over, turns him around, and points
at their simple double bed a few feet in front of them.

"Here's the bed you will sleep in, with me. You've slept
there every night for five years now. You'll like it. It's very
comfortable."

He nods and walks forward and gets into bed.

MOTHERING

Parenting seems to come full circle nearer the end of life. My
parents raised me. My children taught me how to parent—

because none of us know what we're doing when we begin. We learn on the job. We sort of know only once we're done . . . and we're never done. In the learning though, I have more of what I need to be a parent to my parents, to be a mother to them now.

We're back to that again, this mothering, this fathering. Naturally, I have a lot to say about mothering. I wrote a little Mother's Day piece back in 2015 that captures much of what I feel about the role. Reading it now, I see a weakness in my writing.

I tend to finish my ideas, my stories, with a trite, happy little ending. An uplift. Take the loose pieces and wrap them up at the end, tied with a bow, a flourish, to make it nice. Why? Why do I do this? It's too sweet, I know it. This wrapping up is not necessary.

I want to make it nice for people. I do. A people pleaser? Yes, though a surly one.

I know that things in life are left jagged and hanging sometimes. Often, actually. Messy and ugly and half-done, I know. Good writers leave the ambiguous, don't tell people what to feel, don't try to fix it or make it nice. They push you to the edge and just leave you there, which is real, and smart. I admire that. But I can't do it.

This fixing of things is a problem mothers especially have. We're often fixers, we women. Whether mothers or not, women do a lot of mothering of the people around them—hopefully not in the controlling way of the dreaded overbearing-mother stereotype. But women often feel compelled to try wrapping up loose ends. I suppose we shouldn't do that, probably don't even need to—yet still we try.

It's like a modern-day version of "to clothe the naked," one of the charitable works of mercy. The "naked" we might clothe are not often literally lying naked in the streets in our era. However, figuratively, metaphorically, women everywhere, especially mothers, see and clothe the naked all the time. We cover people when they feel naked. Cloak what someone finds shameful. Enwrap another in reassurance. Turn a blind eye sometimes, to "not notice," to excuse. Shelter a person exposed. Bring mercy to a situation left jagged and hanging.

Wrap. Enfold. Swaddle. Cover. Embrace. Wait. Wrap things up and tie them with a fucking bow. And a kiss on the cheek. Clothe. Women can be conniving and petty too of course, capable of being manipulative and cruel—all of that. But still, we often look to clothe others. Maybe this is our weakness, a fault . . . or maybe it's our strength, a superpower. Or both.

> "Goodnight, sweetheart."
> —me, to Mom, on the phone late one
> night, startling myself with the use of an
> endearment reserved for my children

> Mom didn't notice. I could tell.

DEATH

So my Dad died in June 2022, the day after his eighty-sixth birthday.

It was sudden and unexpected. Maybe death always strikes us that way. There was a sudden weakness, a collapse at home, a fall, a hitting of his head, my mom calling an ambulance. A sickened state, a virus that had briefly brought the world to its knees, and him too. A body frail and struggling, teetering toward not surviving. A decision made to keep him comfortable and let him go.

The days that followed are a blur, of his frail, little wife being brought in, of all of us in gowns and masks and gloves, of her stroking his face and telling him, "I always loved you, from the moment I first saw you." Of his grandchildren, my children, each phoning to say loud greetings of love and caring, in forced-cheerful voices over speakerphone, Dad's face lighting up, repeating their names back in greeting, more quietly with each one as the time passed. Of hard phone calls made in an echoey, industrial bathroom with its harsh light. Of his son, my brother John, arriving within forty-eight hours, after a multi-leg journey from Australia, in time to call out, "G'day, Dad! It's John here," to have Dad's eyebrows rise up along with a small mouthing of his son's name, the word *John*, as they held hands. Of my practical, kind brother Allan sitting quietly with Dad for hours, over days, right beside him. Of my nurturing, generous sister Joanne, a nurse, wiping Dad's face and moisturizing his lips, fussing and arranging things just so. Of my pragmatic husband, Marcel, doing things behind the scenes, driving people around, bringing sandwiches, making calls, even taking Mom home and tucking her in one night— making me grateful again to have married someone who isn't necessarily "nice" all the time but, more importantly, is good.

Every time I left Dad I'd spend time doing the weird thing I've always done when I *need* to remember something, in case he died before I came back. I'd intentionally look, to really *see*, to remember all I could about the moment, to not hurry or pass anything by, since each departure might be the last time I saw Dad. And one of them was.

I looked right at his face, stroking his beautiful brow and tracing his eyebrows. I really, really looked at his hands. Dad had beautiful hands, with graceful, long, tapered fingers, which even in these dying days he placed, slightly interlocked, upon his chest, as he always did while engaged in attentive discussion with me, or anyone else. My actions were a defense against a rising panic that I might forget exactly him, in the weeks following the moment I left the room. An OCD of love. Love crashing.

One of these times alone with Dad, as I began my departing ritual, another departing ritual happened along. The local parish priest suddenly appeared in the curtained space, flustered by the procedure involved in entering and garbing up, and by the insistence that was required in order to bring his blessing kit along. He had come to do Anointing of the Sick, or Last Rites, as it used to be called. We offered words of greeting to one another, then he opened the kit and began setting up his stuff.

A calmness settled in.

There, amid the metal and plastic, the sterility and equipment of a cramped, shared hospital room, some grace and mystery befitting the beauty of our sacred humanity entered, like angels breaking in. I loved the silk of the purple stole the priest placed around his neck to mark the administering of an occasion, an event; the heavy, dark green paper of the prayer booklet he handed me; the pure element of blessed water, water Dad spent innumerable joyful moments of his life swimming in, used now to bless him once again. The laying on of our hands, in blessing upon this good man, praying words for forgiveness and of gratitude and praise. We joined Dad with our eyes closed too, in a quiet moment spent, of humans convening together with God. I felt gifted, a peace in my distress, a daughter taking part in blessing her own father on his way, as he hovered between this earthly life and the transcendent. A sacred moment, like birth. The afternoon light, from the window to the sky and through his neighbour's curtain, lit the space softly, as I was blessed in the anointing of my father's hands with holy oil, "for all the many good works done with them over his long life, our brother Peter."

At the very end, Dad left this world on his own one afternoon, while his attentive family were all out of the room.

Peter Ereth Home Purves
June 2, 1936–June 3, 2022

HOPE

MIZPAH

Back in 1960, my grandfather, William Winter Purves Sr. (there's a Jr. living in Australia these days), wrote a letter of welcome to my mother when she and my father became engaged. The letter, a poem actually, was sent across the world to Canada by ship. He signed off with the expression *Mizpah*, a Hebrew word for "watchtower", used in the Book of Genesis of the Old Testament to refer to a place and to words spoken there:

> *May the Lord watch between me and thee, when*
> *we are absent one from another.*

Years later, I became steady pen pals with his wife, my nana, Robena Emily. She too signed off her letters to me with the same *Mizpah*. Nana and I sent numerous letters, via airmail by then, back and forth between New South Wales, Australia, and my hometown in British Columbia, Canada, and later, Vancouver.

Dad used the word *mizpah* with me as well, on notes and

letters. While I was still living at home, Mom came across a greeting card featuring the expression, which she had laminated for me as a keepsake. Later I propped the card up on the dresser in my bedroom when I went away, off to university, or while travelling, or living away from home. There it sat, as a talisman marking this idea of our time away from one another as being watched over and blessed.

That mizpah of watched-over space apart from Dad feels vacant now and lonely since he died. For now, it sits empty, holding only a massive ache, "with sighs too deep for words." Our souls are not separated, thank God, but the rest of us is, and it's not possible to say how much I miss him. I cry a lot, with grief that Dad is gone from me here, and in finally unloading some of the sadness I'd piled on the shelf during his changes of dementia.

I sense the space will fill with memories of my beloved Dad over time, as a chance thought, a happy event, a shared inside joke, a cherished exchange, falls softly into the blessed space between us without being swallowed up by sadness. I will hold close each exquisite memory that rests there and wait for more to come. As with happiness, it seems we cannot urge this process along, or bid it happen at will. Time and openness and attentiveness will help, I think.

Mom is living her mizpah apart now from her life's love of sixty years. She's spiraled away from us, struggling against an unwell state, immersed in a shadowy place where it's difficult to get to her, or help her. For now, our conversations go round in circles, a two-way helplessness, ending where we started, or even backward a bit. We try, but it's frustrating and makes each of us lonely. I miss Mom these days, miss the way we've always been together. That grounded, real, competent woman and I, we understood each other.

Our love is what we cling to and hold up. The love Mom

and I share these days is an unclad love, naked and demanding, like a wet toddler standing screaming in a drained bath-
tub. This bare love is real though, as real as the soft, lovely
kind. Maybe more so.

Mom is trying hard, brave woman. We pray our way
through, receive tiny little lights, and keep going, as families
do. I can see Mom finding her way back, being lifted little by
little, weaving her way out of a dense fog of what might be grief
in one of its many disguises.

Mom's seniors' mental health worker recently said to her,
"You are doing your best, Marie-Annette—and that is enough."
That struck me deeply: *and that is enough.*

How do we convey this to our teenagers? Our young
adults? Hell, even our children these days? To ourselves too.
Do your best: that is enough.

You are enough.

Hope abounds all around us. There's hope to be found in
the blessed space between each of us and those we care for and
love—the love we've shared with others forms bridges of shining hope that traverse the "watched-over" space.

REVIEW OF CHAPTERS

Let's review what we have learned so far.

Babies blow your life apart and become your obsession. They are adorable and an unfathomable amount of work. Babies are portable though and can't fight back very hard, so are fairly easy to take places. You see the personality of your baby in the first few months. Get to know it, as you'll be seeing that for the rest of your life. Babies are an explosion of development. They can command a roomful of adults while only able to sit, smile, and babble incoherently, which is impressive. We love babies. Their clothes are cute too.

Young children are delightful, mobile menaces, equally adorable but able to fight back pretty hard. They learn to speak, then won't stop talking, which helps you know where they are. Most of what they do is insane, and soon you begin to feel insane too. Just a little break makes you feel better, and before long, you miss them. They are bewitching and small, but are heavy, exhausting work. Young children say funny things that are remarkably logical. Your arms become strong while caring for young children. Young children learn incessantly and make a lot of mess, and we love them.

Children are real and pure and mostly nice. If all is going well, they are without airs and beginning to realize they're not, in fact, the centre of the universe. They are odd, surprisingly complex creatures, and engaging conversationalists. They can wear the exact same clothes for days and are usually fairly open about how they feel. Children need to move a lot and are naturally curious if not dulled by too much direction. They come up with super-great ideas. Children are smart and will push you around if you let them. Don't let them. You get glimpses of what a child might be like as an adult, but then again, you have no idea. Children are forthright, fresh, and more honest than adults are. We love them.

Teenagers are complicated, difficult, deeply earnest on the inside, and hungry. They resist and strain against us, pushing away to become themselves; they are not us. They're frequently withdrawn but occasionally talkative. When they are talkative, it is helpful if you don't talk, because they need you to listen. Teenagers grow and change so much that you glance up, sometimes startled to see a person you momentarily do not recognize as your child. Teenagers can be extremely kind but often are not. They still need you, very much. You both have to sneak that in, the needing of one another. Teenagers frequently piss us off, but we love them.

Adult children are excellent because they join the force of humanity that gets most of the work done. Adults are really, really good at an amazing array of things, your child included. Hopefully you've established enough shared understanding and affection to have a fairly solid relationship. You need to work on that relationship more than you might have originally thought. With adult offspring, you occasionally "forget" somehow that this person *is* the child you once held. Being with your adult child, whom you like a lot (who used to be your baby) can be the most satisfying of experiences you'll ever have. We don't notice adults enough because they're everywhere, doing everything. All of them are somebody's baby though, grown up. We appreciate adults, and we love them.

You may have elderly parents, or be an older adult yourself now. Elderly people feel the same about themselves as they did when they were thirty, and matter to themselves exactly as much as you matter to yourself right now. Aging body parts begin to hurt, things easily done become difficult, and dear friends die, which is all a drag. It's a challenge being old; you've got to be tough. Elderly people stay vibrant by being active and enjoying hobbies and favourite music, outings, and get-togethers with good friends . . . sort of like everybody. We worry about aging parents, about their safety and well-being, but ideally, people are free to be somewhat unsafe at any age. Older people enjoy reminiscing and have earned the right. Ask elderly persons what they think about things. You'll often be blown away by their answers, and should say to yourself, *Hey, dumbass, did you think they'd live this long and not know stuff??* We admire elderly people, and we love them.

That pretty much covers it.

CONCLUSION

There is no conclusion to this book. How can there be? My story is still unfolding, and so is yours. And we never know how our stories will go.

I finally know what this book is about though.

Here we are, all together on the bench, staring expectantly at one another. We humans, parents and otherwise, are always seeking, hoping for, looking to what might be, straining to see the thing ahead. Yet, apparently all we have to grapple with and offer one another is right in front of us, here and now. Just this. Now.

Wherever you are, that is what you have. That's all any of us has ever got: right now. Wherever you are in your story, be right there. Be fully and completely there, as best you can manage, there in the ever-changing times of your ordinary, enchanted life. Now is the moment, "now is the acceptable time."

We are all different, and we are all the same.

We are good and bad, both, all of us.

We are oh so tough and frightfully fragile, each of us beautiful and broken and idiotic.

The world we live in is one of art, politics, technology, religion, and economics. But even more so for each one of us, at its essence, this life is a grand adventure of love. Much of that love, for good or for bad, happens within our families. Family is both burden and treasure—in that, we are all the same.

Our families love us when no one else will.

And even when your family doesn't, or won't, or can't, you are still loved. You were loved first, thought of before you even came to be. You didn't will yourself into being—neither did your parents really. You were brought into being by a Creator who chose you to exist and loves you without reservation, without condition.

You are a heartbeat of God. Crazy I know, but true: lovable you, wonderfully made.

Give that love away, even when it's difficult. When we do so, we become more.

Each of us has the capacity to be wonderful and horrid. It's better if we face that, parents and kids, non-parents and non-kids. *You* are probably not all that terrible, but if you have been, or are, people change, all the time. Actually, not so much change as turn, turn in another direction—the same person, only going another way.

It's the turning that matters—how we respond to our terribleness and what we do with our goodness. Limitless grace and mercy abound though, more than enough for all of us, redemption all over the place.

By the way, and cosmically less important, I love you too. That sounds super-weird I know, but it's really not if you believe what I believe about you. You are of infinite value; you have boundless potential. You are worthy. You are a thing of beauty; you have a story to tell. Knowing this about you has made all the difference in my life—for that I am grateful.

I have loved writing this book with you. *Loved.* Thank you. Such a joy. I will miss this.

Good luck with that thing you have to do. I know you can do it. I have great faith in you.

XO

PS. Give my love to your family.

ACKNOWLEDGMENTS

My heartfelt gratitude to:

Dale Telfer, for his honest critique and unreasonable amount of encouragement of my writing. Dale made me believe a book could be possible, which was "gold, Jerry, pure gold."

Daphne Gray-Grant, for her guidance to "get it done," through her program titled just that, and for her patient answers to my thousand and one questions. Daphne is a fountain of knowledge, calm encouragement, and kindness.

Jonathan Burke, Neil de Gelder, Mark Goudie, Christine Mayston, and Brenda McLean for giving me their precious time and carefully considered feedback as "beta" test-readers. The insights of this lovely group of people, combined with their willingness to engage in the risk of being honest, became *the* difference-maker of betterment for this book.

Warren Clark, for being a source of inspiration and helpful conversation early in the writing process.

Lewisia Dvorak, my cherished new daughter-in-law, for her inspired assistance in helping design my book website, and Dustin Groÿ, website developer, for making it happen.

Adam Dvorak, for his regular, patient assistance with all things IT, because I remain useless in that regard.

Girl Friday Productions, of my publishing imprint GFB, for being exceptional in all the ways we have come to not expect companies to be. In particular: Christina Henry de Tessan, VP of Strategic Partnerships, for taking a chance; Georgie Hockett, Marketing Director, for helping ensure that my book doesn't enter the world shy and lonely; and Emilie Sandoz-Voyer, Publishing Director, *Apparently*'s publishing manager, for being such a talented book-whisperer and lovely person to boot.

Eva Dvorak, for designing and managing my book's social media because I was not able to.

Far too many people than are possible to list here, for their goodness and support. You are not named here but your names are etched on our hearts.

Victor and Helen Dvorak, Marcel's parents, for being a backbone of prayer for our family.

Peter and Marie-Annette Purves, my parents, for creating the beautiful world my world was shaped around.

Emily, Adam, Madeline, Eva, Levi, and Veronica Dvorak, my children, for the content and for their regular input of knowledge, opinion, advice, and help throughout the entire writing and publishing process. I thank these beautiful people for story-detail clarifications, slang review, cultural insights, subtitle vetting, non-alarming newsletter formatting, cover design and promotional text feedback . . . but mostly for allowing me to write our stories. And for the hype support. Let's goooooo!

Marcel Dvorak, my husband, for his delight in, and exuberant support of, this book. Marcel provided me generous freedom to do this, never once asking to read any of it, yet all the while bursting with pride and startling insights about my book he'd never read. I am bowled over by Marcel's outrageous display of trust in me. I'm glad I married him.

Ultimately, I thank God for everything. All of it.

"What shall I render to the Lord for all His bounty to me?"
Psalm 116:12

ABOUT THE AUTHOR

Sue Dvorak is a small-town girl who moved to the city, becoming a physiotherapist, a wife and a mother—eventually of six. Spending years wrestling with her children and the goal of living in the moment, Sue has a fondness for involving herself in things that tend not to pay but are otherwise rewarding. She lives in British Columbia with her husband, Marcel, an orthopaedic spine surgeon. Their children are the sort of people you'd lean on in a bind. They currently work as a civil litigation lawyer, an entrepreneur physicist, an infants' child- and youth-care worker, a student of veterinary medicine, a business startup team member and a nearly graduated biological environmental scientist.

www.ingramcontent.com/pod-product-compliance
Lightning Source LLC
Chambersburg PA
CBHW030355130626
46549CB00004B/1506